BOOKS BEFORE PRINT

MEDIEVAL MEDIA CULTURES

Medieval Media Cultures offers analyses of how individuals interacted with written, visual, dramatic, and material media in medieval and early modern cultures, as well as how modern scholars interact with the remnants of medieval and early modern cultures via written, material, and now digital and electronic media.

This new series in media literacy welcomes proposals for monographs and essay collections in the fields of digital humanities, mapping, digital text analysis, games and gaming studies, literacy studies, and text production and interaction. We are especially interested in projects that demonstrate how digital methods and tools for research, preservation, and presentation influence the ways in which we interact with and understand these texts and media.

BOOKS BEFORE PRINT

ERIK KWAKKEL

For Ruth

British Library Cataloguing in Publication Data
A catalogue record for this book is available from the British Library

Cover image: Leiden, Universiteitsbibliotheek, VLF 94 (ninth century).
Photo by the author.

ISBN (HB): 9781942401612
ISBN (PB): 9781942401629
e-ISBN: 9781942401636

www.arc-humanities.org

CONTENTS

FILLING THE PAGE: SCRIPT, WRITING, AND PAGE DESIGN

ENHANCING THE MANUSCRIPT: BINDING AND DECORATION

READING IN CONTEXT: ANNOTATIONS, BOOKMARKS, AND LIBRARIES

THE MARGINS OF MANUSCRIPT CULTURE

CONTEXTUALIZING THE MEDIEVAL MANUSCRIPT

Frontispiece. Leiden, Universiteitsbibliotheek, BPL 14 D, thirteenth century. Photo by Giulio Menna.

LIST OF ILLUSTRATIONS

Various photographs in this book were taken and generously provided by colleagues, credited in the captions where they appear in the book. Images without attribution to a photographer were supplied by libraries or downloaded from their digital repositories. Public domain images are marked as such in the captions and their sources are identified. All other photographs were taken by the author with a Canon Eos 600D camera and a Sigma DC 18–250 mm lens.

PREFACE

As a scholar of medieval book culture I handle manuscripts (handwritten books made before the invention of print) several times per week. I cannot help but speed up as I make my way to the Special Collections Library. What will the object I called up from the vault look like? What might it let me discover about its past? As soon as I touch the manuscript it attacks the senses: its pages are "velvety" to the touch, they sound crackly and tired when I turn them, and they present a musky scent that is unbeatable if you like old books. As the manuscript starts acclimatizing to the warmer and moister air outside the vault, the tips of the pages begin to curl—although not usually as much as the ninth-century manuscript on the cover of this book—as if to encourage me to keep going. I find the whole experience simply magical, each and every time.

It is this feeling of magic and excitement that I am trying to convey in the book you are holding. This volume is intended for those who want to learn about medieval manuscripts and are new to the topic, or perhaps have some prior knowledge. In fact, I designed it to serve three different audiences. First and foremost, it is intended as an introductory tool for undergraduate courses in such disciplines as History, English, Medieval Studies, and, of course, Book History. I taught many such courses during my five-year tenure at the University of Victoria, Canada (2005–2010), and I wished a general introduction like this had been around to accompany the more specialized books I generally used. Graduate students, too, can benefit from this book, even if they already know the feel and scent of a manuscript. It introduces them to a wide array of real-world case studies, which adds depth to existing knowledge and expands it further. Finally, the book also reaches out to non-experts outside academia, a growing—and most rewarding—audience for research undertaken by academics.

Because these primary audiences are non-specialists, I have opted for a casual narrative, avoided jargon where possible (beyond the essential terms introduced in the Introduction), and refrained from using footnotes unless truly necessary: they are added only to reference quotations, online resources (usually image databases), and scholarly studies if the text borrows directly from them. To open avenues of further research, a list of relevant literature is provided at the end of this volume. Many of these titles have appeared on the reading lists of my manuscript courses and have proven to be both useful and accessible.

The contents of this book first appeared on my blog, medievalbooks.nl, which I started in 2014 with this book in mind. The original posts have been significantly modified. Certain case studies had to be dropped because the accompanying images could not be reproduced in print (libraries often charge substantial fees for this). Moreover, new cases were introduced where it helped to clarify the discussion. For the same reason, a number of case studies were contextualized differently. For pedagogical reasons, I have kept the brevity and the thematic approach of the original posts intact rather than blending them into larger chapters. While this would have produced a more traditional book format, I think non-expert readers, especially students, are helped by a presentation in shorter chapters fitted within thematic clusters. This thematic engagement with the material is enhanced by the bibliography at the back, which provides recommended literature for each section.

The transition from digital to print medium would not have been possible without Jenneka Janzen (Leiden University), who suggested numerous changes to the original text, identified many of the replacement images, and copy-edited the chapters. I am grateful to Leiden University's Faculty of Humanities, my previous employer, for the grant that made it possible for her to support me this way. I also wish to thank Anna Käyhkö (Helsinki), Jenny Weston (Victoria, BC, Canada), and especially Giulio Menna (Leiden) for letting me use their photographs. I am also indebted to Leiden University Library, who allowed me to freely photograph and publish anything I wanted from their manuscript collections. I was also able to use my own images taken in Erfgoed Leiden en Omstreken (Heritage Leiden and Region); Bibliotheca Thysiana, Leiden; and Regionaal Historisch Centrum Limburg (Limburg Regional Historical Center), Maastricht. I owe a debt of gratitude to Ed van der Vlist (curator of medieval manuscripts at the Royal Library, The Hague) and Nicolas Bell (librarian at Trinity College, Cambridge) for providing images from their respective manuscript collections for free and without reproduction fees. Their generosity enabled the inclusion of several chapters.

Finally, this book could not have been produced without institutions that have placed their digital image repositories in the public domain. I have included such materials from the online image repositories of the Beinecke Rare Book and Manuscript Library, Yale University; Boston Public Library; the British Library's Catalogue of Illuminated Manuscripts; Houghton Library, Harvard University; Metropolitan Museum of Art, New York; National Archive, The Hague; University of Pennsylvania Libraries, Philadelphia; and Walters Art Museum, Baltimore. Their belief in making manuscripts digitally accessible for free enabled me to illustrate this publication—which carries almost 130 images—at no cost. This book celebrates these and other forward-thinking institutions that so generously offer their digital photographs to be enjoyed, studied, and published without restrictions.

Vancouver, August 27, 2018

ABBREVIATIONS

BL	British Library
BPL	Bibliotheca Publica Latina
BUR	Burmannus
KB	Koninklijke Bibliotheek
KBR	Koninklijke Bibliotheek van België/Bibliothèque royale de Belgique
LTK	Letterkunde
SCA	Scaliger
UB	Universiteitsbibliotheek
VLF	Vossianus Latinus Folio
VLO	Vossianus Latinus Octavo
VLQ	Vossianus Latinus Quarto

GENERAL INTRODUCTION

EXO

Fugientibusq; egiptijs occurrerunt a-
que: ꝛ inuoluit eos dñs ĩ medijs flu-
ctib3. Reuerseq; sunt aque: ꝛ operuerũt
currus et equites cũcti exercitus phara-
onis·qui sequẽtes ingressi fuerãt mare: nec unus quidẽ supfuit ex eis. Filij
autẽ isrl̃· pgrexerũt p mediũ sicci mari?:
ꝛ aque eis erãt quasi pro muro·a dex-
tris et a sinistris. Liberauitq; dominꝰ
ĩ die illo isrl̃ de manu egiptiorũ: ꝛ vide-
runt egiptios mortuos sup litus maris: ꝛ manũ magnã quam exercuerat
dñs cõtra eos. Timuitq; pp̃ls dñm: et
crediderũt dño· ꝛ moysi suo eiꝰ. XV
Tunc cecinit moyses ꝛ filij isrl̃· car-
men hoc dño: et dixerũt. Cante-
mus domino. Gloriose eni magnifi-
catus est: equũ et ascensorem deiecit in
mare. Fortitudo mea ꝛ laus mea dominꝰ: ꝛ factus est michi in salutẽ. Iste
deus meus et glorificabo eũ·deus patris mei: ꝛ exaltabo eũ. Dominꝰ quasi
uir pugnator· omĩpotens nomen eiꝰ:
currus pharaonis·et exercitũ eius pie-
cit ĩ mare. Electi principes eiꝰ submersi sunt ĩ mari rubro: abissi operuerũt
eos: descenderũt in pfundũ quasi lapis.
Dextera tua dñe magnificata ẽ in fortitudine: dextera tua dñe pcussit inimi-
cum: et ĩ multitudine glorie tue depo-
suisti adũsarios meos. Misisti iram
tuã· que deuorauit eos sicut stipulã:
et in spiritu furoris tui cõgregate sunt
aque. Stetit unda fluens: congregate
sũt abissi in medio mari. Dixit inimi-
cus. Persequar ꝛ cõprehendã: diuidã
spolia: implebit aĩa mea. Euaginabo
gladiũ meũ: interficiet eos manꝰ mea.
Flauit spiritꝰ tuꝰ· ꝛ operuit eos mare:
submersi sũt quasi plũbũ ĩ aquis ve-
hemẽtib3. Quis similis tui ĩ fortib3 dñe?
Quis similis tui magnificꝰ ĩ sanctitate:
terribilis atq; laudabilis· ꝛ faciẽs mirabilia? Extendisti manũ tuã: ꝛ deuorauit eos terra. Dux fuisti in misericordia
tua: pp̃lo quẽ redemisti. Et portasti eũ
ĩn fortitudine tua: ad habitaculũ san-
ctũ tuũ. Ascenderũt pp̃li ꝛ irati sũt: dolo-
res obtinuerũt habitatores philistijm.
Tunc cõturbati sunt principes edom:
robustos moab obtinuit tremor: ob-
riguerũt omẽs habitatores chanaan.
Irruat super eos formido et pauor in
magnitudine brachij tui. Fiant im-
mobiles quasi lapis· donec ptrãseat
pp̃ls tuus dñe: donec pertranseat populus tuꝰ iste quẽ possedisti. Introduces eos·et plantabis in monte heredi-
tatis tue: firmissimo habitaclo tuo qđ
operatus es domine. Sanctuarium
tuũ domine: qđ firmauerũt manꝰ tue.
Dñs regnabit in eternum ꝛ ultra. In-
gressus ẽ eni eques pharao cũ currib3
et equitib3 eius in mare: ꝛ reduxit sup
eos dominꝰ aquas maris. Filij autẽ
isrl̃ ambulauerũt p siccũ: in medio eiꝰ.
Sumpsit ergo maria pphetissa· soror
aaron· timpanũ ĩ manu sua: egresseq;
sunt omẽs mulieres post eã cũ timpa-
nis et choris: quibus pcinebat dicẽs.
Cantemꝰ dño. Gloriose eni magnifi-
catus est: equũ et ascensorẽ eius deiecit
in mare. Tulit autẽ moyses isrl̃ de mari rubro: ꝛ egressi sunt in desertum sur.
Ambulaueruntq; trib3 dieb3 per solitu-
dinẽ: et nõ inueniebãt aquã. Et uene-
runt in marath: nec poterant bibere a-
quas de marath· eo q essent amare.
Unde ꝛ congruũ loco nomẽ imposu-
it: uocans illũ marath id ẽ amaritu-
dinẽ. Et murmurauit pp̃ls cõtra moy-
sen dicẽs. Quid bibemꝰ? At ille clama-
uit ad dñm. Qui ostendit ei lignum:
qđ cũ misisset ĩ aquas· in dulcedinem

Figure 1. Leaf from Gutenberg Bible, ca. 1455. Boston, Public Library, Rare Bks Q.450.5 Folio. Public domain. Source: www.digitalcommonwealth.org.

Books Before Print

It is easy to forget, but there were books long before Johannes Gutenberg started printing them in the middle of the fifteenth century. Books before print—commonly called "manuscripts" or, fancier, "codices"—were first made in the Latin West during the fourth century CE, when they started to replace the revered roll, a process that took until well into the fifth century. This transition was prompted by the growing length of texts, resulting from the increasing popularity of Christianity, a religion built on long stories and lengthy discussions. So when in ca. 1455 Gutenberg's Bible rolled off Europe's first printing press (a craftily converted wine press) the "new" object he produced had actually been around, in handwritten form, for over a thousand years.

In fact, if we look closely at Gutenberg's printed bible (Figure 1), we have to conclude that it looks almost *exactly* like the handwritten bibles produced by scribes in his vicinity, especially the large lectern bibles. As a businessman, Gutenberg knew not to change the look of books and potentially upset his clientele of readers. And so he adopted the manuscript's relative dimensions (the width of the page being 70 per cent of its height), layout (two columns), materials (like scribes, Gutenberg used both parchment and paper), reading aids (chapter titles, running titles at the tops of pages), and even the shape of handwritten letters: his printed *textura* was a direct copy of the written version used by scribes. In this early period of print the similarity to the handwritten book was so profound that one wonders if readers could actually see the difference, or if they even cared. The only real novelty, using moving type instead of a quill to produce letters, is difficult to observe unless you have an expert eye.

This book is devoted to the millennium of the quill, the era of the ancestor of the printed book, and, specifically, the manuscript (from the Latin *manu scripta*, "written by hand"). Most chapters tap into what is arguably the most notable feature of manuscripts: their individuality. While printers, producing several hundred copies at the same time, targeted a generic audience rather than a specific person, medieval scribes usually knew who would ultimately read the books they were making. After all, the manuscript was either produced for the scribe himself (for personal use), for the institution he belonged to (in many cases a monastery), or for someone who purchased his services commercially (after the year 1200 books were increasingly copied for profit), in which case the reader was a client and often known by name.

This familiarity between scribe and reader turns out to be a major factor in the physical appearance the manuscript ultimately received, as this book shows. Significant time and resources were required for its creation: a production time of half a year was not uncommon and the book could cost as much as a car does today.

This implies that medieval scribes would have, for the most part, produced a book that reflected the wishes of the person who would use the object; the manuscript's first user, that is, for even in the Middle Ages there was a lively trade in second-hand books (see Chapter 29). When the scribe produced a book for personal use, if he had the resources and materials, he was able to construct an object that reflected his own preferences and needs in every respect: from writing support (paper or parchment), type of script, and page layout, to decoration and type of bookbinding. Members of religious houses (monks and nuns) or other institutions (city or royal administrations) usually produced manuscripts that reflected the customs or regulations of their institutions, so here too the appearance of the manuscript is closely connected to its intended reader. Paying customers, the final major group of book recipients, were most persistent about the features of their books. We cannot blame them, for they paid a lot of money to get exactly what they wished. The arrangements they made with hired scribes were even put down in contracts.

It is important to realize (indeed, it is the premise of this book) that medieval manuscripts were not designed randomly, but that their features reflect how the original reader wanted his or her text "packaged" materially. To put it differently, material features are "cultural residue," tangible traces of the rationale behind the manuscript's intended use.[1] For example, small manuscripts may reflect a need for portability, and those with running titles point to a need for speedy access to information. Further, large margins point to a need to add notes to the page, and luxurious decoration suggests conspicuous consumption. Thus, material traits not only speak to the appearance of books before print, they also act as a conduit to medieval reading culture, and indeed more broadly to communication before the coming of print. It is for this reason, the revealing nature of the material book, that the physicality of the manuscript is given the central place in this publication: each chapter is rooted in observations related to material features, from parchment holes and the shape of book clasps to letter styles and the size of margins.

What is a Manuscript?

There have already been various references to "the manuscript," and many more are to follow. However, exactly what *is* a manuscript? The short answer to this query is simple: it was the first version of a book that the world saw. Yet this somewhat vague answer generates new questions: what is a book? How do we define it? And when was it born? To put the main object of this book into perspective, it is useful that we address these seemingly simple questions in more detail.

1 Kwakkel, "Decoding the Material Book."

A good exercise for the purpose of defining the object studied in this publication is putting the following query before Google: "What is the oldest book in the world?" We are immediately provided with a broad range of possible answers. Some are flawed. First of all, many websites confuse "book" with "text." The website Answers.com reports: "the oldest book in the world is the Bible." Still, a book and a text are actually very different things: like a glass filled with milk, content and container are not one and the same. A book contains a text, carries it, and gives it shape, but it is not its equivalent. Equally incorrect are websites whose claims are based on the premise that a book is a printed object. Thus, the oldest book in the world must surely be the Gutenberg Bible (the oldest printed book in the West, from ca. 1455) or the Buddhist Diamond Sutra (the oldest printed book in the East, from ca. 868). No, it's clearly neither of these.

More carefully phrased answers can be equally confusing, even when provided by reputable institutions. When the British Library purchased the St. Cuthbert Gospel, the seventh-century copy of the Gospel of John found in St. Cuthbert's coffin when it was opened in 1104, both the press release of the library and newspapers claimed this was "the oldest European book to survive."[2] The rationale behind this claim is that this is the oldest book to survive *in its original binding*, as the press release explains. While this nuance is welcome, the verdict feels forced. The thing is, many medieval books were designed and used without a binding, which raises the question of whether the binding should even be made part and parcel of the conceptual "book." Notably, if bindings are taken out of play there are other books older than the St. Cuthbert Gospel, such as the sixth-century illustrated *herbarium* (a text about herbs) at Leiden University Library, which includes texts by Pseudo-Apuleius (VLQ 9).

The question of what, precisely, constitutes a "book" also lies at the heart of another prominent result in our Google search. The oldest book in the world is an object that consists of six bound sheets of twenty-four-carat gold written in a lost Etruscan language in around 600 BCE. The sheets are (at my time of writing) thought to make up the oldest such work of multiple joined pages, and are now housed in Bulgaria's National History Museum in Sofia. The following assessment of the museum is significant: similar sheets are scattered throughout the world, but those are not linked together.[3] A book, the underlying premise suggests, is an

2 See the press release, "British Library acquires the St Cuthbert Gospel—the earliest intact European book," British Library Press Office, www.bl.uk/press-releases/2012/april/british-library-acquires-the-st-cuthbert-gospel--the-earliest-intact-european-book. See also, for example, this news article: Kennedy, "British Library seeks £9m to buy oldest book in Europe," *The Guardian* online, www.theguardian.com/books/2011/jul/14/british-library-seeks-buy-oldest-book.

3 "Unique book goes on display," *BBC News*, May 26, 2003, http://news.bbc.co.uk/go/pr/fr/-/2/hi/europe/2939362.stm.

object that consists of multiple leaves bound together. So far, so good: we have started our initial descent towards our answer.

Unfortunately, the shiny Etruscan object cannot be called "the oldest book in the world." The reason is that it consists of *unfolded* single sheets (golden plates, actually), which are held together by two rings. However, the codex (the book before print and therefore the oldest type of real book in the world) is not an object that merely consists of a bunch of leaves. It is, by contrast and definition, built from double-leaves: sheets that are folded and set together into gatherings or "quires." Looking for the oldest book, then, we should look among objects made from bendy, foldable writing material, such as papyrus (made from the papyrus plant), parchment (animal skin), and paper. Of these three writing supports, papyrus is the oldest. Papyrus was used in four formats for different purposes:

i. Unfolded sheets, used for notes and documentary purposes
ii. Rolls
iii. Book-like objects made up from groups of unfolded single sheets ("singletons")
iv. Regular books made from quires ("codices").[4]

The oldest book must be made of papyrus, since it is the oldest material and has been used for folded leaves. Which papyrus book could it be, however? Our search is made easier by the fact that very few ancient papyrus books survive. There are some specimens from western Europe dating to the seventh or eighth century CE, such as a codex made at Luxeuil or Lyon that is now divided between the Bibliothèque national de France in Paris (lat. 11641) and the Bibliothèque de Genèva (MS lat. 16).[5] As we have seen, there are older surviving parchment examples, so these western papyrus codices do not get the award for oldest book in the world.

Problematically, the really old specimens, some made over four millennia ago, are fragments from once-complete sheets (Figure 2). It is their fragmentary nature that constitutes the last—killer—hurdle on our way to finding the oldest surviving book. From a papyrus fragment we cannot, unfortunately, deduce—at least as far as I know—if it originally belonged to an unfolded (single) leaf or a folded (double) sheet. While catalogues might tell us that a papyrus fragment was part of a codex, in other words, that it belonged to a book made from quires, we cannot know for sure if this was the case. Consequently, unless it announces itself with sheets featuring sharp centre folds, the oldest book in the world will remain

---

4 Johnson, *Bookrolls and Scribes* (rolls); Mudridge, *Copying Early Christian Texts*, 39–42 (codices).

5 Genèva lat. 16 and Paris lat. 11641 have both been digitized by the Virtual Manuscript Library of Switzerland (e-codices), and can be found at www.e-codices.unifr.ch/en/bge/lat0016 and www.e-codices.unifr.ch/fr/list/one/bnf/lat11641.

Figure 2. Ancient papyrus fragment, ca. 2030–1640 BCE. New York, The Metropolitan Museum of Art, Papyrus 09.180.535, recto. CC0 1.0 Universal. Source: www.metmuseum.org.

hidden in its vault, deprived of its prize. In other words, while the nature of the manuscript book can be defined quite precisely, when the concept of the book was born remains unknown.

Producing the Medieval Book

Even with its origins sometimes obscured during centuries gone by, the manuscript is a great topic of study. The object never bores because it can be explored from many different angles. Before doing so, however, it makes sense to take a look over the shoulder of the scribe to see how the book before print was made (for convenience, scribes are identified as "he" in this book, and while women also made books, the large majority of scribes were men). Without knowing how manuscripts were made, it will be hard to understand the case studies presented in the chapters. The production process of handwritten books is quite different from that of its successor, the printed book: different tools were used, and manuscript production also included stages not encountered in the era of print, such as pricking and ruling each page. The following section concisely describes the various stages in a manuscript's production—from first conception by the scribe to

Figure 3. Hole in parchment with traces of hair, ca. 1100. Leiden, UB, BUR Q 1, fol. 97v. Photo by the author.

the post-production finishing touches by the reader—while highlighting common terminology in bold typeface.[6]

Writing Support: Parchment and Paper

For much of the Middle Ages—that is, up to ca. 1300—animals were the main ingredient of a book. What was frolicking in the meadow in May could in June become a bifolium in a bible. The skin of animals (usually calf, goat, or sheep) was turned into **parchment** through a tedious (and smelly) process, after which the treated material was cut or folded into sheets. Remaining hair, missed by the crescent-shaped cleaning knife (***lunellum***) of the parchment-maker, sometimes reminds us of the manuscript's former life (see Figure 3).

The quality of parchment sheets varied considerably: like people today, not all medieval creatures had perfect skin. Some cows loved to scratch their itch by rubbing against trees, while others were particularly prone to insect bites. We

6 This part of the General Introduction borrows from *Quill: Books Before Print* (www.bookandbyte.org/quill) which I built in 2013–2014 in collaboration with Giulio Menna (photography). The text was significantly modified for inclusion in this General Introduction.

encounter these defects as we read Jerome or Chaucer: they appear on the page as tiny holes, gaps, and dark patches (see the images in Chapter 31). Parchment quality was also affected by how well the scribe prepared the surface: the best sheets were sanded just long enough and have a deep off-white colour, perhaps with just a touch of yellow. They feel like velvet and make a slight rustling sound when the page is turned—whispers teasing the impatient reader.

When parchment was in short supply, for example, because the monastery ran out of animals, there were various solutions available to the scribe. The first was recycling: the scribe turned to a book that was no longer in use and scraped the text off its pages, after which he simply reapplied text of his own. Such recycling resulted in a **palimpsest**, a manuscript that held a removed **lower text** and a newer **upper text**. It was not a perfect solution. The ink of the reapplied text often did not stick to the page very well. Moreover, the older reading often still peeks through (see Figure 127 at p. 246). Though uncommon, palimpsests are important artifacts, especially those from the earlier Middle Ages: underneath the old text an even older work is buried. There are cases in which the lower text only survives in one overwritten copy. With today's digital photography the lower text can sometimes be rendered visible again, which makes studying these books like digging for treasure.

There was another option when the scribe was in need of alternative writing support: he could turn to the scraps that were thrown in the bin during the production of parchment sheets. When the scribe cut sheets out of the processed animal hide, he would normally use the best, central, part of the skin; the area I like to call the **prime cut**. This meant steering clear of the skin's outer rim, because this region was usually stretched thin and translucent, and the ink did not hold very well there. These **offcuts** can be easily recognized by their defects, such as translucency and uneven pages (Figure 4 and Figure 94 at p. 182). Small books were made from these scraps, usually standing no taller than 160 mm, but the material was particularly popular for note-taking (see Chapter 22).[7]

In the twelfth century a new writing support arrived in Europe: **paper**. Originally imported from the Arabic world by merchants, from the second half of the twelfth century paper was also produced in European mills, first in Italy and Spain (twelfth century), then in France (fourteenth century), and finally in England and Germanic countries (fifteenth century). The new material was initially used exclusively for documentary purposes, such as account books and letters, and not for literature. In a remarkable shift of scribal practices, in the fourteenth century scribes across Europe began to use paper for manuscripts. Conservative scribes,

7 Kwakkel, "Classics on Scraps."

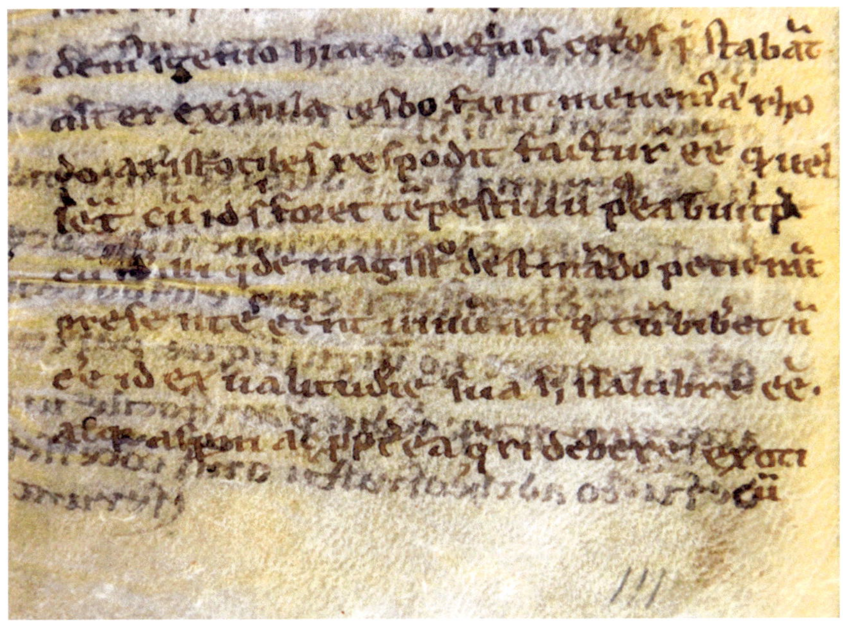

Figure 4. Translucent leaf made from parchment offcut, ca. 1150–1200. Leiden, UB, BPL 1925, fol. 111r. Photo by the author.

especially monks, ignored the new material during the first century after its introduction, while more liberal book-makers, especially those who wanted to economize, embraced it immediately. Paper became a more affordable (and sometimes more plentiful) alternative to parchment. Although paper made the production of manuscripts somewhat cheaper, handwritten books still remained costly. As the book historian Malcolm B. Parkes put it, "Books were always a luxury in the Middle Ages, but the production of cheaper books meant they could become a luxury for poorer people."[8]

If you look carefully at a medieval page that is made of paper you might notice a shape hidden inside, pressed right into the paper, such as the head of an ox, a bell, or a jester. These hidden "drawings," which show themselves when you hold a light behind the page, are called **watermarks** (Figure 5).

They are a by-product of the paper production process. The papermaker used a screen to scoop up the cloth mush from which paper was made. Water was pushed through the screen, with the mush on top, and drained out of a roster or sift below, leaving behind the pulpy layer that would be dried to form a sheet of paper. Stitched

8 Parkes, "Literacy," p. 564.

Figure 5. Watermark, fifteenth century. Leiden, UB, BPL 304, fol. 142v. Photo by Giulio Menna.

to this screen was a figure made of thin metal strings. Each papermaker had his own "logo" with which he branded his product. Because the screen was replaced every few years and the figures or logos were handmade, the watermarks from a single mill vary slightly over time. Today's databases of these unique watermarks, identifying which logos belonged to which paper mill at specific dates, makes them a handy tool for dating medieval paper manuscripts.

Quires and Bifolia

The **quire** is the building block of the manuscript. Quires were produced from folded sheets called **double-leaves** or **bifolia** (singular **bifolium**). The bifolium consists of two **folia** (singular **folium**), although in Anglo-American scholarship the term **folios** (singular **folio**) is also in common use. Each folium has two pages, one on the front of the leaf (**recto**) and one on the back (**verso**). When you look at the top or bottom of a manuscript you can easily spot the individual quires, which are all nestled up inside the binding (Figure 6). A medieval book could consist of as many as twenty of these gatherings, although many contain fewer than ten. The bifolia that made up a quire were cut out of the processed hide; depending on the size of the manuscript, a skin produced one, two, or even three bifolia. Alternatively, the hide could be folded, depending on the planned dimensions of the manuscript,

Figure 6. Quires visible at tail of manuscript, fourteenth century. Leiden, UB, VLF 33. Photo by Giulio Menna.

either once (producing a **folio** format manuscript), twice (**quarto**), or three times (**octavo**). Unlike with print, these three denote the **natural size** of the parchment sheet (i.e., how many bifolia were taken out of the skin), not how large the book is. Because of the considerable variation in the dimensions of skins, a parchment sheet in natural octavo could be taller than its counterpart in natural quarto.

Looking closely at the binding of the book, each bifolium appears to embrace its neighbour, bonding together to produce a strong quire. How many bifolia were used for a quire depended on different factors, including the moment and location of production. Copyists in twelfth-century England, for example, frequently opted for six double-leaves, while their continental counterparts almost never did: they usually favoured four. Some late-medieval manuscripts contained quires with a very high number of bifolia. The small-sized Paris Bibles of the thirteenth century, which were made from extremely thin parchment, contained up to eighteen bifolia simply because this would ensure the quire had a somewhat regular thickness, which was necessary for a cohesive and strong binding. Even thicker quires of twenty-four leaves are met in account books produced by chancery clerks, and in the literary manuscripts that they sometimes copied for payment.

To make sure that each finished book ended up with all quires in the correct order, after about 1300 the scribe often wrote the first word or two of the next quire at the bottom of the previous quire's last page (**catchwords**). If the catchword at the end of quire 1 matched the first words of quire 2, the pair was put in the correct sequence, and was therefore ready for binding. If not, the binder had to search his desk for the correct quire. Scribes further helped binders by adding **quire signatures**. Up to around 1300 these were simply Roman numerals placed in the lower margin of the last page of the quire. In the fourteenth century a different system emerged whereby each bifolium was given a letter and a number (a1, a2, a3, a4, b1, b2, b3, b4, etc.) at the bottom of the page at recto. These numbers identified the location of each double-leaf in the manuscript (the quire signature in the fourth bifolium was sometimes a cross). Despite these efforts, binders would sometimes bind quires in the wrong order anyway.

Preparing the Page

Before a scribe could begin to fill the quires with text, the **layout** of the page needed to be designed. Preparing the page was a labour-intensive process, especially when the scribe had opted for a complex layout with multiple columns. It was important to get it right, however, as a messy layout would produce a messy book. How a page was designed depended on a variety of factors, including the number of required text columns, the space left blank for decoration, and the presence of marginal commentary and reading aids (more about these in a moment). The most basic layout consisted of a single column of text. These are frequently encountered in books of hours, for example, because these are usually smaller books.

The design materialized when the scribe started to prepare the sheets. Every single word on the page was written on a ruled line, like we usually do today. To produce these lines, the scribe pricked tiny holes in the outer margins (**pricking**), as well as in the upper and lower margins. Lines were then drawn between these holes (**ruling**), usually with the help of a straightedge: the horizontal ruling guided the text lines, while the vertical ruling indicated where each line began and ended (Figure 7).

Until the early twelfth century the ruling was done by pressing down on the parchment with a sharp object, producing a "furrow," and on the other side of the folium a "ridge," that would guide the scribe's pen. This is called ruling in **dry point**. In the first half of the twelfth century this method was replaced by drawing lines with a piece of lead, which left more visible traces on the surface of the page (ruling in **plummet**, as seen in Figure 7). From the fourteenth century the ruling was also executed with ink, usually in brown or black, but sometimes in colours like red or purple.

Writing the Text

Skins were prepared, bifolia were cut, pens were sharpened, and inkpots were filled. All these activities would be in vain were it not for the single event that

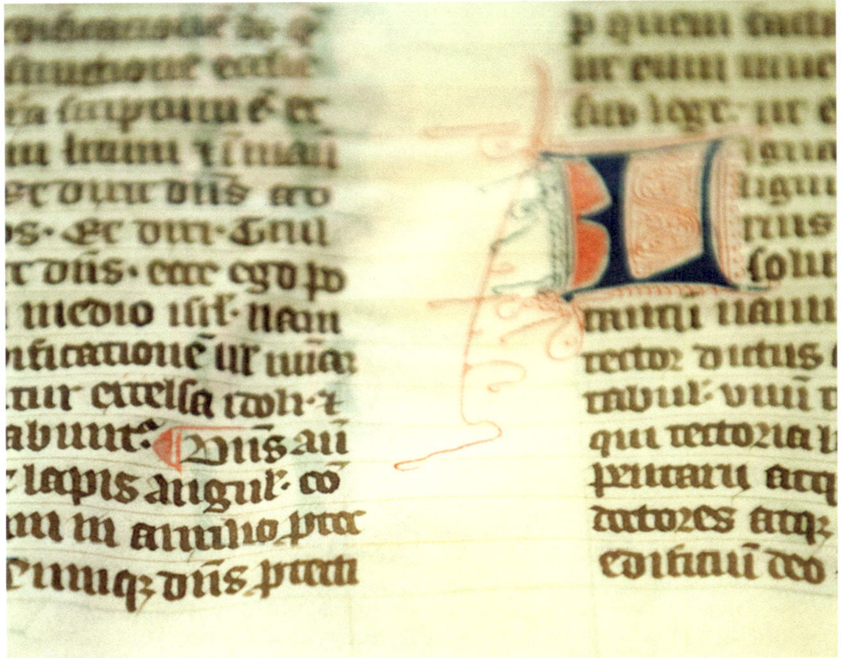

Figure 7. Horizontal and vertical ruling, pencil, fourteenth century. Leiden, UB, VLF 5, fol. 15r. Photo by Giulio Menna.

inspired them: writing down the text. Writing a medieval text with a quill is hard work. "Three fingers write, but the whole body toils," the monk Eadberct wrote at the end of a law manuscript he had just finished copying (St. Gall, Stiftsbibliothek, Cod. Sang. 243, p. 254).[9] Because of how the nib was cut throughout much of the Middle Ages, the medieval pen could only move downwards, which meant that letters had to be broken up into multiple pen strokes. (Cursive script, which appeared in the thirteenth century, was written with a thinner pen, which facilitated upward movements as well.) Consequently, writing was a very slow process: depending on the quality of the letter, a bible could take a full year to complete. Having completed their work, scribes sometimes wrote a colophon underneath the last line, for example, stating the year and location of production, or that they deserved a drink (see Figure 37 at p. 66).

9 Cod. Sang. 243 has been digitized by the Virtual Manuscript Library of Switzerland (e-codices), and can be found at www.e-codices.unifr.ch/en/list/one/csg/0243.

Figure 8. German-style Pregothic script, twelfth century. Leiden, UB, BPL 2514: A 19, fol. 1r. Photo by Giulio Menna.

Medieval **script**—the scribe's handwriting—is the material representation of a text. How this text appeared on the page depended entirely on how the scribe operated and on the context of production. If he was inexperienced, or experienced yet hasty, it may be difficult to decipher his handwriting. If he was undisciplined, the wrong words may appear on the page. Yet if he was paid well for a book project, or if it concerned a book that was to be gifted to a benefactor, the scribe often produced excellent handwriting. Two other variables are at play in the execution of the letterforms: where and when the scribe was trained. German scribes, for example, had a very distinct and recognizable way of producing letters (Figure 8), but so did their counterparts in England, Italy (seen in Figure 12 at p. 19), and southern France (seen in Figure 35 at p. 62). Moreover, script developed continuously, which allows experts to date a manuscript, usually within about a quarter of a century from its production. This is especially handy since the title page had not been invented yet; it was introduced by the second generation of printers in the late fifteenth century.

An important feature of medieval text is the presence of **abbreviations**. The modern English language is filled with them (app, maths, TV), but medieval scribes abbreviated far more words, and in much more complex ways. The most

Figure 9. Marginal quotation marks, possibly from the eleventh century, in a ninth-century manuscript. Leiden, UB, SCA 28, fol. 36r. Photo by Giulio Menna.

common abbreviation symbol is the *macron*: a line that represents the letters *n* or *m*. Thus the Latin word *omnia* (all) was usually written as "omia" with a line (called a macron) over the letter *m*. Another popular abbreviation is the 7-shaped symbol for *et* (and). Its predecessor, the ampersand (&), we still use today. The number and type of abbreviations in a medieval text varied; manuscripts with liturgical texts usually have very few abbreviations, but they are abundant in university textbooks.

Another important element of medieval texts is **punctuation**. Much of our modern punctuation was invented by medieval scribes, although the marks used were often different. In the Middle Ages, the period at the end of a sentence, for example, was often expressed by symbols that look like our comma or semicolon. Where the marks were placed was often different too. Medieval quotation marks, for example, were usually placed in the margin and not in the actual text (Figure 9). Moreover, the symbol is repeated over and over again for each line of the quotation: when the symbols stop, the quote is over.

To write down the text and its punctuation, scribes had to constantly adjust the nib of their quill by cutting it into the right shape. A deformed nib would not supply an even flow of ink, which resulted in letters that were not fully formed. To test that the nib was in good shape, scribes scribbled a few swirly lines or short words on a blank leaf, or sometimes even a decorated letter or a drawing (see Figure 39 at p. 70). We usually find these **pen trials** in the back of the book. The most famous pen trial written in Dutch is a poem jotted down by a monk who laments how all birds are building nests, but that he, alas, is not (Oxford, Bodleian Library, MS Bodley 340). It shows that anything goes for a trial.

Aids to the Reader

Having completed the text, the next stage ensured that it could be used efficiently. Medieval scribes recognized that readers may have needed some help finding their way through the book or within the texts it contained. Over time, a number of tools were invented to this end. They proved so useful that we still use many of them today. To make these **reading aids** stand out on the page they were commonly written in a different size script or colour ink than the surrounding text. Red, for example, is an excellent colour for attracting attention. In manuscripts it was used for the **rubric**, from the Latin word *rubor*, meaning "red." Placed at the outset of each chapter, rubrics indicated to the reader what the following chapter was about (see Figure 63 at p. 119). Some were very short and simply stated "about such-and-such," while others were quite elaborate—spoilers, even—which revealed in detail what the reader was about to read. The red ink sets the words apart from the black or brown words of the main text. Moreover, the bright colour on an otherwise dull page (as many medieval pages indeed are) acted as a reading aid: it helped the reader find certain information in an efficient manner as they flipped through the book. If red was not available, scribes would write the chapter titles in a different style of script to make them stand out from the main text.

Most aids, however, owed their effectiveness to the position they took on the page. The most notable reading aid is found in the top margin. Its main purpose was to indicate to the reader where in the book he or she was. These **running titles** have a long history. They are encountered in manuscripts made as early as the sixth century. Early examples merely reveal the given book within the text, stating, for example, "Liber primus" (Book 1). In the textbooks of the new universities of the late twelfth century, running titles became more sophisticated. They would often provide the reader with the full title of the text written on each page. Moreover, the presentation of the running title became smarter as well. It was split up and spread out over both top margins of a book opening: half of the text title on the left page, the other half on the right page. Another early adopter of this clever type of running title was the Paris Bible, a popular tool among preachers on the road (Figure 10). Like students, they needed to find texts and passages quickly to do their work. In the printed Gutenberg Bible these running titles were still added by hand, as seen in Figure 1 at p. 1. There we read "dus" which accompanied "exo" on the facing page; combined, they spelled the title of the second bible book, "Exodus." (Also executed by hand are the red letter T, the blue and red Roman numeral XV, and the red accents in the capitals.)

While running titles told the reader what text was found on a particular page, the **chapter number** narrowed down the contents even further. As

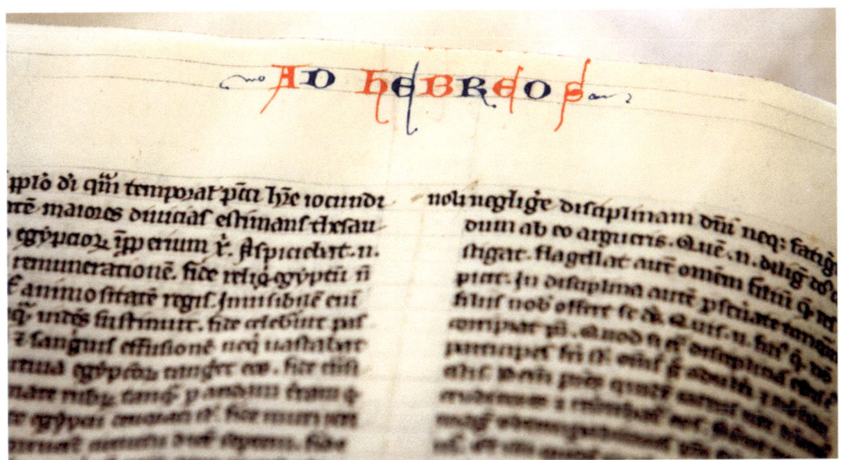

Figure 10. Running title, thirteenth century. Leiden, UB, BPL 14 D, fol. 482v. Photo by Giulio Menna.

with many other reading aids, the practice of numbering chapters goes back to the Carolingian era. They appear to have become standardized much later, however; perhaps as late as the twelfth century. In the thirteenth century, a bible redaction was made in Paris, the already-mentioned Paris Bible, wherein chapter numbers became consistent, which was not the case before. This meant that two individuals, each with their own Paris Bible copy, could refer to Genesis 15 and would be talking about the same part of the text for the first time. Many works used in universities had an additional tool to define the location within the text even more precisely: the **paraph**. Before ca. 1200 this aid indicated the beginning of a new section, a paragraph. At the universities, however, paraphs indicated the beginning and end of a smaller section called the *lectio*, a short text segment that was read aloud by the teacher as the starting point of class discussion.

A final aid is found in the corner of the page: the **page number**. Until the invention of the page number, readers had no means of finding a particular page in the book quickly. The system medieval scribes came up with is slightly different from our modern pagination. Only one side of each leaf was given a number, meaning that medieval foliation referred to not one but two pages. As a result, we have to indicate at what side of the folium a page is found: the front (*recto*) or the back (*verso*). Scribes first used Roman numerals, like the number 34 (xxxiiij) seen in Figure 11; the penciled "36" seen there is modern and includes two flyleaves that were not counted by the medieval scribe.

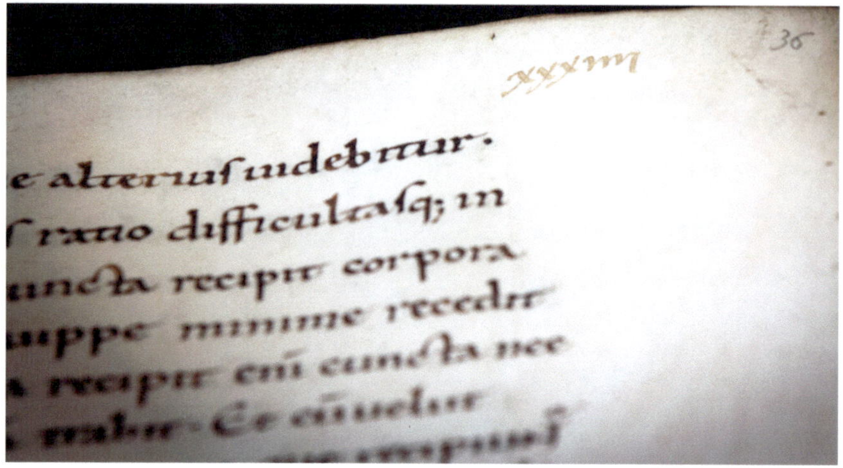

Figure 11. Fifteenth-century foliation in brown ink in an eleventh-century manuscript. Leiden, UB, VLQ 10, fol. 36r. Photo by Giulio Menna.

In the fourteenth century, scribes switched to Arabic numerals, which had come into regular use by then. It is in this century that foliation is more commonly encountered. Scholars at the university, for example, found it easier to reference information on certain pages if they were numbered. The sequential numbering of leaves also allowed for the production of more detailed subject indexes and tables of contents. Finding information was now as easy as one, two, three.

Correcting the Text

Having written the pages and prepared them for use, all that remained was to correct everything that was copied. While a bible may take a year to produce (copying the text and installing the reading aids), a mistake could be made in a split second. Hasty scribes and those who did not understand the text they copied tended to make many mistakes, but even artisans who carefully copied their text were unable to produce a flawless text. Correcting the text—scouting for flaws and fixing them—was, therefore, a key stage in manuscript production. There were various ways to do so: some techniques were subtle and left no traces, while others were more severe interventions which remained visible to the reader.

A common scribal mistake was accidentally skipping over a word or even a full sentence. When the scribe noticed that text was missing he usually inserted the missing words next to or above the line where they were needed. The reader would know when to read them from the context: when something was missing he or she

Figure 12. Annotation with tie mark "I," thirteenth century. Leiden, UB, VLF 3, fol. 14v. Photo by Giulio Menna.

would search nearby for the missing link. However, if the omission encompassed one or more lines it could be challenging to determine at which point they should be read, and the correction may not have fit between the lines of text. In such cases the scribe would reach out to the reader and connect the marginal insertion to its proper location with a symbol called a ***signe de renvoi*** or **tie mark**. These were usually simple symbols, such as crosses, lines, and sequences of dots. In Figure 12 the Roman numeral I connects the main text and the gloss: the number is placed in front of the marginal notation and superscript after the first word on the page. It is not difficult to recognize here the ancestor of our modern footnote.

If the wrong word or sentence was copied, however, eradicating the mistake took considerably more effort. In such cases the scribe resorted to his knife. Dried ink could be scraped off the page with the knife's tip (**erasure**). Once the words were removed, the correct reading was placed in the gap, a process called **writing on erasure**, although mistakes were usually never fully deleted. If you look carefully, you can often still see the outlines of the original text, much like in a palimpsest. Moreover, the surface of the corrected spots usually feels slightly softer, which gives away that the scribe intervened with his knife.

Most flaws encountered when scribes corrected a manuscript could and would be fixed immediately. In some cases, fixing mistakes took time. The monastic scribe may have taken a moment to consult with somebody in his vicinity—a monk whose Latin was better—or look up a difficult word in a glossary. Such time-consuming fixes were usually done after the text was fully copied out. In these cases the

Figure 13. Initial with penwork flourishing, fifteenth century. Leiden, UB, VLQ 4, fol. 78v. Photo by Giulio Menna.

scribe left blank spaces in the text to reinsert the verified words at a later stage. When he finished copying, his text could have been riddled with such ***lacunae***, standing at the ready to receive the new readings. The practice of using lacunae is particularly common in autograph copies, texts copied down by the author that created them. Translators, for example, often needed some time to find equivalents for words that were rare or unusual.

Decorating the Book

After each of the described production steps were completed, it was time for finishing touches. A fair number of medieval books contain some kind of decoration, which was executed by the scribe or by a specialized artisan in his vicinity. There is a considerable variation in the style and quality of decoration; for books produced commercially, the decoration contributed significantly to their cost. At the lower end of the scale is **penwork flourishing**. This style of decoration, introduced in the late twelfth century, typically involves thin lines, usually in red and blue, drawn with a pen rather than a brush (Figure 13).

The swirly lines form lively patterns with unexpected twists and turns, creating miniature mazes in which your eyes easily get lost. If you look carefully you may recognize familiar objects: a tree, the moon, pearls, a smiling face. Some of these playful elements typify local styles, allowing us to tie a manuscript to a specific country, city, or even religious house.

More elaborate than penwork flourishing is the **historiated initial**: a letter inhabited by a scene, usually related to the text that accompanies the initial. In Figure 14, the large P initiates the name Paulus (Paul), the author to whom the following section of the bible was attributed. To mark the beginning of the text, the decorator extended the P and applied colour and gold to it. Contained in the

Figure 14. Historiated initial letter "P" (for *Paulus*, St. Paul), thirteenth century. Leiden, UB, BPL 14 D, fol. 458v. Photo by Giulio Menna.

letter is St. Paul himself, presented as a soldier of Christ. In his hand rests a large sword, his standard attribute in medieval decoration, and his head is clearly bald, which also aids in his identification. Like penwork decoration, historiated initials supported an important function besides beauty: to help the reader navigate to the beginning of a new section of text.

At the upper end of the luxury scale is **illumination**: sophisticated little paintings that include gold. In a process called **gilding**, the decorator would apply an ultra-thin film of flattened gold, which looked not unlike our modern tin foil, to the page. The initial letter in Figure 15 shows that the golden shapes were not always appended directly to the surface of the parchment, but were stretched over little "hills" of plaster. This way the gold would catch the light from different angles, maximizing its dazzling effect. Gilding not only brought an appealing sparkle to the page, it also underscored that the reader paid a handsome amount of money for the book. If the book was a gift, for example to a king or a bishop, this conspicuous element on the page made the gift all the more impressive—and effective, because the bearer of the gift often wanted something in return.

Figure 15. Gilding, fourteenth century. Leiden, UB, VLF 5, fol. 1r. Photo by the author.

Miniatures are often the most elaborate decoration found in a medieval manuscript. They encompass scenes for which a significant amount of space, and expense, was reserved. Some are boxed in by a frame, while others appear to float on the page. Their size, quality, and level of detail can vary widely. Books of hours normally contain at least one full-page miniature, and often several. Some of these were mass-produced and could be picked out by a client as he ordered the book. More common are smaller miniatures of half a page or less (see Figure 19 at p. 29). These were normally added after the text was copied: the scribe would bring his completed quire to the decorator, who would subsequently work his magic.

Binding

The very last step in the production of a medieval manuscript was **binding** the quires together (if the reader opted to do so, because it appears that some manuscripts remained unbound, at least for some period of their lives, as **booklets**). If the book was made commercially, the client brought the completed quires to a binder to review the available options. The cheapest possibility was the **limp binding** (Figure 16). Its most notable feature is the absence of wooden cover boards, which explains its name. Instead, limp bindings are mere sheets or layers of plain parchment wrapped around the quires without the protective

Figure 16. Limp binding, fifteenth century. Leiden, UB, BPL 2483. Photo by the author.

support of these boards, commonly made of oak. Manuscripts in limp bindings can be compared to today's paperbacks.

The quires in these bindings—usually a small number—are attached to the outer parchment at the spine with thread, which is often visible on the outside. A limp binding resulted in a lighter manuscript, which made it easier to transport. This type of binding also decreased the cost, given that wood and fine leather coverings were not needed, and that the binding process was less time-consuming. This is probably why this type of bookbinding was so popular among medieval students.

Many medieval bindings, however, made use of **wooden boards**, placed on the front and back to protect the stack of quires, as we see in hardcover books today. The quires were then stitched to thin leather thongs or ropes made of plant fibre, which were pushed through channels drilled through the edges or tops of the boards.

Figure 17. Bookbinding without its leather cover, fifteenth century. London, Wellcome Institute, Archives and Manuscripts, WMS 5262. CC BY 4.0. Source: www.wellcomelibrary.org/collections/digital-collections.

The straps were fixed into the wood with pegs or wedges, as seen in Figure 17 (note the white leather thongs to which the quires are stitched). This method produced a surprisingly firm binding—although a heavy one—that lasted for centuries. Giant Bibles, which can stand at half a metre tall, can weigh as much as twenty-five kilos: today they might require two library staff members to carry the manuscript to your table.

Medieval books are a joy to look at even when they are closed. High-end bindings in the later Middle Ages had **blind-tooled** decoration stamped in the leather (see Figure 41 at p. 74). The motifs used in this type of decoration can sometimes help us relate a binding to a certain atelier or city. Some even tell us who the binder was. "Godefridus me fecit" (Geoffrey made me), says a binding produced by Godefridus de Block, a fourteenth-century binder in Brussels (now Brussels, KBR, 2877–78). Moreover, various shiny add-ons could be attached to the covers. The most pronounced of these are called **bosses**, which are metal studs attached to the boards; they held the surface of the covers off the lectern or bookshelf to prevent damage to the expensive leather. Binders tended to protect the corners of the book, and also placed "feet" at the bottom edges of the cover, which protected it from damage when placed on a shelf or lectern (Figure 46 at p. 83). The most common binding furniture are **clasps**, interlocking pieces of metal that kept the book closed (Figure 44 at p. 80). These were especially needed for parchment manuscripts because, unlike paper, parchment has a tendency to expand and curl, which can push the book open. A clasp secured the book closed when not in use, protecting the text inside. Lastly, and very rare, are **treasure bindings** which feature precious metals and gems, used to cover books that needed to look handsome and rich, such as gifts to a royal or a gospel book used for altar display.

Post-Production Activities

Users often modified manuscripts post-production, bringing them even further in tune with their specific needs. They added **bookmarks**, for example, to guide them to the beginning of a favourite chapter or significant section of the book (see Chapter 16). Sometimes flowers or leaves were used as makeshift bookmarks. More permanent and secure, however, are bookmarks that were attached to, or even part of, the page (Figure 73 at p. 136). Some bookmarks are fragments of manuscripts later readers deemed redundant, from which they were cut as a form of recycling. Whatever form they take, bookmarks are important to book and literary historians because they show which passages were deemed important by book owners, even though it is usually difficult to identify the person who expressed his or her interests with these add-ons.

While the bookmark guided the reader to an important chapter or text, the ***nota* sign** marked a significant passage or sentence on the page. From time to time readers noticed something in the text worth highlighting. In such cases they wrote the Latin "nota" in the margin. While some of these *nota* signs may have served as a reminder to cross-check something, others command a more generic "take note!" to the reader. The sign is not written like a normal word; rather, its four letters are reshuffled and stretched so as to form a variety of unique symbols. This was perhaps done to distinguish a reader's own chosen passages from those marked by the book's other users, such as his brethren in the monastery.

The ***manicula*** (Latin for "little hand") was another means to do so; these signs are, generally speaking, drawings of little hands with pointing fingers. As with *nota* signs, the execution of *maniculae* varies considerably (see Chapter 15). Readers may have had their own unique design to distinguish their hands from those of other readers. The hands are sometimes accompanied by short notes, which the reader may have written in response to the text. As with bookmarks and *nota* signs, *maniculae* show us what information was deemed important or relevant to people long ago. In that sense they lend a helping hand to the book historian as much as they once did to the medieval reader.

While we are taught not to write in our books, medieval readers had no problem writing in the margins, which they usually did with regular ink or, exceptionally, with a piece of lead. In fact, the majority of manuscripts contain some sort of marginal additions added by later readers. Some of these **glosses**, which clarify words or phrases, add alternative interpretations, or "dialogue" with the main text, are extensive. If a scribe knew the reader would add such substantial marginal glosses,

Figure 18. Detail from heavily annotated page, ninth century. Leiden, UB, VLQ 18, fol. 2r. Photo by the author.

he could opt to reduce the **textblock**, the area of the page containing writing, thus effectively extending the margins. Such marginal glosses are usually written in a smaller script (Figure 18).

More extensive notes were sometimes written on tiny paper or parchment slips, or ***schedulae*** (strips) as they were called in medieval documents. These were made of the bits and pieces cut off the edges of a skin to make it into a bifolium (as described previously on p. 10). Students are known to have used them to take down notes in the classroom or when they were studying a text at home (for an in-depth discussion of *schedulae*, see Chapter 23). Few of them survive today. Not only were they easily lost, but many of them were actually thrown out, a fate usually shared by our modern day "sticky notes." In some manuscripts they survive simply because they were tucked between the pages and forgotten.

This Book

The central focus of this book is the materiality of manuscripts and what it teaches us about the culture of producing and reading books in the age before print. This publication not only orbits around the material features of manuscripts, but it also discusses the motivations behind their inclusion. While the person or team that made the manuscript could potentially cycle through each of the production stages, in practice they often skipped one or more, as the chapters which follow illustrate. Scribes did so for good reason and this book will delve into those reasons as well.

As explained in the preface, this book aims to provide an introduction to manuscript studies to those who have little or no knowledge of medieval manuscripts. The format chosen for this book leans heavily on providing short and well-illustrated narratives based on real-world case studies, which were mostly encountered in my own research. These "excursions" are built into a framework that consists of five important dynamics of medieval manuscript culture. *Filling the Page* discusses how manuscript pages were designed and filled with text, and it deals with the motivations scribes had for doing so in the way they did. *Enhancing the Manuscript* subsequently shows how the looks of medieval books were enhanced, both on the inside and outside, through decorations and bookbinding. The third section, *Reading in Context*, focuses on the interaction between readers and their books, and especially on the traces such interactions left behind on the page. *The Margins of Manuscript Culture* expands our view and introduces some less common artifacts from medieval written culture, from unusually shaped books to paper and parchment strips carrying text. *Contextualizing the Medieval Manuscript*, finally, discusses a broad range of topics devoted to the cultural context of manuscripts, from their location of production to their sales as second-hand copies, and ultimately to their destruction in the Early Modern period, when handwritten books became obsolete and recycled, as the concluding chapter shows.

FILLING THE PAGE: SCRIPT, WRITING, AND PAGE DESIGN

Figure 19. Professional scribe and client? Ca. 1400–1410. Los Angeles, The J. Paul Getty Museum, MS 33, fol. 3r. Public domain. Source: www.getty.edu/about/whatwedo/opencontent.html.

INTRODUCTION

Reading was—and is—the ultimate reason for producing and purchasing a book. This opening section of *Books Before Print* therefore gravitates around key issues related to the transfer of text from the exemplar (the original placed in front of the scribe as he made a copy) to the sheets that were prepared to receive it. Focusing on layout and script, which are the material results of this migration of text from original to duplicate, this first section shows how the medieval page was designed and filled with text. The chapters in this section not only discuss the decisions made by the scribe—what script to use, what quality the script would have, how large the margin would be—but also address the rationale behind these decisions. As becomes clear, some decisions were made without further thought: the scribe simply did what he was trained to do. Others, however, reflect conscious decisions, for example, because the scribe knew, or heard, what function the book would have once it was completed.

The first two chapters home in on the actual process of writing down words with a quill. **Chapter 1** shows how medieval letters were created from multiple strokes and what their construction tells us about the moment of production. As is explained, a script family is a style of handwriting shared by scribes in a given time period, region, or sometimes individual religious community, and its execution varied across time and geographical space. To show this, the chapter introduces the three most commonly used book scripts of Europe and shows how their letter shapes changed over time. While the three scripts are regarded as different families, each having their own distinct set of features, they actually share a great deal of paleographical (script) traits.

Chapter 2 discusses a specific dynamic of writing: it highlights strategies available to scribes to abbreviate the words they were copying. Here, too, lie important clues related to the background of both the maker and reader of the manuscript.

Abbreviations only work, of course, if the reader can solve them. Abbreviation signs in manuscripts therefore confirm the close relationship of the scribe to the reader of the book he made: after all, the maker of the manuscript would only have included abbreviations which he knew the future reader was familiar with. The chapter also introduces a peculiar type of abbreviation: Tironian notes. Having the feel of our modern shorthand, complete manuscripts were written in these abbreviations. Such books could only be read by people who knew this "shorthand," which again shows that the scribe knew who the future reader of the book would be.

Chapters 3 and 4 both deal with page design. **Chapter 3** investigates the areas of the page that were *not* filled with text: that is, the margins. Margins form a key element of the page's design, and by focusing on their size, as Chapter 3 does, we get a sense of the scribe's intentions and the purpose for which he made the book. **Chapter 4** focuses on one specific element of page design, the inclusion of "footnotes," or *signes de renvoi*. This aid to the reader, placed within the textblock when the margins would contain a significant amount of annotations, became an increasingly popular practice as medieval book production developed. As with the shaping of letters and margins, the manner of a footnote's execution can be related to how the book was used. Consequently, it draws the manuscript towards a certain cultural–intellectual environment: the scholarly milieu of the emerging university. The presence of these marginal notes often coincides with special design features, such as extended margins. Thus, this chapter shows that page design was a package deal: sparked by the manuscript's function, the scribe came up with a format that included a variety of features and tools he thought, or was instructed, would be useful to the reader.

Chapters 5 and **6**, finally, attempt to gauge what we can learn about the manuscript and its producer from the first and last page of the medieval book. Both pages are special in that they provide information on the background or the goals of the scribe. As is shown, the first page is often a blueprint for the whole book. On it the scribe sets the tone by showing the script he will use for the book as well as its quality of execution, while also revealing to the reader what the page layout will look like. Another artisan that participated in the book project, a decorator, is often also introduced on the first page by means of a decorated initial. The last page, in contrast, may hold identifiers that shed light on the background of the scribe: a colophon in which the scribe identifies himself is usually located on the concluding page of the manuscript. It represents the last words of the scribe to the reader, uttered right before he closes the book.

C oncedit neque corporibus finem esse secandis
q uare in utraque mihi pariter ratione uidetur
e rrare atq; illis uira quod diximus ante
a dde quod inbecili animis primordia fingit
s i primordia sunt simili quae praedita constant
n atura atque ipse res sunt aequeq; laborant
& pereunt neque ab exitio res ulla refrenat
n am quid in oppressu ualido durabit eorum
u t mortem efficiat leti sub dentibus ipsis
I gnis an umor an aura quid horx sanguis an os

sensu probanda sunt quę le
guntur: ut iuxta aplica mo
nita. & teneamus quę recta
sunt. & refutemus quę cont
ria ueritati exsistunt. sicq;
in bonis instruamur: ut a
malis illęsi pmaneamus.

Chapter 1

MEDIEVAL SCRIPT

Let's start at the beginning. One of the fundamental features of the book before print is handwritten letters: those carefully crafted symbols that fill up page after page to convey meaning. Each one of us writes differently today, and considering that medieval books were handwritten before the invention of print, it follows that the letters they carry likewise show a great variety in execution styles. This is perhaps the most amazing aspect of spending a day paging through medieval books in the library: the immense variation in how the text was written down, by the hands of medieval people, onto the page.

No surviving artifact underscores this point better than the advertisement sheets of commercial scribes (Figure 102 at p. 196). Many of them even wrote the names of the scripts next to the samples, some in appealing golden letters, like good marketing men. Providing the names of scripts also allowed customers to converse with the artisan in precise—specialist—terms. Figure 19 at p. 29 probably shows such a transaction between a commercial scribe and his client, whose greetings are extended to each other in text strips called "banderols" (about which, see Chapter 12).

In the wild party of letters seen in advertisement sheets, two categories of variation can be observed: first, the shape of medieval letters differs because they belong to different script families; and second, their precise execution varies because the scribes opted for a particular size, thickness, quality, and pen angle. Remarkably, this variation is still preserved in our modern typefaces,

Figures 20 and 21. Top: Text written in Caroline minuscule, ninth century. Leiden, UB, VLF 30, fol. 22v. Bottom: Text written in Pregothic script, datable to 1145–1149. Leiden, UB, BPL 196, fol. 129v. With permission.

which represent families of fonts, and express the variation within these families, concerning size, weight, and angle, for example.

If we forget for a moment that letters themselves convey meaning, these two levels of variation—choice of script and of its execution—comprise perhaps the greatest value to the historian of the medieval book: they show us when a manuscript was made. This information comes in extremely handy considering that the title page was not yet invented. But how does the script expert establish the precise date of production? Welcome to the illuminating world of handwritten letters from the Middle Ages.

Tick, Tock

Medieval script tells time, although not usually very precisely. Let's take a closer look at two important script families from the medieval period: Caroline minuscule (Figure 20) and Pregothic script (Figure 21). The first was created in the late eighth century and became the main book script in the empire of Charlemagne (d. 814). Used until ca. 1100, Caroline minuscule was an elegant script with a particularly round and spacious appearance. Because Charlemagne had conquered a vast territory during his reign, he found himself with an empire of many cultures, each with its own manner of writing. A cohesive and unifying script was needed if his administration was to function properly.

From the middle of the eleventh century Caroline minuscule started to include new letter forms. By 1100 the number of letter transformations had grown to such an extent that the script began to look very different. This new form of writing is called Pregothic script, the second family we are looking at. Ultimately it would evolve into a third family, Gothic textualis, whose development was nearing completion in the early thirteenth century (see for example Figure 25 at p. 42).[1]

Despite the fact that the two script families we are focusing on here are relatively easy to distinguish, merely being able to identify the "family name" is not enough to pinpoint precisely when a book was made. This is because scripts were used for extensive periods of time, up to several hundreds of years. To get a more precise date is more complicated. To deduce when a book was copied, one needs to investigate where in the timespan of a script the sample in question can be placed. Does a style of writing fit better in the infancy of a script, does it perhaps show its middle age, or is it representative of the end of its lifecycle? To answer this question one needs to know how the script in question developed over time. This kind of research is called "quantitative paleography" because it uses a high volume of verifiable data to study medieval script. Thus, it is possible to map how

1 Kwakkel, "Biting, Kissing and the Treatment of Feet"; Kwakkel, "Book Script."

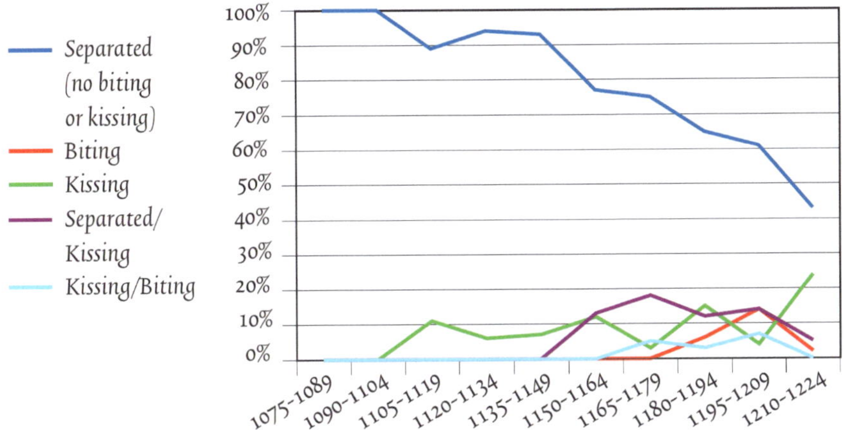

Figure 22. Trends for the letter pair "bo," from Kwakkel, "Biting, Kissing and the Treatment of Feet," p. 208. Open access. Source: www.oapen.org.

Pregothic script evolved by tracking, for example, the letter pair *bo*. The following discussion concentrates on the presentation of the contrary round curves in the heart of this pair: the right side of the *b* and the left side of the *o*.

Figure 21 shows a manuscript written ca. 1145–1149 and the letter pair *bo* is still separated (see line 6, "bonis"). As Pregothic script was developing, however, these two letters came to be placed closer together by scribes. First, they would touch one another, a process I dubbed "kissing," but ultimately they would overlap, which is called "biting."[2] The two letters are placed so close together that they share the central vertical pen stroke: the right side of *b* is also the left side of *o*. The two have literally become inseparable, because separating them would leave one incomplete. This presentation of the letter pair is observed, for example, in the script of Figure 56 at p. 104 (ca. 1205–1210). Note how in "bonum" at the end of line 3 the *bo* pair shares a central column. Biting is also seen here in another letter pair with contrary round curves: *de* (end of line 1, "deus").

We can track this development with hard evidence when we gather data from manuscripts that actually bear a date, which they do every now and then. From this data one can deduce, with quantitative support, when certain features were born or when they died. Data shows, for example, that biting in the letter pair *bo* is first encountered around the middle of the twelfth century (Figure 22, red line).

2 Kwakkel, "Biting, Kissing and the Treatment of Feet," pp. 96–102.

Before this letter pair consistently overlapped, however, scribes placed the letters *b* and *o* so closely together that they kissed, as mentioned (Figure 22, green line). The data in this graph, which was gathered from some 350 dated manuscripts, suggests that this process started very early in the twelfth century. The data also shows that the stage of consistent biting (the red line going up) was preceded by a phase when scribes made the letter pair sometimes only touch, and at other times overlap, both in the same manuscript (Figure 22, light blue line, which goes up before the red line does). In other words, scribes first used a new feature (biting) in combination with an existing feature (kissing) before ditching the latter.

If you look carefully at Figure 56 you see that this scribe not only wrote *bo* in a biting fashion, as discussed, but on the same page he also *separated* the pair (last line, "bonum"). The same goes for *de*, the other "biting" pair we looked at: in line 1's "corde" the letters *d* and *e* are separated. Evidently, this scribe mixes the older presentation with the newer one which is increasingly being adopted across Europe at the time when he copied this manuscript. He, like others of his colleagues, is still on the fence about which presentation to choose.

No Big Secret

The average medieval scribe knew a number of scripts by heart. Commercial producers of books aimed to please a diverse clientele, however, and would therefore have known more writing styles than any other type of scribe, including the monk. The latter was rather conservative: he did not usually have as broad a palette of scripts, and he was probably less inclined to adapt his manner of writing on demand. Still, even within single script families, the average monk–scribe showed variation in the style of execution. Interestingly, he poured something from his cultural–historical background into the shape of letters, revealing to the attentive script expert (called a "paleographer") when he copied his book, even when he did not give this piece of information away explicitly in the form of a dated colophon.

The shape of letters also reveals other things about the scribe, as explained in the General Introduction, for example, where he lived, or that it was a cheap and hasty book project. Unveiling this hidden information in handwriting is difficult, because letter shapes do not easily give up their secrets. Still, the increasing popularity of Digital Humanities, and the efforts of quantitative and digital paleographers to map the development of handwriting and uncover regional variants of scripts with the help of verifiable data, makes it increasingly difficult for scribes to keep their secrets.

Electrix: elextrix; Abene: corrige frenorum;
Signum habentes: serpentem aeneum;
In aqua ualebat ignis: fulgura in pluuia
ad impios missa; ∫ massa uulnerax;
Malagma: multe herbe contrite in unum
Inacerate sine ferro. in mare rubro;
Poderis: uestis est sacerdotum a pedibus;
usque ad umbilicum pertingens: et ibi strin
gebatur cingulo manius subterzore
parte habebatur tintinnabula et ma
la punica; In forsb: iusti: i. loth;
Bona esca manna quae soluebat a sole non ab igne.

DE ECCLESIASTICO:

Euergetis: boni operis; ut factoris;
Scandaligeris: scandalizaueris:
Obductionis: dilectiones. i. mortis;
Inplanauit: seduxit inmisit;
Magnato; magno: Acide; tristae;
Placore: placationem; ∫ aliquando decore
Rusticatio: culturatire / mto sic & colla.
Cacabus: de testa est ducas in canabias habent:.
Ceruicatus: superbus; Inpendiis: rebus;
Calculus: minutissima petra arena;
Alacriter: sine gratia comariter;
Loramentum; ligamentum; Cerritae: petre mol
Infrunite: in frenate; lliores
Platanus: arbor est boni odoris;
Aspectum; speculdur: Calbanx: pigm
Aromatizans; redolens; ∫ tum album
Ungula & guttae: pigmentum de arboribus;
Storax incensum; Nitres; non tardes;
Dorix i. proprium nomen fluminis;
Inormentum; inornamentum;
Aporia: abominatio: subitanea
Torturas: torquem. Solide: fortiter

Lingua tertia; discordiantis lingua tr
Colera; necessa; Auocare; occupare;
Frugis: parcus; Detractione de de t
Infrunita sine freno. t moderatione; id est inc
Equus emissarius: qui mittitur ad ium
Similaginem; genus tritici. Lor funis;
Sophistice: conclusione t reprehensione
Plestice: abundantie t indegeries;
Cyneris: nablis: ut citheris longior
quae psalterium non psalterium est cen g
sit theodorus dix;
Lino crudo: i. uiris de non cocto ueste;
Uasa castrorum: arma et exercitum i. n
celi; dicitur enim quod bella futura possent p
dere in sole et luna; Agonizare; certare
Inpingeris: inpelleris;
Caupo: qui uinum permiscet ad uendend
Accommorante; conhabitantes;
Offusio; effusio; Pululent; crescunt in m

IN LIBRO ISAIAE PROPHETE;

Cucumerarium: hortus in quo cucumer
crescit bona erba ad manducandum
siue ad medicinam; Tugurium: domunca
Uermiculus; a similitudine uermis;
Fissura; scissura diuisura;
Comolitur: exterminatur;
Lunulas: quas mulieres in collo habent
de auro ut argento: a similitudine lune
dicunt dicunt; Discriminalia: an
discernunt capites de auro t argento
Periscelidas: armillas de tibiis;
Olfactoriola: turibula modica de le
ro ut argento mulieres habent pro odo
Murenulas: catenulas;

Chapter 2

CRACKING CODES: ABBREVIATIONS IN MEDIEVAL SCRIPT

Having introduced script, the defining feature of the manuscript, this chapter addresses a ubiquitous feature of medieval handwriting: abbreviating words with specific, recognizable symbols. To a literate person, reading a book is fairly straightforward: just pick it up, flip to the first page, and start reading. However, if you want to read medieval script as a modern reader, there are some challenges to overcome. It turns out you need to decode quite a bit of text first. The first round of decoding happens when your eyes meet the page. As the previous chapter showed, medieval letters are shaped very differently from those today, and some are actually quite difficult to read.

See what happens, for example, when you start reading the famous Leiden Glossary (Figure 23). The paleographer E. A. Lowe defined this script as a pre-Caroline Alemannic minuscule, which means it dates from before the establishment of Caroline minuscule, which developed shortly before the year 800. It is relatively easy to decode Caroline minuscule with our modern brains. This is because early printers in Italy used the script as a model for Roman typefaces, which ultimately became our Times New Roman. Because most people read a version of Caroline minuscule in books or on their computer screens every day, they can identify the letters on a ninth-century page even if they don't know what the Latin words mean. The script in Figure 23, however, is far more difficult to consume, as you may have noticed, because our brains are not used to these letter shapes. Carolingian readers of around 800 would not have found this script illegible because they were trained to read it.

Figure 23. Text written in a pre-Caroline script, late eighth century, Leiden, UB, VLQ 69, fol. 24v. With permission.

However, even when you are able to read a challenging script like this (and one can learn to do so in paleography classes), there is a second coding problem to overcome, which is much trickier: letters and words are frequently abbreviated with symbols. In fact, sometimes a full page or even an entire book is written in this "code." Like any cipher, you can only read it if you know the key. It is this kind of decoding of abbreviated words, some made up of special signs, that stands centre stage here as a defining feature of medieval script.

Abbreviations

Decoding abbreviated letters and common short words is not rocket science, nor would it have been for medieval readers. Some of these abbreviations are actually still in use today, for example, the ampersand (&). Its shape is a blend of the letters e and t (*et*, which is Latin for "and"), although this is less clear in our modern version. Less frequent words could also be abbreviated, but this practice was tricky: the medieval scribe had to judge what abbreviations the book's reader would understand. If he miscalculated, the text could not be decoded. Students and teachers in the emerging universities were masters in coding and decoding words, including those which were heavily abbreviated.

Figure 24 shows the marginal notes to a work by Aristotle made by a medieval student. He abbreviated words like there was no tomorrow: nearly every single one is shortened with special abbreviation signs. It makes sense that students operated this way, because their remarks were originally intended for personal use only. Moreover, shortening text in this fashion saved time and space: coded words were quicker to write, and created room for more coded words.

Tironian Notes

In the Middle Ages a peculiar "language" of abbreviation existed, made up of symbols called "Tironian notes." Even an experienced reader at the time was not necessarily able to decipher this system of shorthand. Rooted in ancient Rome, the language made use of several thousand symbols which abbreviated entire Latin words. The poet Plutarch tells us that Cicero had trained scribes—including his servant Tiro, from which the name of this system derives—to take down dictation at a fast pace.

In the Middle Ages, Tironian notes were used by scholars trained at the highest level. During the ninth century, in the heyday of abbreviating words in this fashion, scholars used them to add comments and criticisms to texts, much like a student did in the university textbook in Figure 24, and for the same reason: to save space and increase speed. Sometimes such marginal additions are substantial, making

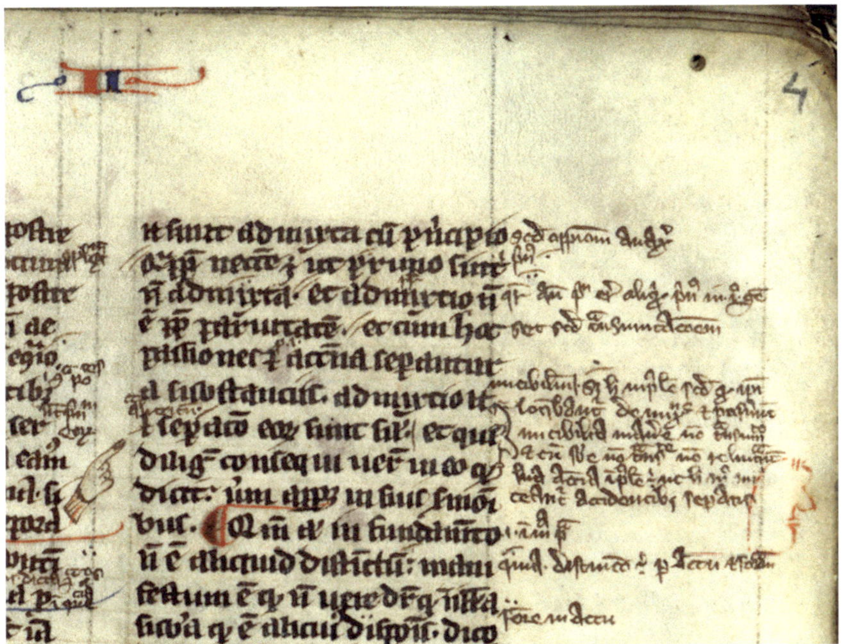

Figure 24. Annotated student copy of Aristotle's *Physics*, ca. 1250–1300. Cambridge, Trinity College, O.7.40, fol. 4r, detail. With permission of the Master and Fellows of Trinity College, Cambridge.

them appear to be drafted in an entirely different language than the text they comment on.

Rarely does one encounter a full text or manuscript copied out in Tironian notes, but it does happen from time to time. The ones I know of are the Psalms, such as Paris, Bibliothèque de France, lat. 190 and lat. 13160, both from the ninth century. Remarkably, the first Tironian note of each chapter is executed in the same style as a regular decorated letter would be: enlarged and painted, as if it were a normal initial. The result, however, is a big and beautiful shape that appears wholly nonsensical unless you are trained to know what it means.

At first sight, it seems an odd practice to write out an entire book in a code that could only be deciphered by scholars who had enjoyed the same high level of training as the scribe. Perhaps these peculiar books were used to train people in the notation system. Monks knew the Psalms by heart, making them the perfect tool to learn the strange alphabet of Tiro. The Latin titles would prompt a memorized text in the reader's mind, after which, perhaps, the symbols would fall into place. It is striking, in this light, that the Psalms, like those in the abovementioned Paris, Bibliothèque nationale de France, lat. 190, are preceded by a kind of dictionary to look up the meaning

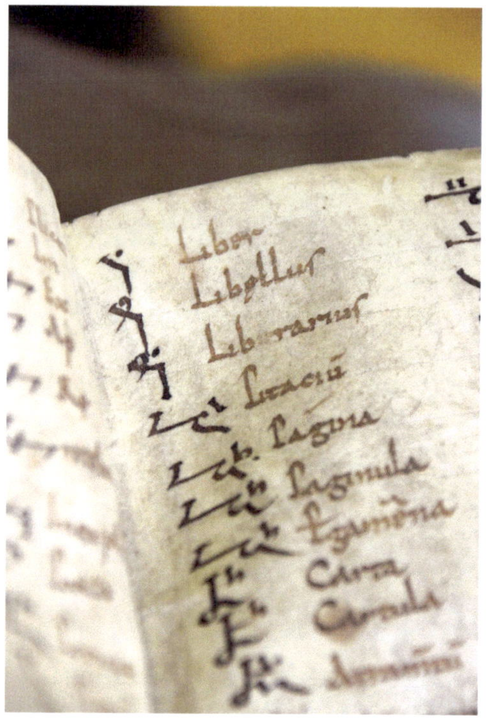

Figure 25. Thematic dictionary of Tironian notes, ninth century. Leiden, UB, VLO 94, fol. 105r. Photo by the author.

of the symbols, just as you would want to do when learning a new language. Several of these explanatory texts survive, including in other manuscripts in the Bibliothèque nationale de France, such as lat. 7493, lat. 8777, lat. 8778, and lat. 8780.[1]

A similar explanatory text is found in a Leiden manuscript. The first entries on the page shown in Figure 25 read *liber*, *libellus*, and *librarius* (book, booklet, and librarian). The symbol for the first looks like a bent line with a dot, while in the second the dot is replaced by a comma, and the third shows both dot and comma: a librarian, after all, looks after both books and booklets. Then follow related words, such as parchment (*pergamena* and, less common, *pitacium*), page, and sheets (*pagina*, *carta*, and *cartula*). As this segment shows, the text is less a dictionary than a collection of thematic word lists.

Uncrackable Code

While not everybody in the Middle Ages would be able to read Tironian notes, many scholars could probably decipher it. However, there is a famous coded book that no one could read but its producer (at least, that is what experts think): the Voynich manuscript, which is written in an unknown alphabet (Figure 26). There is considerable discussion about many aspects of this manuscript, including its precise date and the meaning of the text it holds. The latter is perhaps the most

1 Each of the Paris manuscripts mentioned here is digitized by the National Library of France, and can be found by searching for their shelfmarks at www.gallica.bnf.fr.

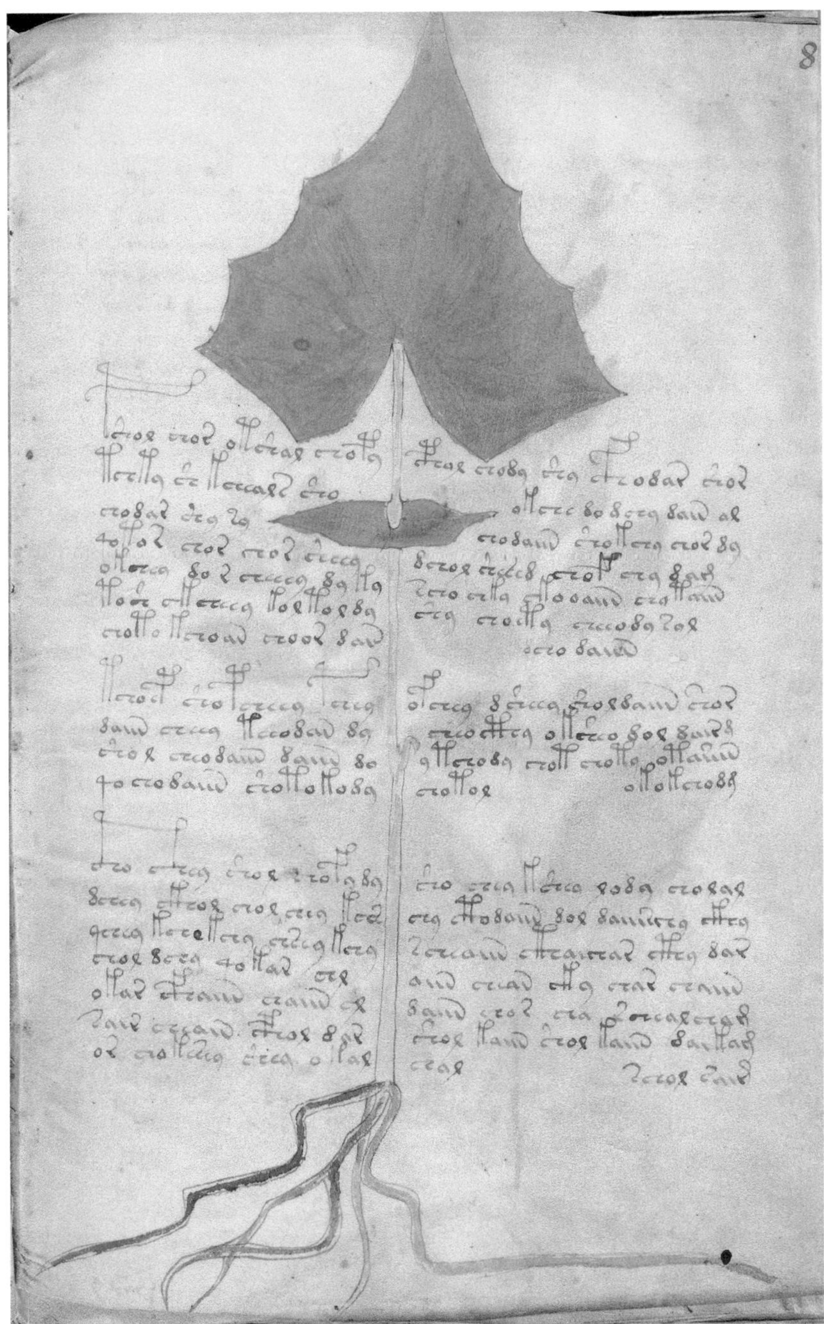

Figure 26. Voynich manuscript, yet to be deciphered, fifteenth or sixteenth century. New Haven, Beinecke Rare Book and Manuscript Library, Yale University, MS 408, fol. 8r. Public domain. Source: http://beinecke.library.yale.edu/tags/digital-collections.

striking aspect of the code in which the text is written: no one has been able to crack it.

The Voynich manuscript has fascinated scholars and non-specialists for a long time. Until 2013, when news outlets claimed the book had a genuine message, it was not even clear if there was meaning behind what looks like madness. Finally, in February 2014, an English professor, Stephen Bax, decoded ten words by identifying certain plants pictured and relating the ciphers to their names. As intriguing as the book is, from a book-historical point of view it is far less interesting than Tironian notes. After all, while the Voynich manuscript appears to be coded in a highly personal way, placing the book in a relatively isolated position, Tironian notes provide an in-depth look into a fascinating world of medieval scholars conversing with one another in what would have been, and still is to most, a secret language. We can, however, decode what they are saying, because the Leiden dictionary and others of its kind give us the cipher.

ΦΛΕΓΟΝΤΑ ΕΡΜΗΝ ΕΡΜΑΝ ΠΑΤΡΟΒΑΝ ΚΑΙ
ΤΟΥϹ ϹΥΝ ΑΥΤΟΙϹ ΑΔΕΛΦΟΥϹ ΑϹΠΑϹΑϹΘΕ
ΦΙΛΟΛΟΓΟΝ ΚΑΙ ΒΗΡΕΑ ΚΑΙ ΑΟΥΛΙΑΝ ΚΑΙ
ΓΗΝ ΑΔΕΛΦΗΝ ΑΥΤΟΥ ΚΑΙ ΟΛΥΜΠΑΝ ΚΑΙ
ΤΟΥϹ ϹΥΝ ΑΥΤΟΙϹ ΑΓΙΟΥϹ ΑϹΠΑϹΑϹΘΕ ΑΛΛΗΛΟΥϹ
ΕΝ ΦΙΛΗΜΑΤΙ ΑΓΙΩ ΑϹΠΑΖΟΝΤΑΙ ΥΜΑϹ
ΑΙ ΕΚΚΛΗϹΙΑΙ ΠΑϹΑΙ ΤΟΥ ΧΡΥ ΠΑΡΑΚΑΛΩ
ΔΕ ΥΜΑϹ ΑΔΕΛΦΟΙ ϹΚΟΠΕΙΝ ΤΟΥϹ ΤΑϹ ΔΙΧΟ
ϹΤΑϹΙΑϹ ΚΑΙ ϹΚΑΝΔΑΛΑ ΠΑΡΑ ΤΗΝ ΔΙΔΑΧΗΝ
ΠΟΙΟΥΝΤΑϹ ΗΝ ΥΜΕΙϹ ΕΜΑΘΕΤΕ ΠΟΙΟΥΝ
ΤΑϹ Η ΠΟΙΟΥΝΤΑϹ ΕΚΚΛΙΝΑΤΕ ΑΠ ΑΥΤΩΝ
ΟΙ ΓΑΡ ΤΟΙΟΥΤΟΙ ΤΩ ΚΩ ΗΜΩΝ ΧΡΩ ΟΥ ΔΟΥΛΕΥ
ΟΥϹΙΝ ΑΛΛΑ ΤΗ ΕΑΥΤΩΝ ΚΟΙΛΙΑ ΚΑΙ ΔΙΑ ΤΗϹ
ΧΡΗϹΤΟΛΟΓΙΑϹ ΚΑΙ ΕΥΛΟΓΙΑϹ ΕΞΑΠΑΤΩϹΙ ΤΑϹ
ΚΑΡΔΙΑϹ ΤΩΝ ΑΚΑΚΩΝ Η ΓΑΡ ΥΜΩΝ ΥΠΑΚΟΗ
ΕΙϹ ΠΑΝΤΑϹ ΑΦΕΙΚΕΤΟ ΧΑΙΡΩ ΟΥΝ ΕΦ ΥΜΙΝ
ΚΑΙ ΘΕΛΩ ΔΕ ΥΜΑϹ ϹΟΦΟΥϹ ΕΙΝΑΙ ΕΙϹ ΤΑ ΑΓΑΘΟ
ΑΚΕΡΑΙΟΥϹ ΔΕ ΕΙϹ ΤΟ ΚΑΚΟΝ Ο ΔΕ ΘϹ ΤΗϹ
ΕΙΡΗΝΗϹ ϹΥΝΤΡΙΨΕΙ ΤΟΝ ϹΑΤΑΝΑΝ ΥΠΟ
ΤΟΥϹ ΠΟΔΑϹ ΥΜΩΝ ΕΝ ΤΑΧΕΙ Η ΧΑΡΙϹ ΤΟΥ ΚΥ
ΗΜΩΝ ΜΕΘ ΥΜΩΝ ΑϹΠΑΖΕΤΑΙ ΥΜΑϹ ΤΙ
ΟϹ ΣΥΝΕΡΓΟϹ ΜΟΥ ΚΑΙ ΛΟΥΚΙΟϹ ΚΑΙ ΙΑϹΩΝ
ΤΡΟϹ ΟΙ ϹΥΓΓΕΝΕΙϹ ΜΟΥ ΑϹΠΑΖΟ
[illegible]
[illegible]

Chapter 3

THE EMPTY PART OF THE PAGE

Filling the page with words and abbreviations is arguably the most important production stage of the manuscript, but there was a task that the scribe had to complete before he could start writing: he had to design the page, meaning that he had to decide how large the page and the textblock on it would be, how many columns the latter would have, and if he needed to leave blank spaces for initial letters to be added when he was finished copying. There was also the issue of the margins, which take up quite a bit of space on the page: how large would they be? How should they be positioned around the edges of the page? And was there any information that they needed to hold?

Margins are a universal feature of books. From the very earliest specimens produced almost two millennia ago to the e-readers we use today, books contain pages that hold both text and a significant amount of blank space. A particularly extraordinary aspect of marginal space is that there is so very much of it in medieval books. My own work on the twelfth century, which reflects broader medieval patterns, shows that pages from that period consist of approximately 50 per cent margin, and in some cases significantly more.[1] This implies, astonishingly, that the majority of medieval books are half empty, despite the fact that parchment was expensive and sometimes even hard to come by. Why is this?

---

1 Kwakkel, "The Margin as Editorial Space."

Figure 27. Leaf from papyrus codex, ca. 150–250 CE. Ann Arbor, University of Michigan, P.Mich.Inv. 6238, recto. CC BY 3.0. Source: https://quod.lib.umich.edu/a/apis.

Inherited Tradition

One answer to this question is a simple one: because this is how books were traditionally made. Medieval scribes adopted a great deal of material features that were first introduced by their counterparts in antiquity. The book as we know it—that is, an object produced from quires—came into existence in the fourth century, as explained in the General Introduction (see p. 2). The pages of the famous Codex Sinaiticus, a copy of the Greek New Testament from around the middle of the fourth century, measures 38.1 cm high × 34.5 cm wide, while the text itself takes up 25 cm × 31 cm. A simple calculation reveals that the text takes up 58 per cent of the page, while 42 per cent is reserved for the outer margins. In other words, a little under half of this magnificent book is empty. Given that the pages were cut by the binder, the margins would have been even larger when it was made.

Going back even further, papyrus manuscripts from antiquity also included a considerable amount of marginal space. Figure 27 shows a page from a papyrus codex written between ca. 150 and ca. 250 CE with St. Paul's Epistles.[2] While the margins have been reduced post-production through damage (the edges of the papyrus eroded), the upper margin, which is largely intact, shows how the scribe reserved ample marginal space. Examples such as this show that the extensive medieval margin is, in one way, simply a continuation of an older practice.

Toolbox

An important reading aid is visible at the top of the same papyrus page: the capital version of the Greek letter Mu (looking like an M), which represents the number forty in Greek. In other words, this is a very early page number (or foliation, actually), an instrument that is apparently some two thousand years old and predates the printed book by over a millennium. The early papyrus page thus highlights that it was convenient to have an empty space around the text: it meant that you could fill it with tools that may be helpful when consulting the book.

There are many other kinds of aids encountered in the margins of medieval books, as explained in the General Introduction, including cross-references to other books or locations in the same manuscript, quotation marks, citations that indicate who the quoted author is, and chapter numbers (see pp. 16–17). A particularly prominent aid is the running title placed in the upper margin, just as you find in today's books, telling the reader which text is on the page before them. The one in Figure 28 is quite pronounced: it reads, in capital letters, "*incipit*

---

2 See the description of P.Mich.Inv. 6238 in the University of Michigan, Ann Arbor, Advanced Papyrological Information System (APIS UM) by searching its inventory number at https://quod.lib.umich.edu/a/apis.

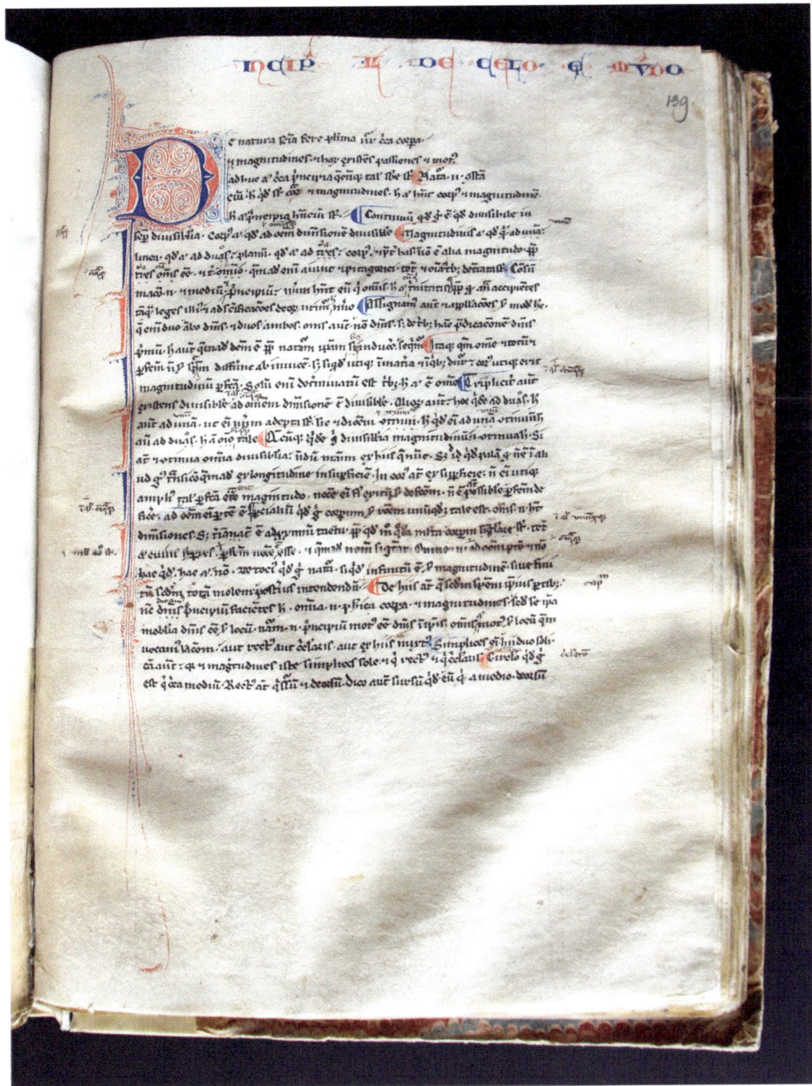

Figure 28. Opening page of Aristotle's *Corpus recentius*, ca. 1250–1300. Leiden, UB, BPL 64, fol. 139r. Photo by the author.

liber de celo et mundo" (here starts the *Book on Heaven and Earth*), which is a work by Aristotle. This manuscript was specially designed for university education, because its margins were equally suitable for yet another task: taking down class notes.

Educational Notes: The Monastic School

While the margin did a good job of accommodating relatively short reading aids like foliation or a running title, it could be challenging to add large amounts of text to the void surrounding the main text. Figure 29 shows a schoolbook from ca. 1100 that was donated to Egmond Abbey near Amsterdam by a certain Baldewinus, who appears to have been a teacher in Flanders.[3] The text in the book, Lucan's *Pharsalia*, was in popular use in the medieval classroom, and it is therefore no surprise that numerous explanatory notes have been added to the text, probably by Baldewinus himself.

There is something special about these marginal notes: they are preceded by symbols that are the precursor of our modern footnote (more about this early practice in Chapter 4). For example, each of the notes in the manuscript shown in Figure 29 starts with a different symbol, which is repeated above the word in the main text to which that particular note refers. However, the schoolbook from ca. 1100 was not really prepared to hold extensive notes, at least not when copied in the relatively large script Baldewinus used. He could have crammed more text in the margins had he copied in a smaller script or increased the number of lines for the marginal text passages (here their number corresponds to the main text), but this was not what he opted for. Perhaps he preferred to have few legible teaching notes, rather than having many notes he could not easily read.

Educational Notes: The University

How things can change in a century! At the medieval university, manuscripts were designed to carry many marginal annotations, which were usually written in tiny letters. None were better suited for this than two textbooks of Aristotle's works, the *Corpus vetustius* (Older Corpus), holding the first (Arabic to Latin) translations of Aristotle produced in the twelfth century; and the *Corpus recentius* (Newer Corpus), which consisted of new translations made by William of Moerbeeke in the 1370s (Figure 29). Both of these editions have a very recognizable layout, as the *Book on Heaven and Earth* in Figure 29 shows (it holds Moerbeke's translation): the main text only takes in a modest amount of the available surface space on

---

3 Gumbert, "The Irish Priscian in Leiden," p. 295.

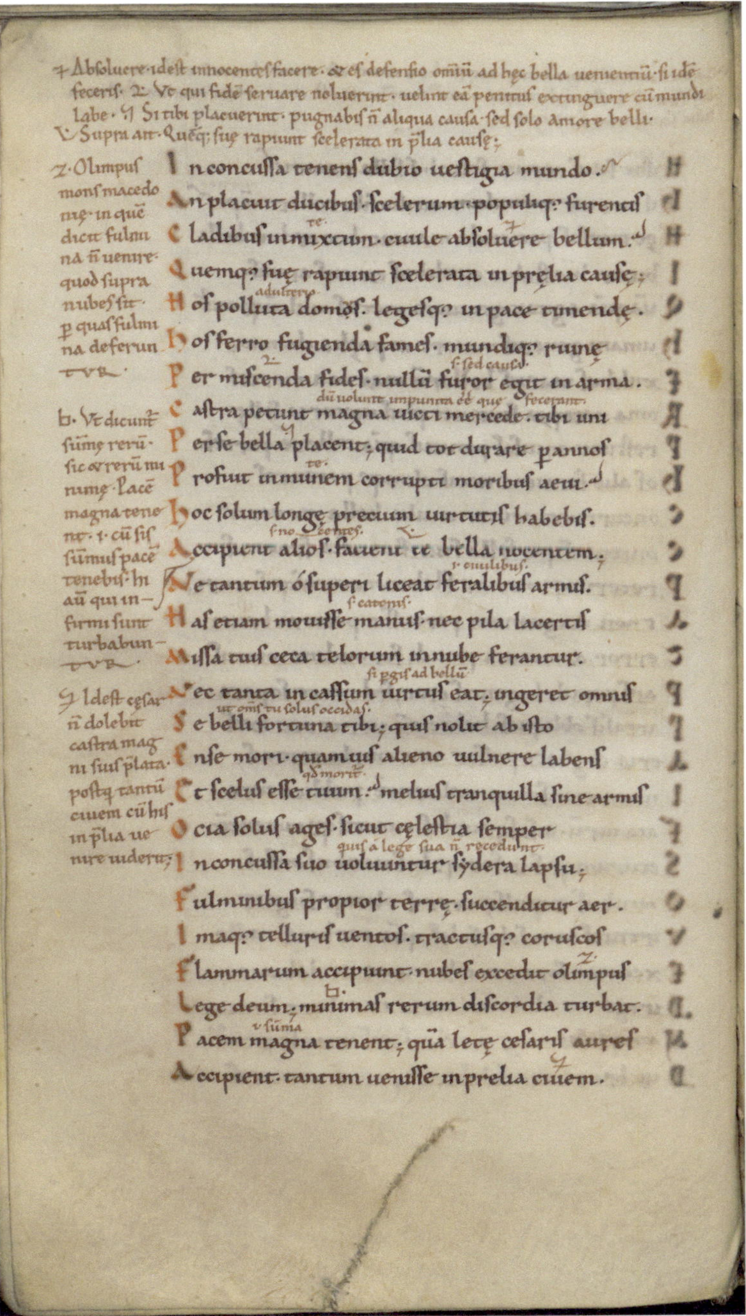

Figure 29. Annotated teaching copy of Baldwinus, ca. 1100. Leiden, UB, BUR Q 1, fol. 19v. With permisison.

the page, usually not more than 30–35 per cent, while the margins are extra large. In fact, given that the page measures 27.8 cm × 20.3 cm and the text 15.6 cm × 11.7 cm, only 32 per cent of the page is filled with Aristotle. In other words, almost 70 per cent was marginal space and could be used for the student's annotations.

Many Aristotle manuscripts prepared for university education (including this one) featured a "zoning" system to accommodate the student's responses to the text. The system consisted of "comment boxes" that were outlined with vertical and horizontal lines drawn in the margin with plummet. The scribe placed long columns on both sides of the text: one or two in the inner margin and two or three in the outer margin. The rationale behind it is that the start of the note could be placed at the same height as the Aristotle line on which it commented; not just once but several times over (as many times as there were columns). Longer comments were placed in the larger blank area of the lower margin.

The manuscript in Figure 29 features a total of three vertical columns (in the photo only slightly visible in the right margin), which is a modest but normal number for an Aristotle manuscript of this size; larger manuscripts could hold as many as five (see Figure 66 at p. 126, which contains 42 comment boxes per page). The student of the codex in Figure 29 did not make a lot of notes, by the looks of it, but used only small segments of two vertical columns for his thoughts, applying a highly abbreviated script to save space.

Figure 30. Monastic teaching manual produced from offcuts, ca. 1000–1025. Leiden, UB, VLO 92, fols. 132v–133r. With permission.

Convention—And Breaking It

As the examples show, the marginal space encountered in medieval books is substantial: it adds up to at least 50 per cent of the page with regular manuscripts, often much more when it concerned a volume made for university education. Evidently, the practice inherited from antiquity was put to good use, because it became the preferred location for tools and notes. As prosaic as it may sound, the rationale behind leaving at least half the page blank—to return to the question posed at the outset—is probably a mixture of tradition and the great benefits that came with substantial empty space.

Some scribes, however, broke with the convention that had emerged, as the manuscript in Figure 30 shows. Like the Lucan manuscript of Baldewinus, this book was made by a monastic teacher too. Unlike Baldewinus, however, the teacher who copied the classical excerpts in Figure 30 opted to include as little marginal space as possible. The reason for this is revealed by the writing support that the teacher used (he probably copied it himself): scrap parchment—"offcuts"—left over after the regular sheets were cut from the animal skin (see p. 7). This was evidently a low-end book that was made cheaply. Thus it made sense to fill the page to the max and get as much mileage out of the scraps as possible. Leaving half the page blank was the rule, but not if other motivations had priority.

SCI REMIGII.

AB IPSO INCHOANT

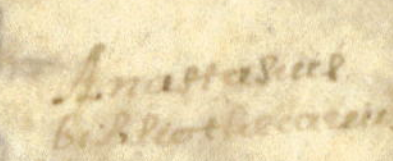

EATUS

PETRUS
APOSTLS
ET PRIN
CEPS
APOSTO
LORUM

ANTHIOCAENUS
filius Iohannis
prouintiae
galileae . uico
bethsaida .
frater
andreae .
Primus sedit
cathedra
episcopatus
in anthiochia
annos
. VII .
beatus
hic petrus in
gressus in urbe
roma .
nerone cesare .
Ibiq; sedit cathe
dra . episcopa
tus . annos
. XXV .
mens . II .
dies . III .
Fuit autem
temporibus .

Chapter 4

FOOTNOTES BEFORE PRINT

As the previous chapter showed, the margins were the go-to place if you had critical information to add to the text, for example if you were a student or a scholar. There is something else that is frequently found in the margin of medieval books: the footnote. As it became more common to add scholarly information in the margins, so too did the need increase to have logistics in place to deal with this extra information. An especially important challenge to overcome was to relate a marginal note directly to the words in the main text to which it pertained. While connecting main text and marginal comment—the essential function of the footnote—was an eleventh-century practice, as the previous chapter showed, in the thirteenth century, when universities were established all over Europe, the sign truly came into popular use. In this scholastic age the footnote also changed appearance in order to create a more efficient linkage system of text and marginal notation. This chapter deals with these changes while presenting a brief history of the footnote in the era before print.[1]

Disconnected

The crux of our footnote system is the presence of a symbol that connects the note to the relevant location in the text. Curiously, in the Middle Ages it was quite common *not* to have such connections in place, especially, it seems, in the earlier centuries. When few remarks were added to the page, a reader could deduce with relative

1 For the post-medieval history of this aid, see Grafton, *Footnote*.

Figure 31. Interlinear compensation for omission of "beatus" in column 2 near green letter "H," ninth century. Leiden, UB, VLQ 60, fol. 9r. With permission.

ease to which passage a marginal note referred. It helped in this respect if a text was widely read or known by heart, as many medieval works were. In such cases the note instantly made sense because the reader was already familiar with the referenced literary context. Moreover, as long as notes were few and short, a reader could simply insert them—interlineally—over the relevant word or passage. In Figure 31, for example, somebody wrote "beatus" (blessed) over the name Peter, compensating for an omission in the text (second column, line 14, near the green letter H).

In this system the position of the remark clearly identified the word to which it referred. However, as the number and size of such comments increased, it became impossible to place them between the lines. The great blank space provided by the margins was now drafted into service. It is here that the absence of a proper reference system was most sorely felt. As the marginal body of remarks and critiques began to accumulate, the page became a messy place, a labyrinth in which it became impossible for readers to find specific pieces of information (see, for example, Figure 18 at p. 26). Enter the footnote.

Dots and Lines

Connecting a marginal remark to the relevant passage in the text was usually done with a duplicated symbol, called a *signe de renvoi* (sign of return) or tie mark: one was placed in front of the marginal note, the other near the word or passage that the remark commented upon.[2] While it is hard to deduce a clear pattern of development, it appears that in the early stages of using such footnotes, scribes and readers resorted to plain symbols rather than letters or numbers. The symbols varied considerably in shape and sophistication. At the most sophisticated end of the spectrum we encounter elaborate, space-absorbing symbols, such as a large crossed out "7" with a curl extending from its top. In Figure 32 it appears both next to the marginal note and above the word to which it pertains, "civem," in the last line. The 7-symbol is part of a system of unusual tie marks that appear to have been made up by the scribe himself (another highly individual system is used by the scribe in Figure 18 at p. 26).

More commonly encountered are less complex symbols, which could be added to the page much more quickly and which took up less space. Dots and lines are particularly popular elements of such footnote symbols. Interestingly, they were first used not to connect comment and text, but as an insertion mark that added an omitted line into the text. The missed line of text was written in the margin, accompanied by one of these simple symbols. The symbol was then repeated in the text

---

2 Budny, *Assembly Marks.*

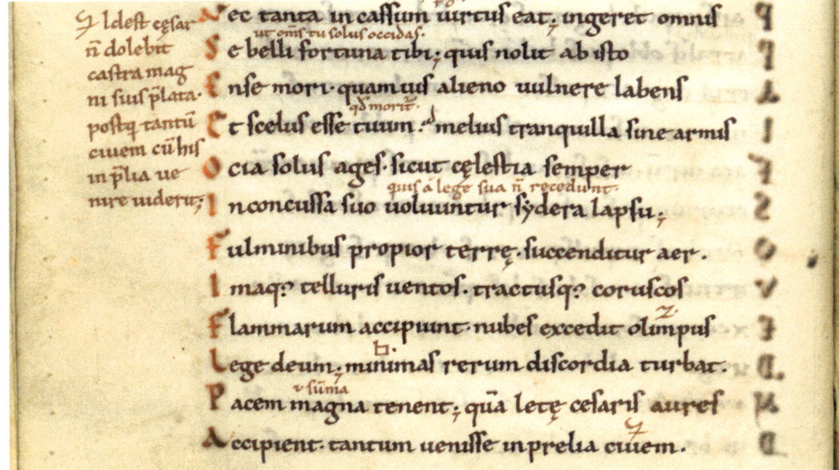

Figure 32. Tie mark resembling "7," seen both in margin and over last word of page ("civem"), ca. 1100. Leiden, UB, BUR Q 1, fol. 2v, detail. With permission.

itself, at the location where the line belonged. This omission mark may well be the origin of the footnote system that emerged over the course of the Middle Ages, and that we still use today, almost unchanged.[3]

Scribes used different versions of the line-and-dot symbol. In fact, they had to if they were to produce unique ties between comment and text. When dots were used, their number would increase as more notes were added. Alternatively, the position of the dots could be varied, so that they formed unique patterns. In Figure 24 at p. 41, for example, various creations are encountered, and each looks a bit different: some reference marks consist of a single dot, others have two; in some the dots are placed over a line, in others beneath one. In what is an unusual find, on the flyleaf of a manuscript in Leiden we see a scribe practising his own range of line-and-dot symbols, probably to test his pen (Figure 33). It showcases some of the variants in the footnote palette of the thirteenth-century scribe.

Letters

Closest to our modern system of footnotes, finally, is the use of letters to tie a marginal remark to its proper location in the text. In some manuscripts, particularly

3 For more on this mark, see Lowe, "The Oldest Omission Signs."

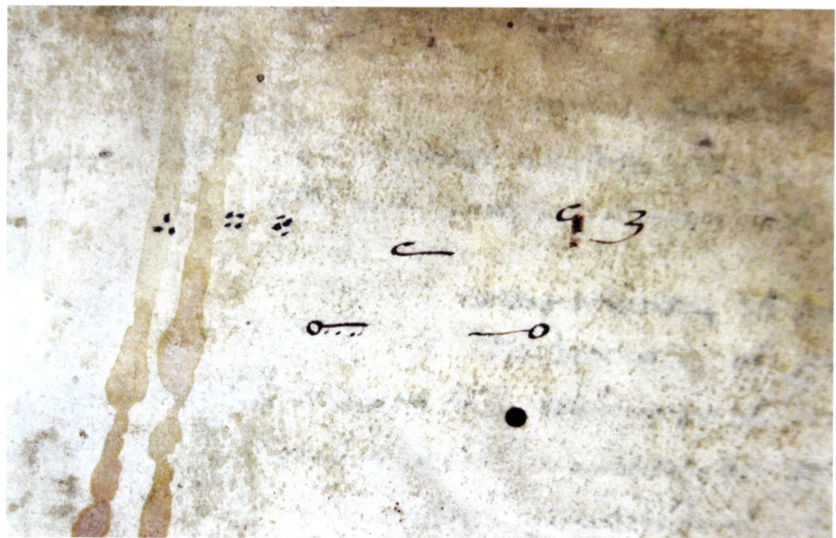

Figure 33. Collection of tie marks, probably pen trials, thirteenth century. Leiden, UB, VLF 69, fol. 2r. Photo by the author.

of the twelfth century, we see the entire alphabet running down the margin. These books were usually made for teaching: the instructors who used them, typically in a monastic school, had many things to explain to their students, as the notes show. It made sense to organize such added information in a clear manner, and the alphabet came in handy in this respect. Some pages contained more footnotes than there are letters in the alphabet, which challenged the system. In such cases the user added extra line-and-dot symbols.

Numerals

So where are the medieval footnotes that make use of numbers, like we do today? Curiously, these are not found in manuscripts. This makes some sense, however. Roman numerals would not be suitable for the task. Placed out of context, as a symbol initiating a segment of text (i.e., the marginal comment) they would easily be mistaken for a letter, which, graphically speaking, they are. Moreover, Roman numerals would quickly take up a lot of space, which is certainly not what you want in a reference symbol—in fact, this chapter has shown there is development towards more space-efficient footnote symbols. Arabic numerals were not widely used in Europe until the fourteenth century and they were still far were less popular than Roman numerals well into the late Middle Ages. Readers may not have felt comfortable enough with these new numbers to use them in the margin (some scribes in the late Middle Ages were still confused by the concept and use of zero). The leap from alphabet to numerals—from the medieval to our modern system—appears to have been taken in the age of print.

VITA PLINII EX CATALOGO VIRORUM ILLUSTRIUM TRANQUILLI

PLINIUS SECUNDUS

novocomensis equestribus militiis industrie functus, procurationes quoque splendidissimas atque continuas summa integritate administravit et tamen liberalibus studiis tantam operam dedit ut non temere quis plura in otio scripserit. Itaque bella omnia que umquam cum Romanis gesta sunt xxxvii voluminibus comprehendit. Item naturalis historie xxxvii libros absolvit. Periit clade Campanie. Nam cum Misenensi classi preesset et flagrante Vesubio ad explorandas propius causas liburnicas pretendisset, nec adversantibus ventis remeare posset, vi pulveris ac faville oppressus est, vel ut quidam existimant a servo suo occisus, quem deficiens estu ut necem sibi maturaret oraverat. Hic in his libris xx milia rerum dignarum ex lectione voluminum circiter duo milium complexus est. Primus autem liber quasi index xxxvii librorum sequentium consummationem totius operis et species continet multorum.

PLINIUS SECUNDUS

Vespasiano suo salutem. Libros naturalis historie novitium Camenis Quiritium tuorum opus, natos apud me proxima fetura licentiore epistola narrare constitui tibi iocundissime imperator. Sit enim hec tui prefatio verissima, dum maximo consenescit in patre. Namque tu solebas putare esse aliquid meas nugas, ut obicere molliam Catullum conterraneum meum, agnoscis et hoc castrense verbum. Ille enim ut scis permutatis prioribus sillabis duriusculum se fecit quam volebat existimari a vernaculis suis et famulis. Simul ut hac mea petulantia fiat quod proxime non fieri questus es in alia procaci epistola nostra, ut in quedam acta exeant, sciantque omnes quam ex equo tecum vivat imperium triumphale et censorium tuum, sexiesque consul ac tribunicie potestatis particeps, et quod his nobilius fecisti, dum illud patri pariter et equestri ordini prestas, prefectus pretorii eius omniaque hec rei publice et nobis quidem qualis in castrensi contubernio. Nec quicquam in te mutavit fortune amplitudo in his nisi ut prodesse tantundem posses ut velles. Itaque cum ceteris in veneratione tui pateant omnia illa, nobis ad colendum te familiari audacia sola superest. Hanc igitur tibi imputabis, et in nostra culpa tibi ignosces. Perfricui faciem nec tamen profeci, quoniam alia via occurris ingens et longius etiam summovens ingenii fascibus; fulgurat in nullo umquam verius dictatoris eloquentie tribunicie potestatis facundie. Quanto tu ore patris laudes tonas, quanto fratris amas. Quantus in poetica es. O magna fecunditas animi: quemadmodum fratrem quoque imitareris excogitasti. Sed hec quis possit intrepidus estimare subiturus ingenii tui iudicium provocatum? Neque enim similis est condicio publicantium et nominatim tibi dicantium. Tum possem dicere quid ista legis imperator? humili vulgo scripta sunt, agricolarum opificum turbe, denique studiorum otiosis. Quid te iudicem facis? Quia hanc operam cum diceret noemas in hoc albo maiorem te sciebam quam ut descensurum huc putarem. Preterea est quedam publica etiam eruditorum reiectio. Utitur illa et M. Tullius extra omnem ingenii aleam positus, et quod miremur per advocatum defenditur: Nec doctissimis. Manium Persium hec legere nolo, Iunium Congium volo. Quod si hoc Lucilius qui primus condidit stili nasum dicendum sibi putavit, Cicero mutuandum, presertim cum de re publica scriberet, quanto nos causatius ab aliquo iudice defendimus? Sed hec ego mihi nunc patrocinia ademi nuncupatione, quoniam plurimum refert sortiatur aliquis iudicem an eligat, multumque apparatus interest apud invitatum hospitem et oblatum. Cum apud Catonem illum ambitus hostem et repulsis tamquam honoribus ineptis gaudentem flagrantibus comitiis pecunias deponerent candidati, hoc se facere pro innocentia rebus humanis summum esse profitebantur. Inde illa nobilis M. Ciceronis suspiratio: O te felicem M. Porci, a quo rem improbam petere nemo audet. Cum tribunos appellaret L. Scipio Asiaticus, inter quos erat Gracchus, hoc attestabatur vel inimico iudici se probari posse. Adeo summum quisque cause sue iudicem facit quemcumque eligit; unde provocatio appellatur. Te quidem in excelsissimo generis humani fastigio positum summa eloquentia summa eruditione preditum religiose adiri etiam a salutantibus scio. Et ideo curam que tibi dicantur condigna sint [illegible]. Lacte rustici multeque [illegible] gentes et mola tantum salsa litant qui non habent [illegible] nec ulli fuit vitio deos colere quoquo modo posset. Meque quidem temeritati accessit hoc quoque, quod levioris opere hos tibi dedicavi libellos. Nam nec ingenii sunt capaces, quod alioquin nobis perquam mediocre erat, neque admittunt excessus aut orationes ser-

xxxvii xii lxxvii

Chapter 5

THE FIRST PAGE OF THE MANUSCRIPT

The previous chapters examined in depth two key stages in a manuscript's production: designing the page, and filling it with text. The next two chapters also deal with these features, but they are approached from a different perspective. Our focus shifts from the production process, when the pages were being filled with text, to the completed book as it appears on our desks today. Observing a finished page provides the full picture of the scribe's design efforts: it offers information about him and the plan behind the book project he undertook. Two specific locations are particularly interesting in this respect: the opening page of the manuscript, which first introduces the reader to the book's design (assuming that he or she started at the beginning); and the final page, which closes both the story and the book.

Leaving the concluding page of the manuscript for the next chapter, let's first turn to the opening page. This is an important page, not just for the reader (How does the story start? Where is it set? Who is the main character?) but also for the historian of the book, who asks very different questions. What decisions did the scribe make with respect to script and page design? What does the decoration look like? Ultimately, the first page reflects the book as a whole, because the scribe did not usually change his design halfway through a book project. Adding further value to the first page, owners of the manuscript may also appear there.

Artisans

The most "in-your-face" clue about the people who produced the manuscript is provided by the script. As you open the manuscript and start reading the first page, paleographical information starts to flow. The shape of medieval letters

Figure 34. Erased ownership inscription at top of page, twelfth century. Leiden, UB, VLF 1, fol. 1r. With permission.

Figure 35. Decorated initial in style of southern France, ca. 1150–1175. London, BL, Sloane 2424, fol. 1r. CC0 1.0 Universal. Source: www.bl.uk/catalogues/illuminatedmanuscripts.

transmits two important pieces of information: as Chapter 1 demonstrated, the scribe's whereabouts and "whenabouts." An experienced book historian develops intuition about the date of a book's production: they can usually "sense" approximately when a book was written just by looking at it. It is not unlike a sommelier being able to tell in what year the wine he or she has tasted was produced. A similar feeling produces a sense of the country or region where the scribe was trained, and where he probably produced the book. All this happens at first glance while observing the opening page of the manuscript.

Thus the script in Figure 35, a copy of William of Conches's *Dragmaticon philosophiae*, was copied by a scribe trained in southern France. It is suggested, among other things, by the shape of Tironian *et* (7), which features a firm and remarkably long horizontal top, and a vertical stroke that is set nearly at a right angle (see line 3 below the Q: "*quibus studio et doctrina*"). In other parts of France (and Europe) Tironian *et* is generally written with a shorter top stroke and a much more angled, or even curved, downward stroke.

In fact, according to the description in the online catalogue of the British Library, where this manuscript is held, the art historian François Avril placed the manuscript in Languedoc, in the very south of France.[1] He did so on the basis of the decoration, which is another bookish feature expressing information about the origins of a manuscript. Both the colours of the initial and the frame surrounding it have a southern French feel, showing that both artisans—scribe and decorator—were

1 Sloane 2424 has been digitized by the British Library, and can be found by searching for its shelfmark in their Catalogue of Illuminated Manuscripts at www.bl.uk/catalogues/illuminatedmanuscripts.

probably trained in that region, which means we can probably place the origins of the book there too. The first page is a perfect example of how decoration comes into play when pursuing the origins of a manuscript, because the opening of the text is often decorated, even if the rest of the manuscript is not. The start of the book had to be celebrated, as it were, and experts can deduce where that party took place.

Purpose

More difficult to assess from the first page of the medieval manuscript is the purpose for which the book was made. For this information one may turn to the page's design. The ca. 1100 manuscript seen in Figure 23 at p. 38, featured in the previous chapter, has side and bottom margins that are wider than normal. Originally the margins would have been even larger, because the manuscript was probably trimmed to fit its new binding in the fifteenth century. Such broad margins suggest that this book, filled with Lucan's *Pharsalia*, was designed to be glossed. This, of course, fits with the manuscript's purpose: it was made for a teacher, who placed his personal teaching notes in the margins.

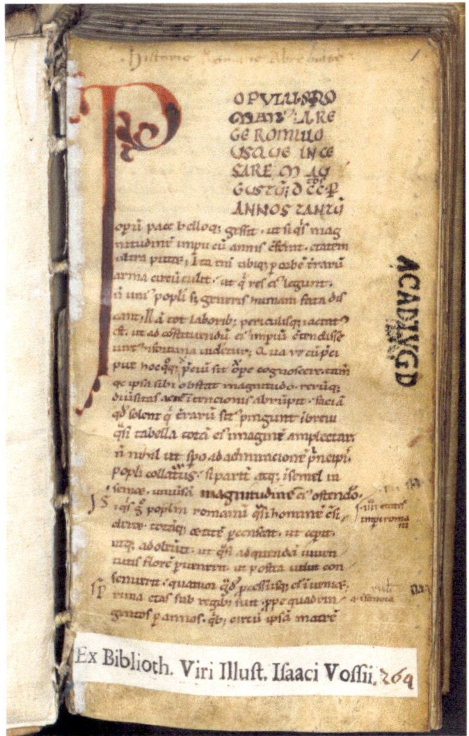

Figure 36. Holster book with classical texts used for teaching, ca. 1100–1150. Leiden, UB, VLO 77, fol. 1r. With permission.

As with layout, a page's dimensions may also provide information about the purpose for which a medieval book was created. Take the ca. 1200 manuscript with classical texts by Lucius Florus and Titus Livius in Figure 36.

The book breaks with the norm of medieval book production in that the page is extremely tall and narrow. This is what we call a "holster book," which is a deceptive name as the object was not fitted in a holster at all (more on this book type in Chapter 20).[2]

2 Robinson, "The Format of Books," p. 54.

Research suggests that this format was favoured by performers, such as soloists in church and actors on stage: the book could be held up and open with one hand, allowing freedom to use the other for different tasks. Similarly, teachers in monastic schools enjoyed the narrow format, which accommodated their walking through the classroom with it.[3] These classical texts formatted as especially narrow medieval books were frequently used to teach Latin grammar to novices.

All this becomes evident as soon as we turn to the page in front of us when we first open the book. In fact, in this case clues about the manner of use can be gauged even *before* we open the manuscript: the very shape of the storage box already suggests that this is a holster book and, therefore, that it was used in a setting of handheld use. Even from inside the closed box the manuscript transmits information about its past.

Owners

The first page may also be key in establishing who owned the manuscript. We often forget that the average medieval book can easily have had ten or more owners. A thirteenth-century manuscript, for example, is currently 800 years old. If the average reading life of an individual was forty years (meaning he or she started to build a library at, say, twenty years of age), we may assume that the thirteenth-century book in question has had twenty different owners. Every surviving medieval manuscript is a second-hand book. It is no surprise, then, that we often find multiple names and *ex-libris* (ownership) inscriptions written down in manuscripts.

This fact is particularly relevant for the present chapter because the names of owners are often encountered at the first page, often at the top. Nobody wants an old ownership inscription in his book, however, and so a subsequent owner of the book in Figure 34 (p. 60) erased the notation from Pliny's *Naturalis historia* with a knife: the only words still legible are "*Iste liber*" (This book), which is the common start of the medieval ownership inscription "*Iste liber pertinent* ..." (This book belongs to ...). A nineteenth-century librarian tried to make the text visible again with a chemical substance known as reagens, which indeed made the text more visible, if only for a short time. It disappeared again soon after, leaving behind a stain and a text that is now almost completely invisible. The Leiden scholar De Meyïer was able to read some of these words: he identified the thirteenth-century owner as the Church of St. Dionysius in Paris (*Iste liber est ecclesie* [*beati*] *dy*[*onisii*]) and

3 Kwakkel, "'Dit boek heeft niet de vereiste breedte'"; Kwakkel and Newton, *Medicine at Monte Cassino*, chap. 5.

could also read the subsequent curse aimed at potential thieves ([*anathema*] *s*[*it*])—curses such as these are revisited in Chapter 18.[4]

The first page was a prime location for ownership details, in part because medieval librarians, who commonly wrote these details down, knew that ownership inscriptions placed on covers or added on flyleaves may disappear when the book was rebound. For the same reason, other information is also found there, including pressmarks—numbers which connected a book to its place in the medieval library catalogue. The letters C and F in the bottom margin of the Leiden manuscript are probably part of such a pressmark.

The practice of putting the owner's name in the front of the book continued in the Early Modern period, and even beyond (for many of us still do it today). Although the manuscript in Figure 34 was once a resident of medieval Paris, near the bottom of the opening page we encounter two of its later owners: the Leiden professor Isaac Vossius (d. 1689) and Leiden University. The latter institution marked the book with a black stamp with the Latin name of the university ("ACAD. LUGD," Academia Lugduno-Batava). Vossius had sold his library to the university, and the white strip of paper marked this fact: "*Ex Bibliotheca Viri Illustris Isaac Vossii*" (from the library of the illustrious Isaac Vossius). Thus, the first page of the Leiden manuscript not only shows us where the book itself was made (somewhere in England during the second half of the twelfth century), but also who owned it in subsequent centuries.

---

4 De Meyïer, *Codices Vossiani Latini*, vol. 1, p. 2.

dyabolicas fraudibus insidere. et minor oneribus
pgrauari. ne male obediendo superbie mag' pa
bus ad dicitur. vnum istis talibus quod dicat esse
faciendum scilicet quod animalia imprudenti
bus. hys enim comparationibus stultos homines
vitam in iutos. ¶ Etiam quod ait in freno ad eq
equum pertinet. frenum enim a fero nuncupatum
dictum est. ferum quippe antiqui caballum dixe
runt. ¶ In camo ad mulum respicit ergo hec
animalia duo supradicta cohibent ista retina
cula. ut ad arbitrium iubentis incedant. Nec
suis voluntatibus efferantur. ¶ Maxilla vero
animalia sunt animalium. quibus esca man
ditur: ut corporis vita seruetur. ¶ Ipsis ergo maxil
las per figuram allegoricam dicit in obedien
tibus debere constringi. id est copias victuales in
parcius dari. ut ieiunior necessitate condu
cti. creatoris subdantur imperio. ¶ Allegoria
est enim sicut iam sepe dictum est. quando aliud
dicitur. et aliud significatur. et quod dicimus
in hac parte dominum christum loqui constringe dicat
patri quia trinitatis sancte vnum velle vna
potestas. vna cooperatio est

Explicit liber seu compilatio Rabani Mau
ri ad ludouicum imperatorem. De na
turis rerum.

Hoc opus est scriptum magister da mi potum.
Dextera scriptoris careat grauitate doloris

Chapter 6

THE LAST PAGE OF THE MANUSCRIPT

The last page of the book is equally telling of the manuscript's history as its first page. Due to its location, however, the end of the book contains very different information than that found on the opening page. The last page represents the closure of a book project, and sometimes the scribe wanted to provide some information about himself or the circumstances under which the book was produced. Given that medieval books lacked a title page, such explicit information is very welcome; it makes the last page an important location for historians of the book. There is another reason, however, why the last page is interesting. At the end of the manuscript we often encounter blank pages, either because the last quire was not completely filled with text, or because a blank flyleaf was added during the binding process. As we have seen when the margins were observed in Chapter 3, such blank spaces were popular locations to write on. So what do we encounter at the manuscript's concluding page?

The Last Page of the Text

The last page of the text was a podium from which the scribe could announce information about himself and his work. While few scribes seized this opportunity, this added information, collected in what we call a "colophon," can enrich our knowledge about a manuscript considerably.[1] Some colophons provide a glance into the reality of the scriptorium or urban workshop, where scribes toiled over their sheets of parchment. Well known are colophons that cry out "Please give

1 Overgaauw, "Where are the Colophons?"

Figure 37. Colophon by scribe at bottom of right column, expressing that he deserves a drink, fourteenth century. Leiden, UB, VLF 5, fol. 174v. Photo by the author.

me a drink!" and "Let the right hand be free from pain!" (*Hoc opus est scriptum magister da mihi potum* and *Dextera scriptoris careat gravitate doloris*). Both announcements are seen at the end of the manuscript in Figure 37, and the scribe probably meant it: the script he used is of very high quality and it must have taken him quite a lot of effort to copy this text.

Particularly telling are colophons in which a scribe opens the shutters and allows us to peek into his working space. The person who copied Giessen, Universitätsbibliothek, MS 945, which contains Justinian's Code in French translation, identifies himself as "*Herneis le Romanceeur*" in the colophon on the last page (fol. 269v). The colophon also includes spam: Herneis invites future readers to come and look him up in Paris, across from Notre Dame Cathedral, if they also want a book like this.[2] There are other cases where a commercial scribe advertises his work. One living in mid fifteenth-century Holland copied the same text, the Historical Books of the Old Testament, at least seven times, meaning that his labour was most certainly a commercial enterprise. Two of these copies include a colophon in which the scribe reaches out to potential buyers. For example, Utrecht, UB, 1006 (4 E 3) states at fol. 124r: "I would be happy to copy the New Testament for payment, because it is beautiful." (*Ic wout hem wel scriven om loen, wanttet een sonderlinge scoen dinc is.*)[3]

While Herneis in Paris was promoting his business to a broad audience who might happen upon earlier works of his, the anonymous scribe in Holland was probably addressing the person for whom he had just copied the Old Testament. When a reader of the Utrecht manuscript reached the end of the last page, he stumbled on the not-so-subtle recommendation cited above. It actually feels like a recommendation in an online shop today: "If you like that book, you will love this one too!" As entertaining as these examples are, the really important colophons are those that contain elements of the modern title page, because it allows us to accurately locate the maker of the book in time and space. The colophon on the last page of BPL 2541, for example, is a rich source of information about how the manuscript came to be (Figure 38).

It states: "This book was written in the year 1484. It was completed on St. Maurice's Day in the city of Susteren, where we were in hiding when our convent had been burnt down." (*Item dit boeck is gescreven Int iaer ons heren MCCCC ende lxxxiiii. Ende geeynt op Sancte Mauricius dach in der stat Susteren daer wi schulende waren al te samen doen ons cloester verbrant was.*) While only a few lines, they provide a wealth of information, not only about when and where the book was made, but also about the life (and suffering) of the scribe, who had recently lost her home in a fire.

2 Rouse and Rouse, *Manuscripts and Their Makers*, vol. 1, pp. 47–48; Busby, *Codex in Context*, vol. 1, p. 42.

3 Cited after van den Berg, *Noordnederlandse historiebijbel*, p. 79n61.

Figure 38. Middle Dutch colophon by scribe who lost house to fire, dated 1484. Leiden, UB, BPL 2541, fol. 347v. Photo by the author.

The Last Page of the Book

The other kind of last page is the actual last page of the book instead of the text. The end of the last page of text sometimes coincides with the end of the book. It frequently happens, however, that the last text page is followed by one or more medieval leaves: either the remaining blank leaves of the last quire, which were left in place as an extra layer of protection for the text, or flyleaves added during the binding process. The latter, usually a single bifolium, were stitched into the binding between the last manuscript page and the cover board. One side would act as an extra leaf (a flyleaf), while the other half became a "pastedown" and was glued to the inside of the book's cover.

Flyleaves can be a feast for the eyes. Not only did medieval users and librarians add notes to them, but they were also a location where scribes tested their pens. The nib of the quill needed to be cut from time to time to keep it sharp. To check if it had been cut correctly the scribe would test his pen by writing down words or short sentences, including *probatio pennae* (literally, "I am testing the pen"). Sometimes a scribe attempted to draw initial letters as he tested his pen, perhaps because he was carefully preparing his pen for such a decorated letter. Just like the script of manuscripts can provide clues about where a scribe was trained, so

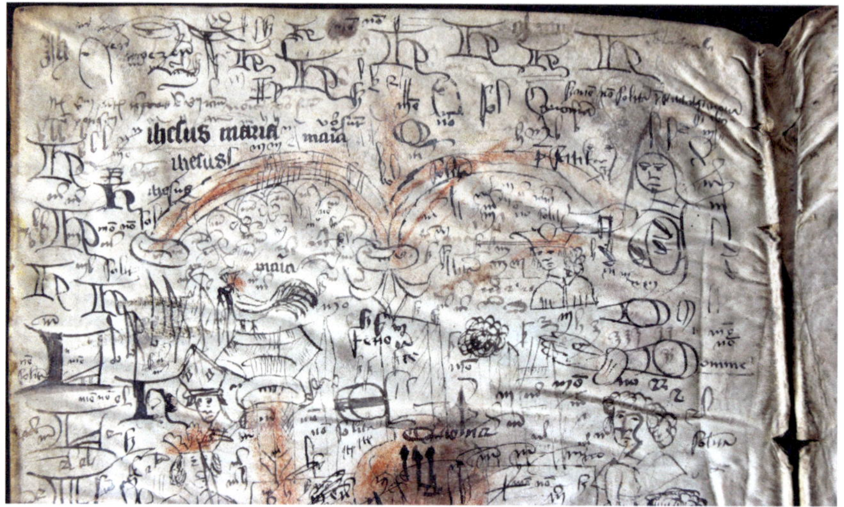

Figure 39. Collection of pen trials, fifteenth century. Leiden, UB, BPL 3327:22, fol. 1v. Photo by the author.

too can pen trials. They can lead, for example, to insights into the "pool" of monks in a certain religious house. Pen trials executed between 1075 and 1150 in two Anglo-Saxon manuscripts at Rochester Abbey, England, show that the members of that community had been trained to write at centres all over Europe: the pen trials have been executed in Dutch, German, and Italian styles of handwriting, revealing that this famous scriptorium was inhabited by a most diverse group of people.[4]

Some flyleaves contain only a few pen trials, while others attracted quite a number of them. An unusually exuberant collection of pen trials is seen in Figure 39, a bifolium that is now separated from the (unidentified) manuscript to which it served as flyleaf and pastedown. Here we see multiple scribes testing their pens, as if the whole scriptorium resorted to this one page. In fact, at least four can be distinguished based on variation in the ink colour. Some scribes wrote down capital letters (*H* and *L* were especially popular), while others preferred to doodle bishops. It is striking how much precision is used in drawing some of the faces, as if the scribe was not just testing his pen but also wanted to see how well he could decorate. Thus, the last page of the book even becomes a practice ground for would-be decorators: it makes for an appealing last look before closing the book.

---

4 Kwakkel, "Hidden in Plain Sight."

ENHANCING THE MANUSCRIPT: BINDING AND DECORATION

Figure 40. Book of hours with chemise binding (discussed at pp. 95–96). The Hague, KB, 135 J 55. With permission.

INTRODUCTION

Picking up where the previous section left off, this section deals with the ways in which the copied manuscript was enhanced, both on a decorative level and with respect to the binding. Decorators and binders have not yet been formally introduced as co-producers of the manuscript. While they were not involved in the production of the book's core, the copied text, their tasks were nevertheless important. The decorator added pen drawings, penwork decoration, or even miniatures to the text copied by the scribe. While these are often pleasing to the eye, their primary function was usually a different one: miniatures and decorated letters acted as signposts and marked important starts and transitions within the text. In other words, the reader's eyes easily fell on these colourful creations and were thus guided to new paragraphs and chapters, or to the beginning of a new text. Because of its function, decoration is yet another way to gauge how the book was used.

The binder, too, had an important role to play in preparing the object that would ultimately end up in the hands of the reader. Bindings held the quires together and turned a pile of leaves into a single entity that could be handled with ease. While it would suffice to have a binding that would merely hold the quires together, additional features were often added, such as protective elements and clasps. Like decoration, such add-ons contribute to our understanding of how the book was used, and even in what kind of environment the user consulted it, such as a private or monastic library, or while out and about. The subtext of this section, then, is to discuss two important stages in a manuscript's production, binding and decoration, while showing how these functional enhancements contribute more broadly to our understanding of medieval book culture.

The first three chapters are devoted to bookbindings and the range of features found on them. **Chapter 7** discusses the materials that were used to cover the binding, from leather to cloth, while **Chapter 8** focuses on the metalwork encountered on some bindings. **Chapter 9**, by contrast, examines the binding not as the product of a binder, but as a device that held critical information about the manuscript to which the binding was added: both owners and librarians wrote information on the leather cover of the binding in order to identify the book's contents. Other logistical information found on bindings, such as pressmarks, may even indicate in what kind of library the book was stored. There is quite a lot one can judge, then, from a manuscript's cover.

The next three chapters focus on decorative elements found on the inside of the manuscript. Three themes are chosen to show not only how medieval book decoration was often carefully considered, but also how iconography (the way in which a scene is depicted) may reflect elements or preferences of the culture that created and used the manuscript. **Chapter 10**, for example, explores the iconographical tradition of Mary's portrayal during the Annunciation, the moment when the Archangel Gabriel revealed to her that she would bear the Son of God. It was customary to show Mary as a reading figure, but medieval decorators had very different ideas about how to do this: some show her modestly handling a single book, while others place her in a library surrounded by multiple volumes.

This versatility is also observed in a special kind of manuscript decoration discussed in **Chapter 11**, which consisted of drawings built up from words. They are often found at the opening of a text, and they reveal to the reader what text he or she is about to read. However, because it concerned the beginning of the text, this title line (the rubric) was often made pretty: this way it stood out and guided the reader. However, when text is turned into an image, especially when an actual scene with humans or animals is created with words, it starts challenging the seemingly clear distinction between text and image. This, too, is discussed in Chapter 11.

Having observed colourful initials and miniatures, this section then turns to another location along the very broad spectrum of decoration. In **Chapter 12** the aim is to highlight a pragmatic use of drawn lines and shapes, namely for the creation of speech bubbles. This is also the first of a handful of chapters in this book that emphasize how many of our modern communication concepts have medieval roots: speech bubbles in manuscripts have a striking resemblance to those in current comic books. **Chapter 13**, finally, highlights a tool that was popular among decorators: the model-book, which provided both inspiration and prototypes for scenes and decorated letters. Many scenes discussed in this section were likely to have been taken from these model-books, which turns them into an important instrument in the creation of manuscripts.

Chapter 7

DRESSING UP THE MANUSCRIPT

Bindings are a key feature of the manuscript. Without a bookbinding, the quires remained individual entities. Curiously, this was sometimes the very rationale for *not* binding a book: some users preferred to keep their quires separate, for example, teachers who needed to bring only part of the book to class.[1] Another important function of the binding was to protect pages from moisture and dust, the dirt of hands and desks, and even the teeth of hungry insects and rodents. From their very early days, books were, therefore, usually given some kind of cover. Medieval bindings generally consist of two components: boards made of wood (but in the late Middle Ages also from compressed paper), as well as a material with which to cover the boards. While the most common covering material was leather, there is great variation in the kinds that were used, as well as how they were decorated. Different readers and reading communities had their own preferences in this regard. Consequently, bindings invite us to "read" the outside of the book for cultural and historical clues.

Wearing Leather

Most medieval bindings are covered with animal skin: it was usually a pig, cow, or sheep that—involuntarily—ended up guarding the manuscript. Leather proved an ideal material for bookbindings. It is flexible enough to cover the stiff boards,

1 Kwakkel, " 'Dit boek heeft niet de vereiste breedte,' " p. 44.

Figure 41. Book of hours bound in Ghent, ca. 1525–1535. Baltimore, Walters Art Museum, W.170. CC BY-SA 3.0. Source: www.thedigitalwalters.org.

but also durable. This means it does an excellent job of protecting the precious cargo it carries, while at the same time adding to the desired appearance of the book. It also repels moisture quite well. This benefit may seem odd from a modern perspective, but it is actually an important consideration: while medieval monks were unlikely to read books in the bathtub (as my spouse tends to do), they did consult them in the cloister, which was a damp environment filled with hallways in the open air. The purple manuscript in Figure 122 at p. 239 demonstrates what could happen to a book in such surroundings. An added bonus of leather was that it accommodated blind-tooled or stamped decoration, which was applied in mesmerizing shapes and patterns. It is hard to capture in photography, but the decoration is still visible in this binding made in 1525–1535 by the Ghent artisan Joris de Gavere (Figure 41).

The oldest book to survive with its original binding still stitched in place is St. Cuthbert's Gospel, which is a copy of the Gospel of John dating from the seventh century. Currently in the British Library as manuscript Add. 89000, it shows just how utterly beautiful (and charming) early medieval leather-covered bindings were.[2] This tiny manuscript was placed in the coffin of St. Cuthbert shortly after his death in 687, and was rediscovered when his grave was opened in the early twelfth century. By then a cult had grown around St. Cuthbert, so the book—in its original binding—was well taken care of. In fact, the binding looks like it was made yesterday.

The use of leather in bindings predates manuscripts made out of parchment. Before parchment became common, books were made from the pith of the papyrus plant. Such papyrus codices were extremely fragile and they needed the protective qualities of leather, which may have started the tradition of using skin for bindings. Given that papyrus fell into disuse after the fifth century (with some exceptions), very few original papyrus books survive. The oldest specimens we have are those in the Nag Hammadi library, which date to the third and fourth centuries. Unlike St. Cuthbert's Gospel, their bindings have no wooden boards. Instead, these are limp bindings: a kind of leather "folder" that was stitched to the papyrus sheets at the fold. Flaps wrap over the fore-edge to protect this side of the book and to keep it closed. The limp leather binding of Papyrus 1442 in the British Library, which dates from 716–717, shows that the covers of papyrus books could also be handsomely decorated.[3]

---

2 The object is digitized and can be found by searching for its shelfmark at www.bl.uk/manuscripts.

3 The object is digitized and can be found by searching for its shelfmark at www.bl.uk/manuscripts. For limp bindings, see Szirmai, *The Archaeology of Medieval Bookbinding*, pp. 285–319.

Figure 42. The "Hairy Blue Register," covered in cow's hair. The Hague, Nationaal Archief, Grafelijkheidsrekenkamer/Registers, 3.01.27.01, Inv. nr. 493 (1510–1540). CC0 1.0 Universal. Source: www.gahetna.nl/en/collectie/archief/inventaris/gahetnascan/eadid/ 3.01.27.01/inventarisnr/493.

Exotic Leather and Hairy Bindings

What to do if you need a leather-covered binding, but there are no pigs, cows, or sheep whose skins can be used for this purpose? This seems to have been the very problem that occupied binders in Iceland. The solution was to use skins from animals that *were* around. Take the Old Icelandic Homily Book (Stockholm, National Library of Sweden, Perg. 4⁰ no. 15), which was copied and bound in Iceland ca. 1200. To do his job, the binder turned to a creature that was available in abundance: seals. Another Icelandic book bound in sealskin is kept at the Árni Magnússon Institute for Icelandic Studies in Reykjavík: GKS 2870 4to, which contains a copy of *Njáls saga*.[4]

---

4 The object is digitized and can be found by searching for its shelfmark at https://handrit.is/en/manuscript/view/is/GKS04-2870. I owe this reference to Sheryl McDonald Werronen (Copenhagen).

The two seal bindings from Iceland clearly show the origins of their cover material: fur is still clearly visible on the binding. While it is rare to encounter hair on regular literary or historical manuscripts, it is more often encountered on archival registers. The one shown in Figure 42 is as good as it gets as far as visible hair is concerned. This "Hairy Blue Register" is kept in the Dutch National Archive, The Hague, and contains accounts for the years 1510–1540 (Grafelijkheidsrekenkamer, Registers, Inv. Nr. 493).[5] The pages of the register are filled with numerous descriptions of expenses. The "hairy" (*ruyghe* in early modern Dutch) in its title refers to the appearance of the volume, which is still covered in cow's hair. It may just be a clever way to identify the book in question, just like medieval archival bindings were sometimes called "red book" or "black volume," which helped to distinguish them from the other books on a shelf.

Cloth

However, not all medieval books were dressed in leather and fur. Less commonly used, probably because it is more fragile, is cloth. Fabric handles the frequent use of a book much worse than does leather. The real-world use of a medieval book was such that it would be pushed back and forth over a wooden desk, which did not contribute to a long life when cloth was used. Towards the late Middle Ages, however, cloth-covered bindings became more common, perhaps because so many more books were privately owned by wealthy men and women, who appear to have enjoyed cloth covers.

The manuscript in Figure 43, known as the Felbrigge Psalter (London, BL, Sloane 2400), has the earliest-known cloth covering. It was embroidered by a noble nun named Anne Felbrigge in the early fourteenth century. The delicate linen has been mounted onto a leather-covered eighteenth-century binding that replaces the original.

These soft and rich coverings suggest that the objects were not consulted on the hard surface of a wooden desk, but on the soft lap of the reader. As with embroidery-covered bindings, which continued to increase in popularity in the Early Modern period, cloth may have been regarded as a more suitable material for private reading, or publicly showing off. In tune with the dress code of their owners, as time went on, books knew when to slip into something more comfortable or something more stylish.

---

5 More information and images at www.gahetna.nl/collectie/archief/inventaris/gahetnascan/eadid/3.01.27.01/inventarisnr/493.

Figure 43. Felbrigge Psalter with earliest known cloth covering, embroidered, ca. 1300–1325. London, BL, Sloane 2400. CC0 1.0 Universal. Source: www.bl.uk/catalogues/illuminatedmanuscripts.

Chapter 8

HUGGING A MANUSCRIPT

We will linger for a while longer in the world of the bookbinding. Wooden boards and leather covers are not the only components of a medieval binding. Sometimes readers asked the bookbinder to add additional elements, some of which were made of metal. Two of these are highlighted in this chapter: clasps and tiny feet. Why were these curious-looking pieces of metal added? And what do they tell us about the manner in which the manuscript was used?

Arm and Hand

While medieval manuscripts were made for reading, the makers of these books also carefully planned how to close them and put them away. In order to preserve the organic parchment pages, it was necessary to keep the volume tightly closed when it was not in use. Not only did this keep moisture out, but parchment also has a natural tendency to buckle, especially when handled at room temperature (see the image on the cover of this book). In fact, parchment pages curl up with so much force that they would push the wooden boards open were it not for this smart device designed to keep the lid on: the clasp (Figure 44).

The clasp is like an arm that extends from one cover to the other. Indeed, I find it hard not to think of clasps as hugging arms that embrace the leaves, safeguarding them from the harsh realities of medieval book use. Clasps protected the pages by generating the pressure needed to keep them fully flat. At the end of the arm a tiny "hand" locks into an extension—we could call it a "handle bar"—as clearly visible in Figure 44. At the same time, it ensured that the book was a firm object that

Figure 44. Clasp, fifteenth century. Leiden, UB, BPL 2579. Photo by the author.

Figure 45. Removed clasp, fourteenth century. Leiden, UB, BPL 96. Photo by the author.

could withstand daily use and abuse, such as being knocked off a desk or shelf in a medieval library.

Generally, two clasps were able to contain the force issued by the buckling parchment of a book. However, it was important to get it right as a bookbinder. When the distance between the one end of the arm (say, the "armpit") and the handle bar was too much, there was insufficient pressure. By contrast, if the distance was too short, the book did not close. Medieval manuscripts that have lost their clasps, which are by far the majority, show what happens to the book when the pressure was too low: unhappy pages with a wavy pattern appeared, as seen in this manuscript that lost its clasp (Figure 45).

Up in Arms

Some readers preferred exotic clasps. A curious specimen is seen in Stockholm, National Library of Sweden, MS A 233 (ca. 1500). The book it helps to close is tiny, made to fit in the palm of your hand. It was designed for the road, containing a portable book of hours (or prayer book) that was carried around by a reader on a religious pilgrimage. The clasp holding it closed is a macabre skull carved out of bone. The theme is fitting for a pilgrim seeking redemption along the dusty roads of medieval Europe. Every time he or she sat down to open the book they were confronted with the future, which looked rather grim: *memento mori*; remember that you will die one day. Better smarten up and keep going.

The exoticness of clasps can also be connected to their number instead of their shape. Clasps are a must for a peculiar binding known as *dos-à-dos* (back-to-back). Such bindings usually hold two books bound together which share the same back board (hence the name), but the National Library of Sweden owns a unique variant that contains no fewer than six books. They are all devotional texts printed in Germany during the 1550s and 1570s, and each one is closed with its own tiny clasp. A book with six arms and hands: it is quite the display of craftsmanship.

Fancy Feet

If clasps can be compared to arms and hands, another feature of the bookbinding must be called "feet." In late-medieval libraries it was customary to store manuscripts on lecterns (see Figures 76 and 77 at pp. 143 and 144, respectively). In lectern libraries, which were found in monasteries and churches, readers consulted books while sitting on—uncomfortable—benches. The libraries were often semi-public, with outsiders walking in and out to consult books. To facilitate such use while making sure none were unlawfully removed, the books were

Figure 46. One of four feet at bottom of binding, fifteenth century. Leiden, UB, BUR Q 1. Photo by the author.

usually chained to the lecterns. Books in lectern libraries were not read on a flat surface: the objects were resting on nearly vertical stands. This kind of use presented a challenge: the shuffling that inevitably happened when the book was read wore out the lower edge of the binding. More importantly, since the medieval book block was flush with the binding, the constant dragging across the lectern as the reader flipped through the book could easily damage the page. A simple tool was invented to prevent such damage: tiny brass studs that hoisted the book up and made it hover, as it were (Figure 46). The feet that are attached to bindings are often worn to a shine, showing just how much the book was used, and how much damage was prevented by the attached feet.

Book historians tend to compare features of the medieval book to body parts. For example, the manuscript's "head" (top edge) is connected to its "spine" (the back) via the "shoulder" (the area where board meets spine). This chapter has added to such bodily analogies: the binding contained arms and feet that helped protect the manuscript during use. As it happens, these particular "body parts" are useful tools for understanding the setting in which a medieval book was used, or even if the owner was, perhaps, a private individual. They also show how in-tune bookbinders were with the needs of readers. They made sure manuscripts could withstand rough consultation, while their designs also left room for a certain amount of personality, as the example of the skull clasp shows.

Chapter 9

JUDGING A BOOK BY ITS COVER

The previous chapters dealt with the construction of the bookbinding: they highlighted the materials used to produce it and gauged how a binding sometimes reveals information about the manner in which the manuscript was used. The present chapter now turns away from the protective design of bindings and turns to modifications that were made by later readers and librarians. That is to say, both groups added logistical information—words and numbers—to the leather cover, usually with the help of pen and ink, but sometimes even with hammer and nail. By the end of the medieval period all sorts of useful information had made its way onto the binding. Some of it was aimed at library use, such as shelfmarks (or pressmarks), the equivalent of our library call number (read ahead to Chapter 17 to learn more about these). The present chapter explores the medieval roots of yet another—and very familiar—tool for finding a specific book: information related to the author and the text displayed on the book's spine and dust jacket. How did the outside of the medieval manuscript communicate what was hidden inside?

Text on Leather

Why make things complicated? The easiest way to identify a manuscript was to simply jot the title on the front cover, straight on the leather of the binding. The manuscript in Figure 48 contains Ovid's *Metamorphoses*. A fourteenth-century librarian wrote the author's name on the back of the book, using particularly dark ink: "*Ovidius Majorus*." The location of this name, on the back, indicates that the

Figure 47. Fore-edge with ownership mark of Jean, duc de Berry, fifteenth century (before 1416). London, BL, Burney 275. CC0 1.0 Universal. Source: www.bl.uk/catalogues/illuminatedmanuscripts.

Figure 48. Leather cover with two titles and shelfmark, fourteenth century. Leiden, UB, BPL 96. Photo by the author.

book was stored with the front facing down, which was often the case in the medieval period. A later librarian wrote the French equivalent of the name right above it (*"Ovid le grant"*) as well as the shelfmark "CCI" (201), which probably linked the book to an entry in a library's catalogue.

Inscriptions like these show that our modern book titles are actually a medieval invention—although because of the lack of surviving original bindings it is hard to know when, precisely, this practice began. Curiously, while the Ovid manuscript was produced in the middle of the thirteenth century, it was not until over half a century later, in the fourteenth century, that the first of the quoted titles was added to its cover (the book is still in its original binding). This tells us that its users in the second half of the thirteenth century were content with a title-less book that provided no clues as to what information it contained. This is all the more striking when you consider that the library that owned the book in question would probably have harboured several dozen others. It sparks a question that is unfortunately rhetorical: how did monks, or the community's librarian, find their way to such "anonymous" manuscripts that did not reveal their content?

Title Labels

Writing text on a manuscript's cover was not easy. The surface of the leather could be coarse and uneven, which may have made it difficult to write the title information legibly. More importantly, when the leather had a dark colour, a black title may simply not be visible. In such cases it made more sense to write the information on a parchment or paper slip—a label—that was subsequently pasted onto the cover, as is still common practice in libraries today. These paste-on labels could be quite extensive. In fact, some book owners preferred to have the entire contents displayed on the outside, even if the book held ten works. As detailed as these labels are, however, they exclusively list the titles of the works contained in the manuscript, not the authors' names. It seems as though the librarians who labelled these manuscripts judged the title, and not the author, to be the most important information for identifying a book.

The Fenestra

Paper or parchment title labels were sometimes placed under a thin piece of animal horn for protection (see Figure 49). The *fenestra* ("window" in Latin) was secured to the wooden cover with nails, as the image clearly shows. This type of cover information can be seen as the next step in the process of providing effective book titles: a clear and permanent label, hammered into wooden boards with nails. It is a far cry from the on-the-fly title hastily written directly on leather.

Figure 49. Fifteenth-century fenestra on a binding from Egmond Abbey. Leiden, UB, BUR Q 1. Photo by the author.

A fenestra is often found on manuscripts that were part of a well-organized library. The one in Figure 49 is from the library of the Benedictine Abbey in Egmond, near Amsterdam, and it provides various pieces of information to the user. It contains Lucan's *Pharsalia*, which the label in the fenestra describes as "*Historia romanorum versifice*," the history of the Romans in verse, which is a good description of the book's contents (we encountered this manuscript in two previous chapters as the teaching manual of Baldewinus). This particular fenestra works in tandem with a shelfmark, which is written on the white label right above it. It reads "Q 2," indicating that the book was placed in the Q cupboard. The use of red ink for the letter Q is significant, because it indicated that the book was housed in a library where the manuscripts were placed on wooden lecterns. The lecterns in this particular library had books on both sides (see Figure 76 at p. 143), as opposed to lecterns with books on one side only (Figure 77, p. 144). The ones on one side were marked with a black letter in their shelfmark; the ones on the other side were fitted with shelfmarks that contained a red letter. This book was apparently the second volume on the "red" side of the Q cupboard. Surviving medieval shelfmarks can tell quite a lot about the library in which the book was originally placed.

Spine Titles

Not only did the front (or back) cover display information about a manuscript's content, such information would ultimately also make it onto the spine, as any modern reader knows. This feature has its own path of development. It all started on the fore-edge, the opposite side from the spine that shows the edges of the paper or parchment pages. Although rare in the Middle Ages, modest decoration was sometimes added to this location from at least as early as the fourteenth century. Manuscript Burney 275 in the British Library shows that medieval fore-edge decoration could serve a functional purpose: Jean, duc de Berry (d. 1416) had his coat of arms painted on the fore-edge of this fourteenth-century manuscript (Figure 47 at p. 86). We may assume the books in his library were positioned with the fore-edge facing outward, as was common practice in many medieval libraries. How impressive his library must have looked to visitors: dozens of precious books, all evidently owned by the duke.

Given that the fore-edge was facing the reader, this location was also the perfect place to write down the title or author of the work contained by the volume. The earliest cases I have encountered date from the fifteenth century, although there may have been earlier examples now lost: fore-edges were often cut when binders in the Early Modern period refurbished books with new bindings.

When books eventually turned their backs to the reader, the title ended up where it is still found today: on the spine. Based on my interaction with manuscripts, this practice was uncommon in the Middle Ages, perhaps because manuscripts were not usually placed with their backs facing the reader. By the Early Modern period, however, it had become so popular that some readers wrote extensive tables of contents on the spines of their books.

The early path towards displaying a book's title, and eventually its author, on the outside is long and winding: first the information was found on the front or back, then on the fore-edge, and finally on the spine. This order is no coincidence, because it roughly reflects changes in how books were stored: first flat (early and High Middle Ages), then upright with the fore-edge facing the reader (late Middle Ages), and finally with the spine facing outward (Early Modern period). What is striking about this brief history of medieval "dust jackets" is that some medieval books were apparently not fitted with a title, at least not right away (like the Ovid manuscript discussed above). In such cases readers or librarians could not tell what texts were found inside a book unless they opened it. That said, frequent users may recognize a certain volume from the features of its binding, such as its colour and decoration or the type of clasp used to close it. Frequent perusing of a library teaches us to judge a book by its covers.

AVE MARIA

Chapter 10

MARY HAD A LITTLE BOOK

Having explored in the previous chapters how the outside of the manuscript was enhanced, it is now time to turn to the inside of the book and see what happened there after the scribe had finished copying the manuscript. The next three chapters each highlight a type of decoration—a decorative tradition, even. The first of these, discussed in the present chapter, shows how the Annunciation scene was depicted in medieval books of hours. The Annunciation tells the biblical story in which the angel Gabriel announces to Mary that she will give birth to the Son of God, Jesus Christ (Luke 1: 26–38). There is something very attractive about these scenes for lovers of medieval books. Especially in the late Middle Ages, Mary is pictured reading when Gabriel breaks the news. The idea was to show her in a holy place engaged in prayer, and to make this connection to the beholder; she was shown with a book, which shows just how important books were for practising religion. In other words, this particular scene invited decorators to depict a reader engaged with a book, in a life-like fashion and to the best of their abilities. While being careful not to take medieval iconography too literally, we are given a glimpse into the practice of reading: how the book was held, what it looked like, and what kind of binding it had.

The Manuscript Tradition

A quick search in public online databases results in hundreds of Annunciation scenes: as of the time of publishing, the British Library Catalogue of Illuminated Manuscripts returned 173 manuscripts, and the French *Inititale* database no fewer

Figure 50. Annunciation scene, ca. 1250. Baltimore, Walters Art Museum, W.34, fol. 31v. CC BY-SA 3.0. Source: www.thedigitalwalters.org.

than 407.[1] These manuscripts provide much information about the tradition of a reading Mary. It is striking, for example, just how many Annunciation scenes depict her with a book, as seen in the Carrow Psalter, a ca. 1250 manuscript from East Anglia (Figure 50), where Mary holds a red book in her hand while greeting Gabriel. It became so much of a tradition, in fact, that after 1300 there are few scenes without a book.

The results from the image databases allow us to gauge in what kind of manuscript the scenes are predominantly found. By far the majority are books of hours, but there is also a fair share of psalters and bibles, as well as some liturgical books such as missals. The most popular vehicle of this scene, the book of hours, is *the* vehicle for texts used in a setting of private devotion: it contains prayers, psalms, the Litany of Saints, the Office of the Dead, and other short texts, which were read several times per day.[2] Many psalters were also used for this purpose, as were some bibles. In other words, the readers of these manuscripts were engaged in precisely the same thing as Mary: praying with a book in their hand.

It is telling for the importance of the manuscript that both Mary and the medieval reader are interacting with it during moments of private devotion. What is also striking is that Mary is shown interacting with the book in different ways. In some cases she is simply holding the object in her hand, either open or closed (as in the Carrow Psalter). In the later Middle Ages, she is usually caught reading, with the book placed either in her hand or on a table or podium in front of her. In most cases Mary is depicted in a room or a building with arches, providing the illusion of a church or private chapel.

While it is really easy to find bookish Annunciation scenes from the later medieval period, when the tradition of a reading Mary was well-established, examples from before 1100 are rare. The earliest I have been able to find date from the late tenth century. One of the oldest is the magnificent Benedictional of St. Æthelwold, which was made in 963–984 for Æthelwold, Bishop of Winchester (Figure 51). Others dating from the late tenth century are found in luxury manuscripts produced in monasteries close to the court of Otto III.

Beyond Manuscripts

Older examples of a reading Mary do exist, but not in books (the sample from the two databases did not return them, in any case). A scene dating to 860–880 is found on the

---

1 The British Library Catalogue of Illuminated Manuscripts is found at www.bl.uk/catalogues/illuminatedmanuscripts ("annunciation") and Inititale: Catalogue de manuscrits enluminés at http://initiale.irht.cnrs.fr ("annonciation").

2 Duffy, *Marking the Hours.*

Figure 51. Annunciation scene, ca. 963–984. London, BL, Additional 49598, fol. 5v. CC0 1.0 Universal. Source: www.bl.uk/catalogues/illuminatedmanuscripts.

earliest surviving ivory *situla*, a bucket for the Holy Water used in the Mass (New York, The Metropolitan Museum of Art, Acc. Nr. 7.190.5).[3] It shows Mary looking up from her book to see the angel Gabriel making a gesture of blessing with his hand. The arch above her suggests she is in a room, a holy space, as seen in so many manuscript depictions. As in many of the images in manuscripts, Mary is shown holding a surprisingly small object in her hand. These are probably meant to represent a portable book, a type of manuscript designed to be carried around.

If we expand our scope and include medieval paintings, we are shown other details of the medieval book as a physical object. Notably, the famous Mérode Altarpiece from the early fifteenth century shows Mary holding a book fitted in what is called a chemise binding (Figure 52).

This type of binding allowed the reader to fold the book into a piece of cloth or leather extended from the binding. Very few have survived from the medieval period, but a particularly well-preserved specimen survives in the Royal Library of the Netherlands in The Hague (see Figure 40 at p. 71). It is fitted around a book of hours that was produced during the 1460s in Valencia, Spain. Measuring only 15 cm × 10 cm, the object is quite modest in size—about the size of a smartphone. Curiously, the Mérode Altarpiece also shows a second book on the table, with a green "bag" underneath it. This bag is another medieval bookish artifact that survives in very small numbers: the manuscript pouch, which was also

3 This object is digitised by the museum and is found at www.metmuseum.org/art/collection/search/464438.

Figure 52. Workshop of Robert Campin, *Annunciation Triptych*, oil on oak, detail, ca. 1427–1432. New York, The Metropolitan Museum of Art, 56.70a-c. CC0 1.0 Universal. Source: www.metmuseum.org.

used for carrying a book around. These bookbindings and bags indicate that the manuscripts Mary uses are portable. More importantly, the beholder would have recognized them as such. By the late Middle Ages, devotional practices had become mobile, and so books used to that end needed to be shown as ambulant. In that sense, the manuscripts depicted in these paintings are very realistic.

The Mérode Altarpiece shows Mary with not one but two books. It appears that this increase started in the fifteenth century and continued into the age of print. A book of hours from an artist known as the "Master of the Polemical Texts" of Bruges shows Mary with three thick volumes, while the famous *Belles Heures* of Jean, duc de Berry, produced by the Limbourg Brothers in the early fifteenth century shows Mary with three books at hand (one placed on a lectern, two inside a compartment), plus a roll (New York, Metropolitan Museum, 54.11a, b).[4] In a woodcut from 1511 by the famous Albrecht Dürer there are at least three books present (New York, Metropolitan Museum, 1975.653.5).[5] Mary is consulting them while sitting at a small lectern (there is probably a fourth copy in front of her), which gives the setting the distinct feel of a library. Considering that she would soon have a child, it makes sense that Mary try to get as much quality time with her books as possible.

4 This object is digitized by the museum and is found at www.metmuseum.org/art/collection/search/470306.

5 This object is digitized by the museum and is found at www.metmuseum.org/art/collection/search/388014.

ihs xps · Matheus homo
incipit euangelii
genelogia mathei

Chapter 11

DRAWING WITH WORDS

This chapter introduces a very different iconographical tradition from the Annunciation scenes in the previous chapter. The kind of decoration discussed here challenges our seemingly clear cut distinction between text and image. By now it is evident that the medieval page was generally filled with two things: words and decoration. Words make up the text, of course, and are executed with pen and ink, while illustrations, produced with brush and paint, decorate the text. There are medieval manuscripts, however, in which this convention is turned upside-down: they contain decoration created by words, inviting the reader to read an image. This intriguing scenario blurs the divide between text and illustration, and it challenges how we define both.

Decoration Forming Words

Decorative elements forming readable text are fairly common in medieval manuscripts. High-quality volumes often open with words—or even a full sentence—that are painted with a brush rather than copied with a pen. The Lindisfarne Gospels, which is perhaps the most impressive manuscript that survives from the early Middle Ages (it was made at Lindisfarne on the coast of Northumberland between ca. 710 and 721), is famous for this mix of words and decoration. The page in Figure 53 shows the *incipit* (the opening line) of the Gospel of Matthew, which is executed with brush and paint: "*Liber generationis Iesu Christi filii David filii Abraham*" ("The book

Figure 53. Lindisfarne Gospels, incipit to Gospel of Matthew, ca. 710–721. London, BL, Cotton Nero D.IV, fol. 27r. CC0 1.0 Universal. Source: www.bl.uk/catalogues/illuminatedmanuscripts.

of the genealogy of Jesus Christ, son of David, the son of Abraham"). Trying to read this sentence is like solving a puzzle.

In spite of the fact that it holds words, this decorative page and the others in the book are commonly discussed within an art-historical context, not as expressions of writing (they are prime examples of Hiberno-Saxon art). This magnificent page blurs the boundary between text and image: it presents something to read, but nothing has actually been written, in the traditional sense of the word, with a pen. The intriguing hybridity forced the user to read a painting.

Words Forming Decoration

Much more unusual is a different mix of text and image: instances where a meaningful scene is made out of words. Delightful examples from manuscript production in the West include that of Cygnus, a swan (Figure 54), taken from a ninth-century copy of Cicero's *Aratea*, on astronomy. The pages in this manuscript show constellations represented as animals and gods according to Greek mythology (the solid red dots in Figure 54 are stars). Curiously, the animal illustrations consist, for the most part, of words written out with a pen.

The text in the swan is not actually the *Aratea* itself, which is found lower on the page, underneath the swan. The animals are instead formed by an explanatory text by Hyginus, called the *Astronomica.* Here, word and image are engaged in a peculiar symbiotic relationship wherein one would become meaningless without the other. Without words the swan, which represents a constellation, would be incomplete; and without the painted top part of the swan, the meaningfulness of the word pattern would be lost.

A similar tradition is witnessed in Torah manuscripts of the tenth century. It introduced a phenomenon called micrography, the art of decorating the page with meaningful text written in tiny letters. By the thirteenth century, Hebrew manuscripts often contained elaborate depictions of humans, creatures, and objects—all made from written words (Figure 55). Jewish religious leaders protested against this practice of drawing with words, as they felt it distracted from taking in their meaning.

See the Music

The notion of drawing an image with words took further steps in the late Middle Ages. By the thirteenth century, for example, we encounter marginal glosses in the shape of objects and people, and sometimes even the entire main text. The fourteenth century Chantilly Codex (Chantilly, Musée Condé, 564) is a particularly

Figure 54. Swan made out of words from Hyginus's *Astronomica*, ninth century. London, BL, Harley 647, fol. 5v. CC0 1.0 Universal. Source: www.bl.uk/catalogues/illuminatedmanuscripts.

Figure 55. Micrography in Hebrew manuscript, ca. 1250–1300. London, BL, Additional 21160, fol. 181v. CC0 1.0 Universal. Source: www.bl.uk/catalogues/illuminatedmanuscripts.

elaborate late medieval variation on this theme. It contains over a hundred polyphonic songs by French composers, including one song composed by Baude Cordier called "*Belle, Bonne, Sage*" ("Beautiful, Good, Wise"). As the Renaissance was nearing, wordplay became a favoured occupation of poets, including in a visual sense. Cordier borrowed the word *Cor* (*coeur*, heart) from his name and used it for the visual presentation of this song, forming the notes and lyrics in the shape of a heart.[1] Cutting-edge design? Hardly. Drawing and writing at the same time was old-school.

1 An illustration can be seen at "Chantilly Codex" in Wikipedia at https://en.wikipedia.org/wiki/Chantilly_Codex.

corde suo non est deus.
Corrupti sunt et abhominabiles facti s̄t
in iniquitatibȝ: non est q̃ faciat bonū.
Deus de celo prospexit super filios ho
minum: ut videat si est intelligens
aut requirens deum.
Omnes declinaverunt simul inutiles fa
cti sunt: non est qui faciat bonum non

Chapter 12

SPEECH BUBBLES

Even more so than before, the decoration style in this chapter blends decorative shapes with functionality. Although it may appear peculiar at first, this chapter is driven by speech. Books are generally quiet objects, apart from the rustling of their leaves as you flip them. The fact that the book is a silent medium (besides audio- and e-books) implies that sound embedded in a text is not heard but read. Generally, this was no problem, except that in book illustrations it was sometimes necessary to indicate that certain words were uttered by certain people. How to show that it concerned direct speech? And how to indicate who said what? Decorators employed an all-too-familiar strategy to deal with these issues: they used speech bubbles. This chapter examines the different ways in which speech was visualized in medieval decoration. As is shown here, they take on different appearances, some of which show a striking resemblance to those encountered in our modern comic books.

Dialogues

The British Library owns a ca. 1300 copy of Jacobus de Voragine's *Legenda aurea*, the most popular collection of saints' lives from the later Middle Ages (Stowe 49).[1] The manuscript contains a number of marginal drawings in which the characters

1 Stowe 49 has been digitized by the British Library, and can be found by searching for its shelfmark in their Catalogue of Illuminated Manuscripts at www.bl.uk/catalogues/illuminatedmanuscripts/welcome.htm.

Figure 56. Man holding banderol, ca. 1205–1210. Los Angeles, The J. Paul Getty Museum, MS 66, fol. 56r. Public domain. Source: www.getty.edu/about/whatwedo/opencontent.html.

Figure 57. Scene with talking travellers in lower margin of manuscript, ca. 1300. London, BL, Stowe 49, fol. 122r. CC0 1.0 Universal. Source: www.bl.uk/catalogues/illuminatedmanuscripts.

are shown talking. In one of them we see a group of people strolling, some of them with a walking stick in their hand (Figure 57). You can almost hear their sing-songs in the background. Curiously, we are looking at a group of travellers conversing in English. What is perhaps even more remarkable is that the words they speak are written out and connected to the mouths of the persons that utter them. In other words, as in modern comic books, there is a visual connection between words on the page and the fictional person that speaks them. Also paralleling modern comic books, the story that unfolds in the Stowe manuscript is funny and familiar.

The following conversation may be overheard. The figure on the left starts with a strange mantra: "They die because of heat, they die because of heat." Then the two young people on his right speak, probably addressing their father, who is walking behind them: "Sir, we die of cold!" The father, carrying a heavy toddler, orders them to stop whining: "Behold your little brother in front of us, he is only wearing a hood." (He is right, because the child is otherwise naked.) Then the toddler speaks, uttering universal toddler sounds: "Wa we." Finally, the two children in the back come into play. "Sir, I am carrying too much weight," says the one on the left. The one on the right closes the conversation by comparing his own misery to that of his brother and father, stating "It is not they who carry the heaviest burden."[2]

The Middle English scene is recognizable to many of us. We are shown a family en route to an unknown location. The young ones are verbally poking at each other,

2 Identification of these figures' roles and a translation of their conversation is here paraphrased from that offered in Freeman Sandler, "Pictorial and Verbal Play," pp. 52–68.

and complain about the temperature and the weight of their suitcases. It is the medieval version of a modern parent's nightmare: being on the road with a crying toddler and whiny kids that egg each other on. "Are we there yet?" The most notable feature of the scene, however, is the ease with which we can reconstruct the dialogue—thanks to the graphic support.

Banderol

Books before print used yet another method to make a silent figure on the page speak: the banderol. This clever device gave the decorator the ability to make someone deliver a short statement. Short, because it had to fit on a tiny roll. In Figure 56 (p. 104), for example, we see a fool repeat the words whispered in his ear by the devil: "There is no God" (*Non est deus*). The speaker holds the tip of the scroll in his hand, so as to claim the words as his own, while the angel above him tries to dissuade him of this error.

Such points of contact (the narrator holds the scroll or touches it) were particularly important when an image presented more than one speaking person. It allowed the viewer to identify who was saying what. Alternatively, and particularly interesting in light of the comic book parallel, is that the banderol was not always held in or close to the speaker's hand: it could also flow from his or her mouth on a white scroll. While such cases are less common, they have a strikingly modern appearance because the banderol creates the illusion of a real text bubble. Not all banderols present such a "live" text. Some label a scene, while others clarify the identity of a person.

No Bubbles

Then there are, finally, manuscripts where direct speech is written in mid-air, unsupported by a banderol or a bubble. In order to relate the uttered text to a given person, the scribe wrote the lines in such a way that they appeared to flow from the speaker's mouth. The resulting wavy lines of text dance across the page. An example is seen in Karlsruhe, Badische Landesbibliothek, St. Peter Perg. 92 (Figure 58). This miniature is part of a cycle on the life and work of the scholar Ramón Llull (d. 1316). Here he is shown conversing with Thomas Méysier, his student and disciple. The images in the cycle were made under personal supervision of Thomas, who also compiled the contents of the manuscript, which presents a compilation of Llull's work called the *Electorium parvum sue breviculum*.[3]

---

3 A study and facsimile of this manuscript is available in Römer and Stamm, *Raimundus Lullus*.

Figure 58. Ramón Llull and student engaged in discussion, after 1321. Karlsruhe, Badische Landesbibliothek, St. Peter Perg. 92, fol. 11v. CC BY-SA 3.0 DE. Source: https://digital.blb-karlsruhe.de.

Over a big and authoritative pile of books we see master and student engaged in a lively discussion. Arguments fly across the page. It looks like the scribe is trying to help the viewer keep track of the discussion through the use of different colours (red and black). Also, the scribe presents the conversation in such a way that each component begins with a line that sticks out slightly. Cleverly, the extended tip is found next to the speaker's mouth, leaving no doubt as to who is saying what. No bubble required.

Chapter 13

MODEL-BOOKS

Having discussed a variety of decoration styles in medieval manuscripts, the present chapter adds contextual information to the culture of decorating manuscripts. While decorators were creative individuals, they had some help in how to depict certain scenes or decorated letters. They could look these up in model-books, which appear to have been quite popular in the later Middle Ages.[1] A true feast for the eye, these books are filled with drawings and paintings that were meant to show scribes and illuminators how to embellish letters, paint initials, or add large segments of decoration to the page. Within this tradition, two types of model-books can be distinguished. Some functioned as instruction manuals, providing detailed step-by-step instructions for artisans. Other model-books appear to have merely functioned as a source of inspiration: they present a wide array of shapes and drawings from which the artisan could take his or her pick.

The level of sophistication among surviving model-books varies considerably. On the lower end of the spectrum there are pattern books that merely show how to make enlarged letters with some minor flourishing. On the higher end, by contrast, there are copies with rich stand-alone designs and sophisticated historiated initials inhabited by figures and scenes. Evidently the requirements of artisans varied, and, by proxy, so did the taste of medieval readers, for whom these drawings were ultimately meant. It is this variation that makes

1 Scheller, *Model-Book Drawings*.

Figure 59. Page from Gregorius Bock's Scribal Pattern Book, ca. 1510–1517. New Haven, Beinecke Rare Book and Manuscript Library, Yale University, MS 439, fol. 31r. Public domain. Source: http://beinecke.library.yale.edu/tags/digital-collections.

model-books so fascinating, both as physical objects and as cultural artifacts. The following examples illuminate the breadth of the genre and the appeal of these medieval "supermodels."

Plainly Decorated Letters

To start at the lower end of the spectrum, some model-books merely showed book artisans how to draw plain enlarged capitals, the most basic kind of decoration. The book opening seen in Figure 59 is from Gregorius Bock's Scribal Pattern Book, which provides instruction on both fronts. Produced in 1510–1517, the first part of the small parchment book contains a series of alphabets in different scripts, some of which are clearly influenced by print typefaces (New Haven, Beinecke Library, Yale University, MS 439).[2] The second part contains decorative initials arranged in alphabetical order. In the introduction to his manual, Gregorius adds a dedication to his cousin Heinrich Lercher Wyss of Stuttgart, who was scribe to the Duke of Württemberg. The arrangement of the material shows how Heinrich probably used the book: he would thumb through its pages until he had reached either an alphabet or capital letter to his liking.

While Bock's letters are a pleasure to look at, they were not the cream of the crop. More complex, but still relatively plain, are the models provided by a much older pattern book in The Fitzwilliam Museum at Cambridge University (MS 83-1972). It appears to be the oldest surviving pattern book for initials: it dates from ca. 1150 and was produced and used in a Tuscan workshop. Its choices are much more limited than in the previous example: the Cambridge model-book does not provide multiple alphabets, nor does it present a wide range of initials. The same goes for a pattern book from ca. 1425–1475 kept in the British Library as Sloane 1448a: encompassing only thirty-one leaves, the choice is limited to a modest selection of initials that are rather plain in appearance (Figure 60).[3]

Elaborately Decorated Letters

From the more upscale end of the book-making market is the model-book known as the Macclesfield Alphabet Book (London, BL, Add. 88887).[4] It was made and

---

2 This manuscript has been digitized by the library and can be consulted by searching for the shelfmark at http://beinecke.library.yale.edu/tags/digital-collections.

3 The object is digitized and can be found by searching for its shelfmark at www.bl.uk/manuscripts.

4 The object is digitized and can be found by searching for its shelfmark at www.bl.uk/manuscripts.

Figure 60. Page from model-book with alphabets, ca. 1425–1475. London, BL, Sloane 1448A, fol. 22r. CC0 1.0 Universal. Source: www.bl.uk/catalogues/illuminatedmanuscripts.

used in fifteenth-century England, apparently to provide models for decorators and their assistants. The artisans were offered a lot of choice, given that we encounter no fewer than fourteen different alphabets on its pages. What makes this book so special, however, is the quality of and manner in which the letters are designed: their shapes are produced by human figures. As in other model-books that include letters made out of people, the figures are shown in the most uncomfortable positions, as if doing yoga exercises.

A similar subject matter is encountered in the alphabet book of the Italian artist Giovannino de Grassi (Bergamo, Biblioteca Civica, inv. cassaf. 1.21). This book was created at the Visconti court and features both initial letters and standalone drawings. The Visconti were known as important patrons of the arts and so it makes sense that we see their generosity extend into the world of book production. Giovannino was known for depicting exotic animals in their natural habitat, and this book also features such images. His pages provided models for other artists who wished to replicate his realistic depictions.

Border Decoration

Even more sophisticated are model-books that show how to create elaborate decoration that runs in the margin along the length of the page. These border decorations, with their curly leaves and unexpected turns, could be tricky to produce. The Göttingen Model Book, made around 1450, provides a solution to this problem. Its pages show, step by step, how to build a 3D leaf pattern, using both depictions of the various stages and detailed prose instructions, like the following:

> The foliage one shall first draw with a lead or a point. Then one shall outline the foliage with a pen and with very thin ink or with thin black color. Then one shall polish the foliage with a tooth, so that the color can be applied smoothly, but not too firmly. Then one shall paint it with the colors, one side right and the other side left or reversed, with a brush, namely light red and green, that is to say green or slate green: The two colors belong together, one side light red and the turnover green, as shown here, or one side green and the turn-over light red, as you like.[5]

The drawings and narrative clearly complement one another. From time to time the instructions refer to the illustrations, saying something like "as it is shown here" or "as the image shows." A model-book can hardly be clearer than this: while the alphabet books described above were, more or less, simply meant to show possible scenes to include in a manuscript, the Göttingen book really takes artists by the hand and guides them through each step of the production process. The instructions apparently worked well, as is shown by a surviving Gutenberg Bible that contains these very leafy borders (Göttingen, Niedersächsische Staats- und Universitätsbibliothek, 2i Bibl. I, 5955 Inc. Rara Cim).[6]

Pouncing

The tradition of model-books shown here is also encountered in other cultures, including in Byzantine and Arabic book production. The artefact shown in Figure 61 presented Arabic decorators with models of scenes from the New Testament. This specimen is interesting because it presents a type of instruction not often seen in Western copies: some of the figures have been outlined by tiny holes; using a technique called "pouncing," the sheet could be used as a sort of tracing paper (look carefully, for example, at the angel Gabriel, carrying a spear). While this instruction method took all potential flaws and creativity out of the modelling process, it allowed decorators with lesser talents to produce something beautiful.

---

5 Images and an English translation of the Göttingen Model Book are found at www.gutenbergdigital.de/gudi/eframes/mubu/mubufset.htm. The quoted selection is found on fol. 1r. See also Lehmann-Haupt, *The Göttingen Model Book*.

6 Parallels at www.gutenbergdigital.de/bibel.html.

Figure 61. Tiny holes as result of pouncing practice, 1400–1700. New Haven, Beinecke Rare Book and Manuscript Library, Yale University, MS 553, recto. Public domain. Source: http://beinecke.library.yale.edu/tags/digital-collections.

Post-Medieval

Models are crucial in any learning process. Observing how something is done helps you acquire a skill or further develop those you already have. Moreover, there is an additional use for the medieval pattern books introduced above: the beautiful letters and shapes could also be browsed by readers looking for a good image for their newly commissioned book. Patrons visiting artisans' shops could well have been given these volumes to visualize what the decorator was capable of providing, and choose from its pages the styles they wished for their made-to-order book—in parallel to the same patrons visiting the professional scribe's shop to pick out a script.

The practice of providing scribes, decorators, and their customers with models continued until well beyond the Middle Ages. Even in the age of print, books were written by hand, and post-medieval scribes and decorators also needed some help and inspiration from time to time. Moreover, printed books from the fifteenth and sixteenth centuries also included hand-painted decoration and here, too, models were used, as the Göttingen Gutenberg shows.

The sixteenth century is also the age of the *trompe-l'oeil*, which is French for "deceive the eye." This was a very popular genre of painting, because it allowed decorators to play tricks on the reader. They painted an object so real that you would think it *was* real. The champion of this genre was Joris Hoefnagel (d. 1542), whose model-book is seen in Figure 62.

The models in his book include flower stems pricking through the page, bugs that walk among the letters (you have to suppress the urge to wipe them off), and fruit that is so real it makes your mouth water. Combining the two medieval categories of model-books, Hoefnagel's detailed paintings are accompanied by script samples in different styles of writing, which could be used as models by scribes. The one seen here presents a particular pointy type of letter of an

Figure 62. Trompe-l'oeil by Joris Hoefnagel, 1561–1562, additions from 1591–1596. Los Angeles, The J. Paul Getty Museum, MS 20. Public domain. Source: www.getty.edu/about/whatwedo/opencontent.html.

undefined script family. Underneath it a frog is about to jump off the page, while the page holds up two flowers, which are stuck through the surface. To make it even more real, the other side of this leaf shows the tiny parts of the stems that are out of sight here. Evidently, this particular book models an alternative, highly entertaining reality.

READING IN CONTEXT: ANNOTATIONS, BOOKMARKS, AND LIBRARIES

Figure 63. Book carousel depicted in Jean de Meung's *La consolation de Boèce*, fifteenth century (discussed at pp. 218–19). Leiden, UB, LTK 575, fol. 37r. With permission.

INTRODUCTION

Whereas the previous sections of this book were devoted to producers of manuscripts, highlighting the accomplishments and products of scribes, decorators, and binders, the focus will now shift to readers and reading practices. It is much harder to shed light on this dynamic of medieval written culture. Books before print contain relatively few ownership inscriptions of specific medieval owners; moreover, rarely do *ex libris* inscriptions affiliate the manuscript to its *first* owner, the person or community that had the book made. The latter type is most interesting, as the General Introduction explained, because the first owner is the one who influenced (or, in case of a commercial book, even negotiated) the material features of the manuscript. While the next five chapters explore various aspects of reading culture in detail, we rarely encounter "real" readers, people we know by name and can place on the map of Europe.

Even though medieval readers of surviving manuscripts are commonly anonymous, many of them left traces that enable us to gauge why they consulted the manuscript or how they valued the text it held. The first two chapters explore these marks left behind during the act of reading. As **Chapter 14** shows, medieval readers frequently consumed their books with a pen in their hand. This instrument was used to make notes in the margin, verbally attack the author of the text, and correct and expand the text, if needed. Moreover, readers highlighted important passages with special signs. It was so common for readers to engage with the text in this manner that it is indeed quite unusual to encounter manuscripts with spotless margins. While the absence of marginalia does not necessarily mean that the book in question was not read (an incorrect inference found in some studies), a margin that remains empty does limit our ability to say something about the people who read the book in the Middle Ages.

Chapter 15 subsequently highlights a particularly charming marginal addition, one that was deemed so useful that it even made it into the era of print: a pointing hand, or manicula, as defined in this book's General Introduction. The symbol was used to identify passages that mattered to the reader who employed it. To us modern observers, these pointing hands can be turned into an instrument to deduce what a particular reader found interesting or useful about a manuscript by analyzing all passages they mark. It is helpful, in this respect, that the pointing hands are usually personalized: individual readers often gave their maniculae their own distinctive shape. Like the marks discussed in Chapter 14, what started as a reader's response to a text can be turned into tool to understand what motivated medieval people to pick up a certain book, or return to a particular passage in it.

A similar sentiment is encountered in **Chapter 16**, which focuses on an external tool added to the manuscript to aid the reader: the bookmark. Medieval bookmarks, which come in different shapes and sizes, are versatile and extremely useful in spite of their usually plain appearance. They served a variety of purposes, from simply marking the page where the reader left off (as we still do today), to indicating the column and precise line where the reader stopped. Some of them even enabled the reader to mark several pages at the same time. Like maniculae, bookmarks can also be used to explore medieval reading culture: some can be used to gauge what individual readers deemed important in a given manuscript.

The remaining two chapters of this section turn away from marginalia and deal with the contextual dynamics of reading: they discuss libraries as well as the security measures that prevented books from being stolen—a real worry given the value of manuscripts. The first of these, **Chapter 17**, inquires how the books available to a medieval reader were stored. Very few medieval libraries survive in their original state, and none, it appears, from before the fourteenth century. Consequently, our look into the medieval book repository has to be indirect, based on surviving library instruments such as catalogues and pressmarks. The last chapter of this section, **Chapter 18**, turns to the security measures that readers and libraries had at their disposal to prevent their precious books being stolen. Some of these measures make sense and are all too familiar (locking books away in a safe place, for example), while others, like adding a curse to the object, are harder for a modern person to comprehend, although from a medieval point of view they are completely logical.

Zooming in and out, from tiny marginal marks to large rooms filled with books, the five chapters in this section approach the theme of reading from both material and contextual perspectives.

SATYRICON LIBRI VIIII · DE DIALETICA I · DE RETHOR I · DE GEOMETR I · DE ARITHM I · DE ASTROLOG I · DE ARMONIA I

MARTIANI MINEI FELICIS CAPELLE. AFRI CARTAGINIENSIS DE NUPTIIS PHILOLOGIAE LIBRI DUO · DE ARTE GRAM LIB I · LIBER PRIMUS INCIPIT

T uquem psallentem thalamis quem matre camena. Pro
genitum peribent copula sacra deum. Semina qui archa
nis stringens pugnantia uinclis; Coplexuq; sacro dissona
nexa foues. Naq; elmta ligas uicib; mundumq; maritas
Atq; auram mtis corporibus socias. Foedere conplacito sub quo
natura iugatur. Sexus concilians et sub amore fidem. O hymenee decens
Cypridis qui maxima cura es. Hinc tibi nā flagrans ore cupido
micat. Seu tibi qd baccus pat est placuisse choreas. Cantare ad thala
mos seu genitricis habes. Comere uernificis florentia limina sertis
Seu consanguineo gratia trina dedit. Conubiudiuum ē ponēs ce callio
pea. Carminis auspitio te sociata annuerit.

Dum crebrius istos hymenei uersiculos nescio quid inopinum intactumq; moliens
cano respsū capillis albicantib; uertice incremtisq; lustralib; decuriatū
nugulas ineptas aggarrientem pferens martianus intuenit dicens; Quid istud
mi pat qd nondū uulgata materie cantare deppas. Et ritu nictantis antis
titis pusquā fores ędituq; reseras ΥΜΝΟΛΟΓΟΥCEIC. Quin potius edoce
qd apportes. Et quorsū pdicta sonuerint reuelato; Ne tu unquā delipis cęcino
duq; pspicuo operis ΕΓΕΡΙΜΙΟΝ. noscens crepertu scepis. Ne liquā hyme
neo plibante disposita nuptias resultare. Siuero ccepta cuius scaturigi
uena pfluxerint pperus scrutator inquiris. Fabellatibi quā satira
comminiscens hyemali pugilio marcescentes mecū lucernas edocuit nupli
xitas pculerit explicabo; Cū inter deos fierent sacra conubia peraccionis im
dliq; numerose liberiq; pcluies. Ac nepoti dulcium aetheria multitudo.
& int se quodā caeli colcerū ēplexu ac foedere potirent. Psertiq; potissimos

EGERIMION lex nuptiarum

Chapter 14

GETTING PERSONAL IN THE MARGIN

A medieval book was made because an individual or community wanted to read, and own, the text contained on its pages. Some miniatures show readers surrounded by books, as in Figure 63 at p. 119. Looking at this particular scene, one cannot help thinking how contently the man looks at the colourful books in front of him (we return to this person in Chapter 28, where his unusual-looking desk is discussed). However, despite the plentiful books in this miniature, owning books in the age before print was a luxury. Due to the expensive materials used, the cost of a book's production was significant, even if it contained no decoration or miniatures. It may seem odd, then, that despite their expense, medieval readers wrote in their books, voicing their opinions on the text wherever they could, often extensively (Figure 64). In Chapter 2 we saw how scribes extended the manuscript's margins to facilitate marginal additions. Let us now look at the same phenomenon from the readers' point of view. What did they add to the pages in front of them? And what do their additions reveal about their motivations for reading?

Annotations

The most common voices heard on the medieval page come from marginal annotations on the text. While in some manuscripts only a few annotations are encountered in the margins, in others these are filled to the brim, as Figure 64 shows. Readers had different reasons for doing this.[1] While reading St. Augustine, one may suddenly remember a relevant passage in the work of another Church

1 Teeuwen, "Marginal Scholarship."

Figure 64. Heavily annotated page, ninth century. Leiden, UB, VLF 48, fol. 2r. Photo by the author.

Father. With a quick stroke of the pen the reader could place a reference in the margin, perhaps even citing the name of the other authority next to it. Or a quote could be added, either by heart or copied from another book. Monks in particular had access to sizable reference libraries: their contents were true temptations for critical readers seeking to interact with the text in front of them.

Alternatively, a reader may jot down a clarifying word, phrase, or sentence next to a passage that was hard to understand. In Latin books such notes may start with *id est* ("this is" or "this means"). They are particularly common in university textbooks, but are also frequently encountered in books from other environments, including monasteries. Clarifying notes were usually placed in the margin; shorter notes were sometimes scribbled between the lines. More exceptionally, readers drew schemes or diagrams to help make sense of the text.

Highlighting Information

Readers also used their pens to highlight important information. They could do so by drawing lines in the margin alongside the text, as we would do today, but there were also more sophisticated means. A particularly attractive one is the pointing finger, or manicula (see Chapter 15). This particularly expressive signpost comes in different variants. At one end of the spectrum there is the simple hand with its pointer finger extended; at the other end there are hands with elaborate sleeves, or even those with entire bodies attached to them. A less conspicuous way of pointing out important information was to place the imperative *nota* (take note!) next to it in the margin. The manner in which these signs were executed was highly personal: readers made their own customized pictogram out of the four letters of the word (Figure 65).

Figure 65. Nota sign constructed with letters "n o t a," ninth century. Leiden, UB, VLQ 10, fol. 93r. Photo by Giulio Menna.

Critiquing the Text Quality

Marginal annotations sometimes critiqued the text next to which they were written. In Chapter 3 a setting was introduced in which this was a common occurrence: the university. Some Aristotle textbooks carry as many as five blank marginal columns for this purpose (Figure 66). However, there were plenty of critical readers outside the university context. Take, for example, how a Carthusian monk interacted with one late fourteenth-century Dutch Gospel Book (now Vienna, Österreichische Nationalbibliothek, Cod. 12.857). Having already corrected dozens of mistakes, a third of the way into the text he remarked the following with a pen shaking from frustration: "These Gospels have been translated poorly; [the translator] did not understand them very well" ("*Dese evangelien sijn alte matelec gedietscht, diet dede verstont se qualec*," fol. 95v). This particular reader is known for his critical pen. He is also encountered in the margins of a manuscript in the Royal Library in Brussels (shelfmark 2849–51), where he corrected yet another flawed translation, of the New Testament. This time he went about systematically comparing the Middle Dutch to the Latin original. There are hundreds of corrections, and every now and then he exclaims in the margins: "This is how I would translate it in Dutch" ("*Dus soudic dat dietschen*"). Take that, translator![2]

Use or Abuse?

Looking at the input of readers on the medieval page makes for interesting research because it allows us to look over the shoulders of the very people whose books we study. Evidently, some medieval readers read with a pen in their hand, ready and willing to make their mark on the page and in the text. However, the line between use and abuse is thin. Figure 67 shows a page where the name Peter ("*Petrus*") is written in the lower margin. The name is written in a hesitant and uneasy fashion, perhaps scrawled by someone learning to write. Given that this book was produced in a monastic environment, we may well be dealing with a novice (a young member of the community) who had just mastered pen and ink. "I can write," this inscription seems to say, "I am Peter and I can write!" Well, that is great, the modern observer mutters, but why on earth would you try your hand in the margin of a manuscript? On top of that, Peter's fingers must have been rather inky, because the parchment surrounding his name shows a lot of staining. He seems to have been new to the whole pen and ink thing.

---

2 Kwakkel, "A Meadow Without Flowers," pp. 196–97 (2849–51) and 204–5 (Cod. 12.857), both with image.

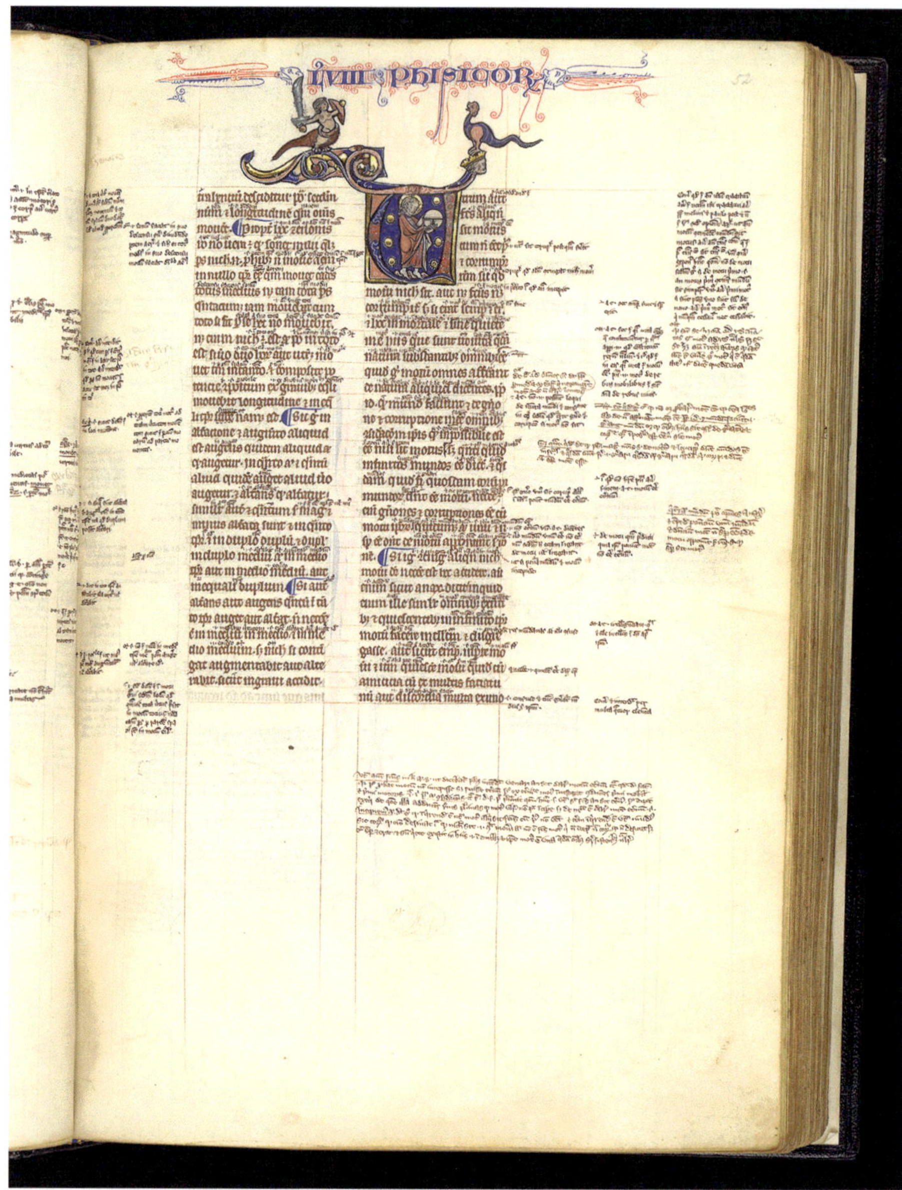

Figure 66. Aristotle manuscript with five vertical annotation columns in margins, ca. 1250–1275. London, BL, Harley 3487, fol. 52r. CC0 1.0 Universal. Source: www.bl.uk/catalogues/illuminatedmanuscripts.

Figure 67. Name *Petrus* (Peter) written in margin, twelfth century. Leiden, UB, BPL 21. Photo by the author.

While we may want to forgive novice Peter for his careless behaviour, there is also deliberate defacement that is more difficult to forgive. With Bamberg, Staatsbibliothek, Msc. Var. 7, an early seventeenth-century fencing manual, a reader has crossed the line between use and abuse.[3] The fencing scenes in the book are illustrated by men who show off various ways of handling their swords—without wearing any clothes. A reader clearly did not like the approach of the decorator and he or she went to great lengths to cover up the private parts of the two opponents. Big fat drops of red wax, of the type used for making seals, were splashed on the page to bring the scenes in line with the standards of the straitlaced reader. No problem to behold two stabbing figures in a battle for survival, but we don't want to see them do it naked. While unforgivable, even this kind of interaction shows us something about readers from the past: some of them were prudish.

3 Leitschuh and Fischer, *Katalog*, p. 501. The digital images of this manuscript have been taken down from the Bamberg website, but a relevant one can be retrieved by searching for "Msc. Var. 7."

23

secundum quod ostendit arist. primo de anima [illegible] tamen actus [illegible] patet [illegible] separare non intellig-
itur et dicit quod [illegible] simplices non potest esse secundum quod loquitur de illa [illegible] simplici que
est forma [illegible]. libro xiii. [illegible] quod ipsa veritas [illegible] eius tres sunt sic materia [illegible] et compositum
non de sola [illegible] nec de sola specie sed de omnibus et [illegible] intellect-
[illegible] et i^o [illegible] magis [illegible] oppositum [illegible]. ut si illa [illegible] principis [illegible]
[illegible]. Error quod necesse est omnis duas esse naturas [illegible] compositas
et [illegible] de [illegible] sicut [illegible] et sensibile et [illegible] et de
[illegible] necesse est quod [illegible] naturam [illegible]
et [illegible] simplicibus quod de [illegible] patet. [illegible] et [illegible] necesse [illegible] non [illegible]
[illegible] sicut [illegible] et [illegible] non [illegible] materia vel
forma [illegible] magis [illegible] et [illegible] sbe
[illegible] de forma quod [illegible] non [illegible] de [illegible]
[illegible] de forma [illegible] sicut [illegible] et [illegible] non negat a boetio
[illegible] exemplificavit quod non [illegible] et i^o non [illegible]
[illegible] Boetius dicit [illegible] magis
esse [illegible] libro xiii. et [illegible] per [illegible] libro 6. Error quod [illegible] quos
aliqua que sunt [illegible] secundum [illegible] carnes et san- ut in
guine sicut [illegible] et animis. non tamen omnia que sunt [illegible] materiam.
libro xiii. Error quod [illegible] que posset esse et non esse [illegible] quod [illegible]
[illegible] ut quod [illegible] formas aliquas [illegible] posse non esse. [illegible]
tam [illegible] nec intelligentias [illegible] esse corruptibilia quod non sunt in se principium no-
[illegible] possent deficere [illegible] diffinitur
secundum [illegible] et quod [illegible] potentie [illegible] influentie. et istud
[illegible] principe in libro de motu animalium. [illegible] xi. metaphysice. libro 9. Error quod anime sensibiles
multiplicantur secundum multiplicationem corporum [illegible] separate [illegible]
et [illegible] separate sequitur [illegible] multitudine in quibus [illegible] quodammodo
sicut si calor ignis [illegible] multa circumstantia amoto calore sine igne
[illegible] illa remaneret [illegible]. similiter si forme [illegible] possent separari a corporibus
eodem modo. unde et anime sensibiles non possunt [illegible] completa
quod sunt [illegible] corporum et in [illegible] intelligentie. libro 9. Error quod [illegible] actus
purus [illegible] intellectus. intelligentia [illegible] et [illegible]
essentia [illegible] in omni [illegible] contra [illegible] omnia [illegible]. Et [illegible]
dicit [illegible] quod [illegible] et eius esse sunt idem. Error quod [illegible] et
[illegible] non [illegible] per formam [illegible] sicut [illegible]. anima et intellectus non sunt [illegible]
[illegible] concomitative [illegible] intellectus materialis semper [illegible] in actu
[illegible] nec de [illegible] possibili. [illegible] intellectus agens [illegible] abstractus
semper [illegible] intellectus materialis semper actu intelligens [illegible] ille qui
actu intelligit. libro 10. Error quod [illegible] magis [illegible] potentia passiva [illegible]
per formam [illegible] que [illegible] prima [illegible] secundum potentiam activam quod [illegible] per [illegible]
i^o physicorum et [illegible] xi. nulla [illegible] potentia activa [illegible] infinita [illegible]
[illegible] potest una forma [illegible]
[illegible] nec [illegible] duas successive [illegible] potentie [illegible] ad magis potens
[illegible] a motore [illegible] ad moriens [illegible] similiter [illegible] forma
[illegible] sunt [illegible] extra suam materiam. et [illegible]

Chapter 15

HELPING HANDS ON THE PAGE

This chapter deals with another marginal notation that reveals reading practices: the *manicula* (Latin for "little hand"). While these helping hands usually have a single purpose—they highlighted an important passage—their appearance varies considerably. This is because there was no standard format for the hand, beyond the point that it had to resemble one. Some were shaped like really tiny hands, for example, while others were quite extensive; some presented just a large finger, while others show hands with an entire arm attached. Since the reader was able to shape the hand and finger as he or she saw fit, we can sometimes recognize a particular reader in several places within a single manuscript, or even within several books of a library. Here we explore the variety encountered in these personal pointers.

Plain Hands

The term *manicula* is somewhat deceptive. Pointing hands are almost never just pointing hands. As mentioned, there are often arms attached, which may even be fitted in sleeves (see Figure 69 overleaf and Figure 24 at p. 41). Sometimes these sleeves are elaborate and realistic, with folds and all. It is an exciting thought that the medieval reader who added a tiny drawing in the margin may simply have looked down and replicated his own arm. And why not? It is not easy to draw a hand by heart, but a model was quite close by. If this is true, we may potentially be able to tell something about the reader's status or background, for

Figure 68. Pointing hand in shape of dragon, thirteenth century. London, BL, Royal 12 E.xxv. CC0 1.0 Universal. Source: www.bl.uk/catalogues/illuminatedmanuscripts.

Figure 69. Large pointing hand with nail, thirteenth century. Leiden, UB, VLQ 99, fol. 10v. Photo by the author.

example, whether he is a monk (wearing a habit) or a private individual. A related point of attention is that some hands look surprisingly natural. The example in Figure 69 has the digits in just the right shape and angle. There is even a fingernail illustrated (if the reader used their own hand as a model, he or she really took care of their nails).

Looking at surviving *maniculae* in medieval books sparks yet another correction: tiny hands are often not really tiny. The one seen in Figure 69 takes up almost the full width of the marginal space. As you would expect, pointing fingers are attached to both left and right hands. Without having done any conclusive research on this, it appears right hands are more common than left ones.

Elaborate Hands

Not all pointing hands look realistic, however. One particular phenomenon is frequently encountered: the pointing finger is stretched well beyond human proportions (as in Figure 70). The reason, of course, is that the tip of the finger needed to point out one particular line, otherwise the system would fail. The fingers of a pointing hand can easily be even more elaborate. Some show a full hand with the fingers fanning out so that several lines could be pointed out. In one

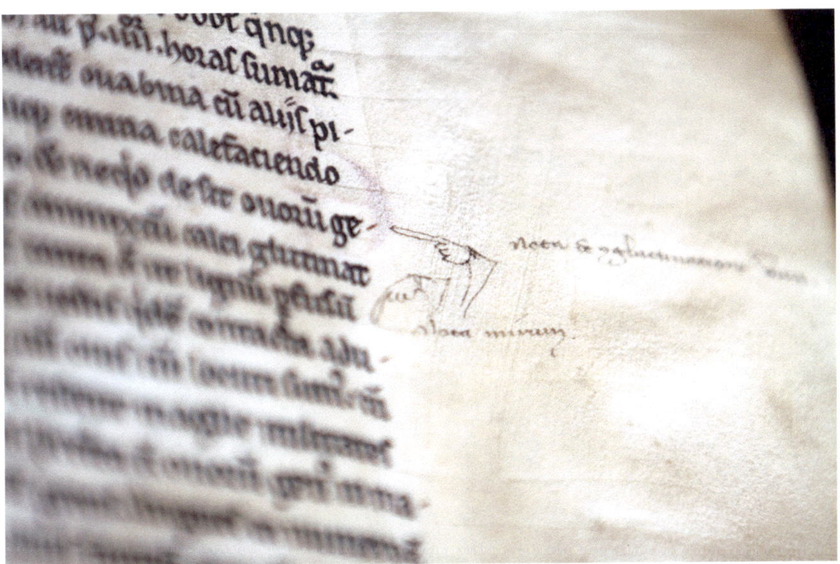

Figure 70. Pointing hand with extended finger, thirteenth century. Leiden, UB, VLQ 4, fol. 104r. Photo by Giulio Menna.

manuscript an octopus was used as a *manicula*: all its tentacles are drafted into service to point out an entire segment of the text that was of importance to the reader (Berkeley, Bancroft Library, MANC UCB 85).[1]

Exotic Hands

Then there are the more exotic hands. Figure 68 on p. 128 shows an arm that is turned into the body of a dragon (right margin). This "hand" is probably not just meant to point out an important passage; it must also have been intended to bring a smile to the reader's face. Notably, while this dragon could have been doodled, others encountered in medieval books were obviously carefully designed and painted. Some of them have a professional appearance, as if the manuscript's decorator—and not the reader—was responsible for placing them in the margin. This would suggest that medieval readers may also have asked artisans to execute pointing hands during production. This is interesting because it means that

---

1 MANC UCB 85 has been partly digitized by the University of California, Berkeley Library, and can be found by searching for its shelfmark in Digital Scriptorium's catalogue at http://bancroft.berkeley.edu/digitalscriptorium.

Figure 71. Traffic light for cyclists in Leiden, the Netherlands. Photo by the author.

readers already knew what passages they would wanted to have highlighted, perhaps because they already knew the text well before owning a copy.

The range of helping hands is remarkable. There were other, easier ways to mark important passages, such as lines and crosses placed in the margin. However, in some cases readers preferred to have a more pronounced signpost. While a tiny line could be overlooked, the hands—particularly large ones, and those executed with colour—really pulled your attention to the text that mattered. That particular sentiment lives on today, given that the traffic light for cyclists in Leiden, The Netherlands, where I used to live, show a *manicula* (Figure 71). "Dear cyclist," the modern version expresses, "push the button if you don't want to wait here all day." Now that is helpful.

fac.

Quod uero gauisum me dico. non dico quasi ppt penuriam. ut s. de penuria tristis. de ipsius gaudeam supplemento. Nam de huiusmodi nec tristari soleo nec gaude. immo in omnib; me equanimiter habeo. Ego enim consuetudine quadam didici sufficiens esse meis in quib; sum. Scio et humiliari. scio et habundare. ubiq; locorum et in omnib; rebus a deo sum institutus. s. et saturari et c. Ut nec habundantia extollar. nec inopia frangar. Veruntamen benefecistis et c. i. inde potius gaudeo quia benefecistis. Nec modo solum. s; antea hac sepe. Quod ait ita. Scitis autem et c. In ratione dati et accepti. i. quando uterq; dat et accipit. ut cum uobis ego dedi spiritualia et uos mihi carnalia misistis. Quod dico. non quia quero datum. i. rem qua exterior homo impletur. et cuius egestate corrumpitur. sed quia requiro fructum. i. bonam et rectam uoluntatem qua interior fecundatur. Unde et dominus in euangelio. non dicit simpliciter qui recipit iustum. sed addit in nomine iusti. Recipere iustum. datum est. In nomine iusti. fructus. Heliam pauisse leguntur coruus et uidua. Sed coruus qui [illegible] in nomine iusti. pauit dato. Vidua qui [illegible] nomine iusti. pauit fructu. hunc ergo fructum magis quam datum requiro. habu[illegible] autem gratia in ratione uita. Vel habund[illegible]m quia multa bona inde peruenirunt. h[illegible] autem. Quasi. Fructum requiro. [illegible] autem. non. Nam habeo omnia et hab[illegible] [illegible] enim et c. In odorem sua[illegible] de uotione. per quam elem[illegible] incensum. Ut; Date [illegible] bit per uobis; Hostiam [illegible] uincere hostes; De[illegible] autem [illegible] me repleuistis; D[illegible] autem et c. [illegible] as suas. quib; u[illegible] merita dat in gloria. in xpisto ihu per[illegible]m omnia. Deo autem et c. Gratia domini nostri i[illegible] xpi sit cum spiritu uestro. ut in spiritualib; h[illegible]deatis. Amen [illegible]

non quasi propter penuriam dico. Ego enim didici in quib; sum sufficiens esse. Scio et humiliari. scio et abundare ubiq; et in omnib; sum et saciari et esurire et abundare et penuriam pati. Omnia possum in eo qui me confortat. Verumtamen bene fecistis communicantes tribulationi mee. Scitis autem et uos phylippenses quod in principio euangelii quando profectus sum a macedonia nulla mihi ecclesia communicauit in ratione dati et accepti nisi uos soli. Quia et thessalonicam et semel et bis in usum mihi misistis. Non quia quero datum. sed requiro fructum abundantem in ratione uestra. Habeo autem omnia et abundo. Repletus sum acceptis ab epaphrodito que misistis in odorem suauitatis. hostiam acceptam deo placentem. Deus autem meus impleat desiderium uestrum secundum diuitias suas in gloria in xpisto ihesu. Deo autem et patri nostro gloria in secula seculorum. Salutate omnem sanctum in xpisto ihesu. Salutant uos qui mecum sunt fratres. Salutant uos omnes sancti maxime autem qui de domo cesaris sunt. Gratia domini nostri ihesu xpisti cum spiritu uestro amen. amen

Colosenses sunt et hii sicut laodicenses asiani et capti erant a pseudo apostolis nec ad hos accessit apostolus ipse sed et hos per epistolam corrigit audierant enim uerbum ab arcyppo qui et ministerium in eos accepit. Ergo apostolus iam ligatus scripsit ab epheso.

Chapter 16

SMART BOOKMARKS

As the previous chapters have shown, medieval readers were pragmatic and they did not shy away from adding things to their books if it enhanced their reading experience. While so far the focus has been on additions to the page, this chapter introduces a physical tool that was sometimes added to enhance the reading experience even further: the bookmark, which, like the *manicula*, had a variety of appearances. Here we look at the various ways in which monks and other medieval readers kept track of the page at which they had stopped reading, and from which they planned to continue reading in the near future. What tools were available for this purpose? And how did these differ from one another?

Static Bookmarks

If certain bookmarks can be called "smart," and some really are, it follows that others were, well, dumb. In bookmark terms that qualifier must go to types that are fixed to one specific page rather than being able to freely move throughout the book. Some of these static bookmarks were extremely easy to produce. All the reader had to do, for example, was attach a string to the corner of the page. A slightly more labour-intensive version of this static bookmark is seen in Figure 73. It was produced by making a small cut in the corner of the page, after which the emerging strip was guided through a small incision, and then folded outwards, so as to stick out of the book. The result was as unmovable as it was destructive to the page. A slightly less invasive version, no doubt preferred by medieval librarians, didn't involve cutting but rather gluing a tiny strip of parchment on the long side of the

Figure 72. Revolving sliding bookmark, fourteenth (?) century. Harvard University, Houghton Library, Typ 277, unfoliated. CC 4.0 International. Source: http://hcl.harvard.edu/libraries/houghton/collections/early_manuscripts/index.cfm.

Figure 73. Page bookmarked with parchment incision, twelfth century. Leiden, UB, BPL 2001.

page. These "fore-edge" bookmarks could even be filled with extra information, such as which section started at the marked location.

Dynamic Bookmarks

Far more "technical" and interesting from a book-historical point of view are bookmarks that could be used at any page of the manuscript because they were movable—let's call these dynamic. An unusual thirteenth-century example survives in what is now Amsterdam, UB, I G 56–57: heart-shaped bookmarks that could be clipped onto a page. Notably, they were cut out of a thirteenth-century manuscript with scissors. The crafty recyclers were twentieth-century nuns who clearly did not appreciate old books. The movable bookmark in Figure 74 was also produced with a pair of scissors, but no manuscript was destroyed to make it. It concerns a bookmark that was placed in a book in much the same manner as we still do today: stuck in the heart of the quire and with its tip sticking out from the top of the book (note the stained left side of the strip). The manuscript in which it survives is a fat German codex from the fifteenth century filled with medical texts (University of Pennsylvania Libraries, LJS 195). The bookmark contains a somewhat cryptic reference to lungs and a substance that needed to be pulverized

Figure 74. Loose bookmark, fifteenth century. Philadelphia, University of Pennsylvania Libraries, LJS 195, unfoliated. Public domain. Source: openn.library.upenn.edu.

(*"Lüngen pulver das güett"*) and it is possible that it was first used as an aide-mémoire before it was turned into a bookmark.[1]

The downside of such stick-in bookmarks is that time tended not to be very kind to them. Since they could be easily separated from the book, many actually were. The solution to the vanishing bookmark came in the form of what is called a "register bookmark." It is, essentially, a collection of cords or thongs attached at one end. This type, which looks like a spider with its legs trapped, could be securely fastened to the top of the binding, so it couldn't get lost. Additionally, the bookmark allowed the reader to mark multiple locations in one book.

Evidently, these two groups of bookmarks—static and dynamic—provided very different approaches to marking information, and thus to a book's use. Readers who used the dynamic type anticipated they would need to retrieve information not from one single page but from several. In other words, movable bookmarks served an audience with a shifting appetite for knowledge, while static ones encouraged a more normative, front-to-back use of a book.

Multi-Dynamic Bookmarks

And then there is, finally, the "multi-dynamic bookmark" (to give it a term). This qualifier refers to the fact that this bookmark is of the moving type, while at the same time it is able to do much more than simply mark a page. The bookmark's use is as simple as it is clever. This becomes clear when we look at the device in action, for example, in this twelfth-century bible in the Houghton Library (Figure 72 at p. 134).

---

1 LJS 195 has been digitized by the University of Pennsylvania Libraries and can be found in its Lawrence J. Schoenberg Manuscripts online repository at http://openn.library.upenn.edu/Data/0001/html/ljs195.html.

As you can see, it consists of two components. As with the register bookmark, it features a string attached to the top of the binding (in this case the string is a strip from a recycled manuscript page). This allowed the reader to mark a certain page. Nothing new here. The second component, however, is what makes this a smart bookmark: a disk with the numbers one to four written on it, fitted in a tiny sleeve looped over the string. The reader would pull the marker along the string until the flat top hit the line where he had stopped reading. The disk could subsequently be turned to the appropriate column—an open medieval book usually showed four columns of text—meaning that the device marked page, column, and line.

Thirty-five or so column indicators have survived from the medieval period, which is quite a lot for semi-loose material that had plenty of time—centuries, in fact—to get separated from the book.[2] This number may indicate, then, that it was a popular device, although it is hard to say how common they were. At any rate, this type of bookmark remained in use during the era of print: one is found, for example, in an incunabulum with sermons printed in 1473.[3]

Bookmarks in Perspective

Different bookmarks point at different ways of consuming the text in a book: unmovable types, like the one produced with an incision in the parchment, marked, permanently, information that the reader anticipated they would need their entire life. The paper slip, by contrast, seems a spur-of-the-moment bookmark, which was produced by quickly grabbing a piece of paper that was nearby. The reader needed to return to this tomorrow, it expresses—but not necessarily the day after. Both the dynamic and multi-dynamic types were "professional" kinds of bookmarks, meant for frequent and heavy-duty use. They were probably available in an environment where texts were studied frequently and where the subjects of such studies changed all the time. It made no sense to use a static bookmark for such circumstances. In fact, permanent markers would arguably be confusing in a setting where books were picked up for different reasons all the time. To each their own bookmark.

---

2 Emms, "Medieval Rotating Column-Indicators" (with inventory of all surviving medieval specimens).

3 See Ferguson, "15th century bookmark with column indicator," *Notabilia* (blog), https://blogs.princeton.edu/notabilia/2014/07/12/15th-century-bookmark-with-column-indicator.

Liber M. Will. Reed Epi Cicestren. quem emit a ven.
pre. dno Thoma Tryllek Epo Roffen. Oretis pro utroque

Contenta

1. Sermones ad diversos status et officiorum genera incerti
2. Statuta Ecclesiae Herefordensis.

XII volume

[illegible]

Liber magistri et scolarium collegii de Trinitatis Cicestr. ex dono venerabilis
patris domini Willelmi tercii Episcopi Cicestr. qui idem collegium a nobili viro
domino Ricardo comite Arundell fundatum de consensu omnium quorum interfuit
auctoritate pontificali erexit. Oretis igitur pro eodem cum benefactoribus eiusdem ac
fidelium animabus a purgatorio liberandis. Et voluntas legantis est quod liber
iste in eodem collegio firmiter cathenetur.

Chapter 17

LOCATION, LOCATION

While marginal scribblings and bookmarks invite us to gauge how readers interacted with their books, this chapter (and the next) turn to another dimension of the medieval reading experience: book repositories. Libraries provide their own view on the practices of reading in the Middle Ages. If we could wander around a medieval library, we would learn a lot about how, precisely, books were consulted and how they were stored. Imagine looking over the shoulders of readers and the earliest curators of manuscripts! However, since very few medieval libraries survive in their original state, such information needs to be deduced from other evidence, for example, from the logistical information placed in books by librarians. Here we explore one of these: the "call number" or pressmark.

The present chapter addresses a seemingly simple question: how did a reader find a specific manuscript in a space that held perhaps several hundred of these objects? So how did medieval readers locate books, especially when they owned many of them? The answer lies in a neat trick that resembles our modern GPS: a book was tagged with a unique identifier (a pressmark) that was entered into a searchable database (a library catalogue), which could subsequently be consulted with a handheld device (a portable version of the catalogue).

Shelfmarks

The most effective tool for retrieving a book in the medieval library was to give it a number and place it in the correct sequential order on the shelf. It is still common

Figure 75. Donation inscription (bottom) and pressmark "*XII volumen*" (middle of page), ca. 1300. London, BL, Royal 10 E.XI, fol. 1v. CC0 1.0 Universal. Source: www.bl.uk/catalogues/illuminatedmanuscripts.

practice in modern libraries and for good reason: as long as the book is put back in the right spot, you are able to find it again quickly. Such book numbers—shelfmarks or pressmarks—come in various formats. The more books a library owned, the more complex the pressmarks became (had to become, actually). The simplest type merely stated that the book in question was the twelfth volume in the cupboard, as seen in the opening of the manuscript shown in Figure 75.

Similarly, in small collections books were marked with single letters. In Bethlehem Priory near Brussels, each item in the small library of Middle Dutch books was given a letter, which was placed on an empty page in front of the manuscript together with a short title. The first volume in this mini library was a late fourteenth-century copy of works by the mystic Hadewijch (now Ghent, UB, 941). On its opening flyleaf (the blank page before the text starts) we can still faintly read "Visiones haywigis. A," showing it contains the *Visions* of Hadewijch and that it is the first book on the shelf (expressed by the letter A).[1]

Larger libraries—with more books than letters in the alphabet—needed a more sophisticated shelfmark system. A particularly clever one is found in manuscripts that were placed on lecterns, like those used in some chained libraries. The shelfmarks might have two components: a letter pointed to the appropriate lectern, while a number indicated the book's position on the shelf. Because manuscripts were placed on both sides of the lectern (Figure 76), a bit of colour was added to distinguish between the sides (Figure 77 at p. 144 shows a lectern library with books on one side). Red letters referred to books placed on the right side, black ones to those on the left (see Lucan's *Pharsalia* in Figure 49 at p. 89). Much like a modern GPS, the tag on a manuscript's cover ties the object to a unique location: it concerns the third book on the right side of the sixteenth lectern.

Inventories

Having a location tag is only useful, of course, if there is a searchable database from which the book's location may be retrieved. How would you otherwise get to Lucan's *Pharsalia* in the library, or even know it is present there? The contents list of a monastic library was usually merely an inventory: scribbled on a blank leaf in a manuscript, it marked the presence of a book, but not its location. While some of these inventories were written out in books (never mind how you would even find them), others were pasted to the wall in the library, like the specimen from St. Jerome's Abbey in Leiden, which measures 80 cm × 59 cm (see Figure 103 at pp. 200–1). The books in this list are numbered sequentially (1, 2, 3, etc.) within

1 Kwakkel, "Ouderdom en genese," p. 135.

Figure 76. Chained library *De Librije* in Zutphen, the Netherlands, sixteenth century, with books placed on both sides of the lectern. Photo by Jenny Weston.

categories such as *libri refectoriales* (books read during meals) and *libri devoti et utiles* (books for personal, spiritual development), as discussed in Chapter 25. However, there is no clear indication as to where each book may be found. Librarians had to wander through the library to find the right section and then start counting to find the book they were looking for, which was not very efficient.

Handheld Devices

The later Middle Ages saw a surge of real catalogues, listing books and their location. From several monastic libraries in the Forest of Soignes just outside Brussels, catalogues survive that actually refer to the sophisticated type of shelfmark seen in Figure 48 at p. 88. The ones from Zevenborren Priory (now Brussels, KBR, II 1038 and 7602, both early sixteenth century) refer to books on both the "black side" and the "red side" of the lectern. The catalogue of the lectern library in another abbey

Figure 77. Cesena, Bibliotheca Malastestiana, fifteenth century. Lectern with shelf beneath the reading surface. CC0 1.0 Universal. Source: Wikimedia Commons (Boschetti marco 65).

in the forest, nearby Rooklooster Priory, is the cleverest of the lot. It comes in the form of a book with a peculiar shape (now Brussels, KBR, II 152). It is long and narrow, a format that indicates it was made for handheld use.

Curiously, the shape of the pages resembles the long inventory slips on the side of book cupboards in chained libraries, fitted in wooden frames. The handheld Rooklooster catalogue must have been copied directly from such slips on the side of the lecterns. What a clever tool the user ended up with. The open catalogue in his hand presented two columns, one for books on the "black" (left-hand) side of the lectern, another for books on the "red" (right-hand) side. Moreover, each column is divided into two halves. The top half lists books placed on the upper shelf of the lectern, the lower half those on the lower shelf, which were placed under the lectern. The Malatestiana Library in Cesena, which opened its doors on August 15, 1464, shows what these shelves looked like (Figure 77).

Standing in front of a lectern with this handheld device, the reader knew precisely which of the volumes in front of them was the one they were looking for: they could identify it without even opening it. Like a modern navigation system, the precise coordinates of manuscripts, as listed in the handheld catalogue "device," directed librarians and readers to works such as St. Ambrose on the Psalms (Black A 1) and Augustine's *Civitate dei* (Red A 5).

1 π

et ne adorarent omne deum excepto deo suo.

A me ergo propositum est hoc decretum. ut omnis populus. tribus. et lingue. quecumque locuta fuerint blasphemiam contra deum sidrac misac et abdenago. dispereat. et domus eius uastetur. neque enim est alius deus qui possit ita saluare., Tunc rex promouit sidrac mysac et abdenago in prouincia babylonis. nabuchodonosor rex. omnibus populis. gentibus et linguis qui habitant in uniuersa terra. pax uobis multiplicetur.,

S igna et mirabilia apud me fecit deus excelsus. placuit ergo michi predicare signa eius. quia magna sunt. et mirabilia eius. quia fortia. et regnum eius regnum sempiternum. et potestas eius in generatione et generatione;

I N NOMINE PATRIS. ET FILII. ET SPS SCI. AMEN.

Quicumque istum librum epistolarum ab ecclesia sancte xpi uirginis Ceciliae. rapuerit. alienauerit. uel quocumque modo fraudauerit. iudicio sancti spiritus perpetue maledictioni subiaceat. & cum iuda proditore domini perpetuo crem etur incendio. nisi emendauerit. aut reddiderit. FIAT. FIAT. FIAT. AMEN.

I TEM AD MISSAM MAIOREM.

LECTIO EPISTOLE BEATI PAULI APOSTOLI AD COLOSENSES;

Chapter 18

COMBATING BOOK THEFT

The previous chapter lead us into the medieval library and we now linger there a while longer. As medieval book repositories grew in size, so too grew security concerns. Making sure your books remained yours was an important part of the medieval reading experience, especially near the end of the period, when libraries opened up their doors to readers from outside the community. Some religious houses allowed people from the outside world to consult books (sometimes they could even borrow them), while the late-medieval city saw the coming of semi-public libraries, which readers could enter if they were granted permission. Given the high cost of manuscripts and the practical problems that arose with replacing a lost copy (it may take half a year to produce one), librarians were really careful about protecting their precious manuscripts. Looking at their options, some strategies are very pragmatic, while others appear wholly ineffective to our modern eyes.

Chains

The least subtle but most effective way to keep your books safe was to chain them to a bookcase. This is effectively what happened in the "chained library." Walking around in such a place is an utterly surreal experience: it looks more like a prison than a library. The chains produce a "cling-cling" sound when you walk too close to them, a sound that must have been familiar to medieval users of these libraries (Figure 79). While there are only a modest number still in existence today, many of the medieval books we consult in modern libraries were once part of such a

Figure 78. Page with book curse, tenth century. New Haven, Beinecke Rare Book and Manuscript Library, Yale University, MS 1000, fol. 27v. Public domain. Source: http://beinecke.library.yale.edu/tags/digital-collections.

Figure 79. Chained library *De Librije* in Zutphen, the Netherlands, sixteenth century. Photo by the author.

collection of "imprisoned" books. Objects that were once chained can be identified with ease, either from the attached chain (not very common) or from the rusty imprint its clamp left in the wood of the bookbinding.

The primary reason for chaining a book was, obviously, safekeeping. Just like phones and tablets on display in stores are fixed to their display tables with straps, these precious medieval books were bolted to the library that owned them. This feature of *stabilitas loci* (alluding to the Benedictine ideal of staying in one location as a monk) turns the chains, or their rusty traces at the upper or lower end of manuscripts' fly-leaves (Figure 75 at p. 140, lower edge), into something interesting beyond the strictly book-historical sense. It shows, after all, that the text inside the object was available in a public or semi-public place, such as a church or a cathedral. In other words, chains (or traces of them) suggest how information was accessed, and potentially by whom.

Book Chests

Not all chained books were part of a "real" library (say, a room with one or more bookcases). The famous seventeenth-century Gorton Chest from Chetham's Library in Manchester shows that books were also chained inside a book chest. This particular example was made in 1658 to contain sixty-eight volumes that were purchased from the bequest of Humphrey Chetham. The lot made up the full extent of the parochial library of Gorton Chapel.

While book chests were common furniture in the Middle Ages, most of them did not actually feature chains. Surviving specimens suggest that the majority were merely wooden boxes, often reinforced, that were fitted with one or more locks. The theft-prevention plan of these chests was simple yet effective: the filled object was too heavy to move or steal, while the locks kept the contents safe from theft. In a sense, the heavily reinforced chest is the equivalent of a modern safe. Similar chests were used for other kinds of precious objects. Sometimes an additional theft prevention strategy was added. The 1296 book provision document of Merton College, Oxford, specifies that the books were placed in a chest with three locks. Keys are to be handed out, it states, to the warden and sub-warden, who would hand them out to fellows of the college against a pledge.[1] A gentleman's agreement to keep safe the college's books.

Smaller chests appear to have been mounted to the walls of cathedrals, such as in Exeter and Canterbury.[2] Remarkably, in Exeter Cathedral one still survives today (Figure 80). The box was designed to contain a single book, which was probably used for services in the nearby chapel, just to the left of the pillar to which the box is attached. Because there are so few left, we know very little about how these boxes worked. How was the book kept safe? Did the box originally have a lock? It seems probable, but if it was there once, it has since disappeared. Moreover, was the ring attached to the wall just beneath the box part of the set-up? Was there perhaps a chain running from there to the book?

Cursing

While we can probably relate to these practical theft-prevention techniques, the third seems a little odd to our modern eyes: writing a curse against book thieves inside the book. Your typical curse (or *anathema*) simply stated that the thief would be cursed, like this one in a book from an unidentified Church of St. Caecilia, now in the Beinecke Rare Book and Manuscript Library at Yale University (MS 1000): "Whoever takes this book or steals it or in some evil way removes it from the church of St. Caecilia, may he be damned and cursed forever, unless he returns it or atones for his act. So be it. So be it. So be it. Amen." (Figure 78 at p. 146).[3] Some of these book curses really rub it in. Here is one from yet another manuscript in the Beinecke Library, MS 214, containing a copy of Peter Comestor's *Historia*

---

1 www.merton.ox.ac.uk/library-and-archives/history.

2 Savage, *Old English Libraries*, pp. 113–14.

3 Cyrus, *The Scribes for Women's Convents*, p. 161.

Figure 80. Book chest mounted to wall in Exeter Cathedral, fourteenth century. Photo by the author.

scholastica: "If anyone should steal it, let him know that on the Day of Judgment the most sainted martyr himself [referring to St. Quentin] will be the accuser against him before the face of our Lord Jesus Christ."[4]

Book curses appear both in Latin and in vernacular, including in non-Western traditions and languages, like Arabic. An Anglo-Saxon curse from the second half of the eleventh century is found in Oxford, Bodleian Library, MS Auct. D. 2.16 at fol. 6v. The inscription on this page records that the manuscript was donated to Exeter Cathedral by Bishop Leofric, followed by a curse against thieves.[5] This combination of curse and donation is encountered more often. An inscription in London, BL, Royal MS 2 C.I, a manuscript copied around 1220, notes that the book was donated to Rochester Priory in Kent by Ralph of Stoke. This information is followed by a short book curse (f. 1r, lower right corner).[6] The recipients of these book gifts felt compelled to treat the gift with extra care—as one would.

Optimism

Book curses raise interesting questions. Were they indeed favoured for books of special significance? Are we to understand their presence as a sign that librarians and book owners really thought the inscriptions were effective? And if they were, why not place them in all books? No matter the answers to these queries, there is a certain optimism embedded in such notations: the writer of the note apparently believed that a gentle (or not so gentle) reminder would deter potential thieves from consequently making off with the object.

The same optimism is echoed by inscriptions that ask the finder or thief of a book to return the object to its rightful owner. A Middle English note in St. Petersburg, National Library of Russia, Lat. F.v.I. N 70, reads: *Ho so me fond er ho so me took I am // jon Fosys Boke* ("Whomever me found or whomever me took, I am John Foss's book").[7] Stolen medieval books were probably not often returned. In fact, the example of John Foss's book gives us reason for pessimism: in the inscription the name is written on an erasure, meaning that the name of a previous owner was erased with a knife. Curiously, this makes John Foss the potential thief of the book. In other words, the thief identifies himself by altering the very book curse that was aimed at people like him. Now that is cunning.

---

4 Shailor, *The Medieval Book*, p. 20.

5 MS Auct. D. 2.16 has been digitized by Oxford's Bodleian Library, and can be found by searching for its shelfmark in their Luna Catalogue at http://bodley30.bodley.ox.ac.uk:8180/luna/servlet.

6 Royal 2 C.I has been digitized by the British Library, and can be found by searching for its shelfmark in their Catalogue of Illuminated Manuscripts at www.bl.uk/catalogues/illuminatedmanuscripts/welcome.htm.

7 Kilpiö, "Two Medieval English Inscriptions."

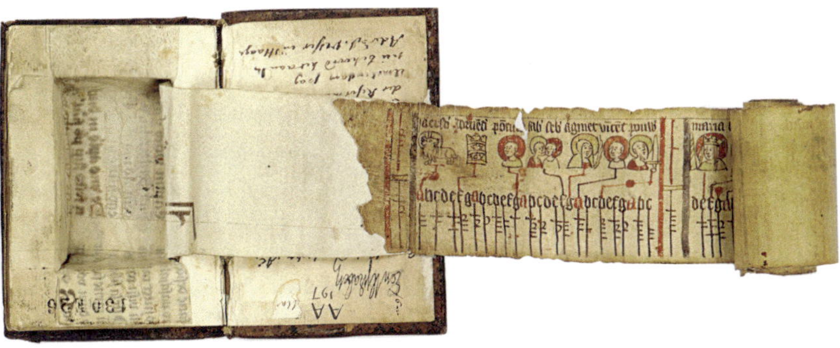

Figure 81. Late fourteenth-century roll kept in book-shaped box, probably from eighteenth century (discussed at p. 160). The Hague, KB, 130 E 26. With permission.

INTRODUCTION

This section deals with exceptional creations of medieval written culture: its focus is not on regular manuscripts, the main object of inquiry so far, but on unusual manuscripts, as well as non-book objects produced with quill and ink. The first three chapters highlight manuscripts that break with the regular material format of such objects. Rules and norms were very important in medieval life, and that extended to manuscript production. Remarkably, scribes often executed various stages of book production in the same manner, even when they were not working in each other's vicinity. We have encountered examples of this in **Chapter 1**, where it was shown that scribes in the same period or region shaped their letterforms in more or less the same fashion. Another example is the uniform use of footnotes in Europe, discussed in **Chapter 4**. While the bulk of medieval manuscripts generally share certain key features, like quires and the proportions of the page, it so happens that some books were designed a bit differently. **Chapters 19–21** introduce three such objects.

As outlined in the General Introduction, the design of medieval manuscripts was usually connected to their intended post-production use. **Chapters 19–21** show that the same goes for bookish objects that were shaped in more unusual ways: here, too, future use was the driving force behind the design, even if it was slightly off mark. **Chapter 19** is devoted to written artifacts that dramatically expanded in size. In addition to the roll, which became bigger as you unrolled it, two types of books are observed: "bat books," which consist of a single sheet that was folded several times over; and accordion books, which are effectively rolls that are not rolled but folded. The two book types are very rare, yet they show the strong connection between form and function. The same goes for the unusual book type discussed in **Chapter 20**, books so remarkably narrow that they break noticeably with the medieval norms of height and width. Although standards for a manuscript's proportions were quite strict, for some manners of use it was necessary to break the rules. The third book type, discussed in **Chapter 21**, is the hornbook. It would be a stretch to call this a real book, even though it carries the name: it consists of a single sheet placed on a wooden tablet with a handle. As **Chapter 21** demonstrates, these not-quite-books had everything to do with reading, as they were held in the hand to teach children to learn to read. Here, too, the manner of use was the rationale behind its peculiar design.

While hornbooks can be called books if we bend the rules a bit—not unlike the people who created them did—it would be a stretch to do so for the creations of written culture introduced in the remaining chapters of this section. They nevertheless matter for understanding medieval written culture because they were made with the same materials (ink, parchment, paper), by the same producers (scribes), and for the same people who read the manuscripts that feature in the other chapters—that is, readers with a variety of backgrounds. In **Chapters 22–25** our view expands beyond the book: the focus is on written artifacts that are flat and consist of a single "page." **Chapters 22 and 23** discuss tiny slips of paper and parchment that were used to communicate messages and to make notes on. **Chapter 22** rifles through the scrappy notes of individuals and their households, while **Chapter 23** handles some notes jotted down by scholars and ultimately meant to be discarded. **Chapter 24** deals with a most rare strip with text: name tags pinned on the clothes of orphans. Combined, these two chapters show that written culture encompassed notably small objects as well. Most of these were ephemeral and eventually lost, although the ones that survive show that these tiny artifacts, too, were versatile and served different purposes.

By contrast, **Chapter 25** focuses on a much larger non-book object: the poster. Ubiquitous in our society, in the Middle Ages there was also a need to display information on the wall. Although equally as rare as the small slips, surviving posters contribute to our understanding of the breadth of written culture. The last component of this section, **Chapter 26**, expands our view even further: it shows how regular objects, such as manuscripts and early printed books, are at home in the margins of book culture because of unusual additions given to them. The examples in this chapter, such as pop-up sundials and calculators with moving disks, are not unlike our modern smartphone apps in that they expand the original intended use of the device.

More so than in other parts of this book, this section ultimately highlights the breadth of medieval written culture: manuscripts were sometimes given unusual shapes and add-ons if their purpose demanded it. Moreover, as this section shows, handwritten books were part of a much broader constellation of products made with quill and ink. In that sense, it hardly seems right to separate books from (or even emphasize them over) other written artifacts, as is common practice in academic scholarship and even in this book. However, this choice is in part pragmatic and sparked by what survives: manuscripts have come down to us in greater numbers than have the artifacts discussed in this section.

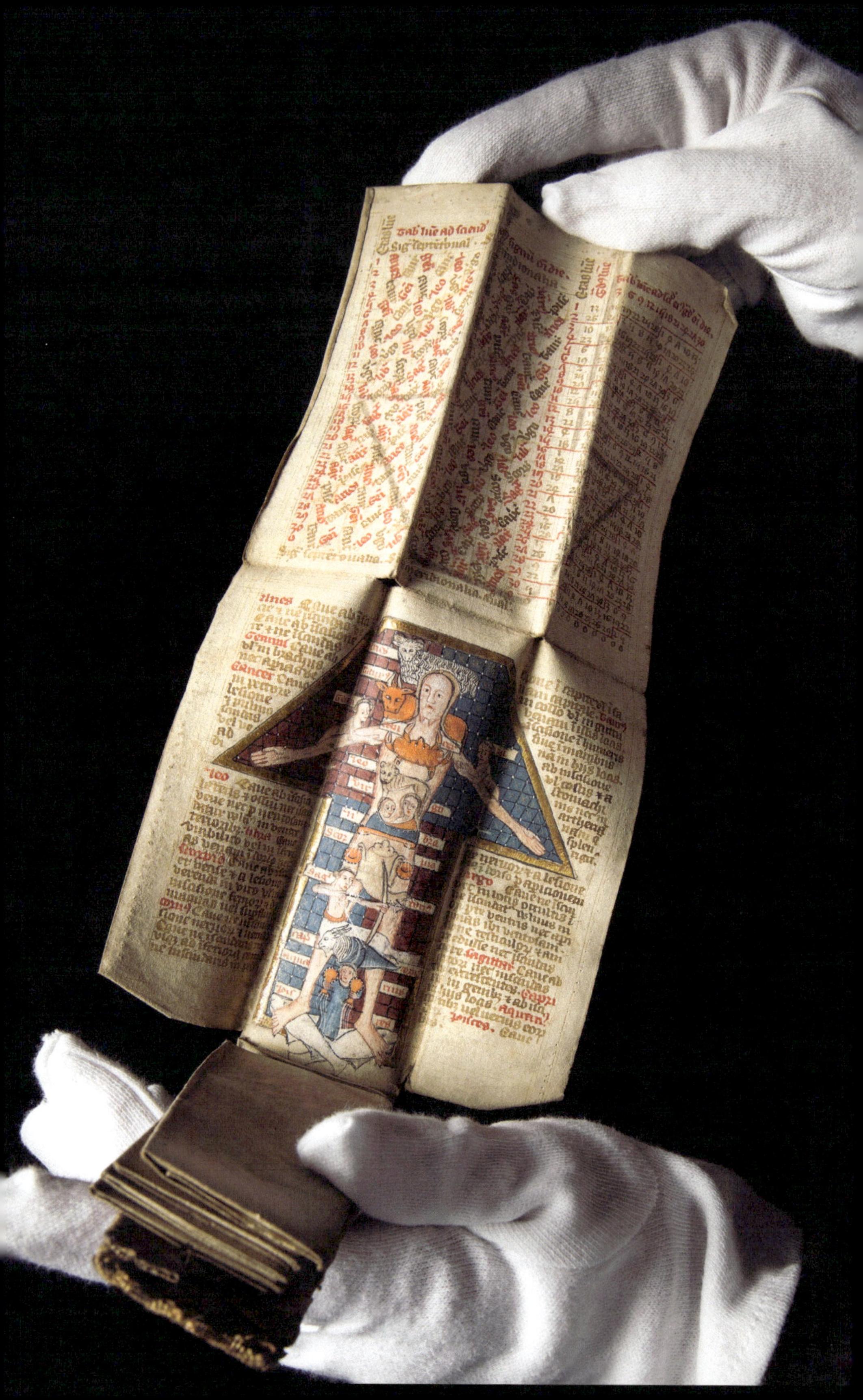

Chapter 19

THE INCREDIBLE EXPANDABLE BOOK

This section opens with a manuscript with a peculiar shape and format. Like most objects, books are confined to the space they occupy, obedient as they are to the laws of nature. That is to say, unlike the Incredible Hulk, they do not expand beyond the limits of their own physicality. This chapter will challenge your beliefs if you agree with this. It draws attention to a manuscript type that *does* expand: with a flick of the finger or a gesture of the hand the dimensions of these special objects increase dramatically, up to ten times their original size—or more. As if defying the laws of nature, this miraculous expansion increased the available writing space in objects that were principally designed to be small and portable. What do these objects look like? And what was the drive behind their production?

Bat Books

Produced in England in ca. 1415–1420, the small manuscript in Figure 82 contains a calendar as well as astrological tables and diagrams. The information was used by physicians to diagnose and prognosticate, while the calendar provided information about religious feasts. The Leiden codicologist Peter Gumbert (d. 2016) coined the term "bat book" for this type of manuscript, alluding to its expanding nature: the book stretched its wings, as it were, when used. Moreover, in an unused state the book would be hanging from the owner's belt in an upside down orientation, like a bat.[1] Gumbert's inventory holds sixty-three items, and many of them look more

1 See Gumbert, *Bat Books*, for an inventory and study of folding almanacs.

Figure 82. Folding almanac, ca. 1415–1420. London, Wellcome Institute, Archives and Manuscripts, 8932. CC 4.0 International. Source: www.wellcomelibrary.org/ collections/digital-collections.

scruffy than the handsome specimen in the Wellcome Library. Folding almanacs were especially popular in late-medieval England, if the surviving specimens form an accurate representation.

These bookish objects are especially interesting from a material point of view. During production, folding almanacs looked very much like a regular book: the scribe filled regular pages with text. However, in a completed state, when the binding was added, the pages were folded in a very clever way, giving them an "unbookish" look. The two different states (a small package when closed, irregular dimensions when unfolded) were chosen with care: closed, it was a portable book that could dangle from the owner's belt, while in its extended state the reader was provided with expansive information at a glance.

The Accordion Book

The almanac in Figure 82 provides six times more writing and reading space in its expanded form, which is quite an enlargement. However, this is still considerably less than another type of expandable manuscript: the "accordion book." An excellent example is Copenhagen, Kongelige Bibliotek, NKS 901, a calendar made in Denmark in 1513. While in its folded state it is as small as a matchbox, it expands to a full page of considerable proportions, comparable to a regular-sized medieval book. Curiously, the calendar has a most unusual way of unfolding: sections of the sheet expand independently, like little flaps from a pop-up book.

The Copenhagen accordion book is a very small, portable object. Even though in its expanded state it becomes much larger, due to the limited length of the object, the expansion still only produces a rather modest writing and reading surface. The remarkable thing about accordion books, however, is that their surface space had considerable potential, despite the puny proportions of their folded forms.

Leiden University Library owns an accordion book from fourteenth-century Russia which is only 12 cm in height (Figure 83). Folded, it shares the approximate dimensions of an iPhone. In its expanded state, however, the book stretches to a breadth of no less than 375 cm, meaning that the surface actually increases by an astonishing factor. The object has a clever design. It presents full pages of text (a calendar as well religious songs), yet each page is folded in half so that the object shrinks in size and forms a longish book. The user could simply unfold the page and the full width of the textblock would then present itself, spreading lines across two half pages, so to speak (note in the image how each line is spread across two pages). There is little gained space-wise, but the book became smaller and easier to carry around in one's pocket.

Figure 83. Accordion book from Russia, fourteenth century. Leiden, UB, SCA 38 B. Photo by Giulio Menna.

Rolls

The oldest expandable bookish object is the roll. Rolls had been in use for a long time by the time the book appeared on the scene in the fourth century, as explained in the General Introduction. During the Middle Ages the roll format remained in use longest in administration. It was not until the late thirteenth century that cities in northwest Europe switched to the book form to record their income and expenses; the city of Bruges still used rolls for this purpose in the 1290s.[2]

Rolls can be quite long. One of the longest that survives from the medieval period is a mortuary roll that was carried to 253 monasteries, convents, and cathedrals across England and France during the 1110s. Mortuary rolls were produced to commemorate the death of a prominent person, in this case Abbess Mathilda of Holy Trinity Abbey in Caen. Like writing a joint birthday card today, clerics in France would add their say to the roll, which grew and grew, until it finally reached a length of 22 metres (72 feet).[3] Chronicle rolls could also be quite long. The one seen in Figure 84 is 50 cm wide and 10.4 metres long (34 feet). The figure shows only a small segment of it, because if the page displayed the entire object the image would only be 1 cm wide.

---

2 De Smet, Vandewalle, and Wyffels, *De rekeningen van de stad Brugge*, pp. 805 (1280–81), 862 (1294–95), 898 (1296–97), and 920 (1300).

3 Friedman and Mossler Figg, *Trade, Travel, and Exploration*, pp. 417–18 (mortuary roll).

Figure 84. Chronicle roll of 10.4 metres or 34 feet (detail), ca. 1470–1479. Boston, Public Library, MS pb Med.32. Public domain. Source: www.digitalcommonwealth.org.

The text contained on the roll, copied in France in the 1470s, is the *Chronique anonyme universelle*, which records the history of the world from Creation until the production of the roll. Besides text, there are quite a few scenes painted on the parchment, including those showing popes, emperors, and the kings of England and France—the usual suspects of such chronicle rolls. The skins of sixteen cows were used for its production: they overlap by about 1.5 cm so they could be pasted together. These full skins each measure around 65 cm × 55 cm, which is about average for northwest Europe, as discussed in Chapter 25.[4]

From time to time unusual rolls are encountered, like the one seen in the Royal Library of the Netherlands in The Hague (Figure 81 at p. 153). This one is special because the fourteenth-century object comes rolling out of a book (of slightly later date), which functions as its sleeve. The end of the roll (which is holding a calendar) is simply pasted into the book. The full roll measures 130 cm (a little over 4 feet). One wonders whether the owner created this remarkable hybrid because it allowed for easy storage on the bookshelf. A book placed among its peers, albeit with an unusual secret tucked away inside.

Doing More with Less

What these incredible expandable books share is an effort to hold a significant amount of text in an object that occupies a modest amount of

4 A description and image of this *Chronique anonyme universelle* roll is available in the Massachusetts Collections Online "Digital Commonwealth" at www.digitalcommonwealth.org/search/commonwealth:np193j76j.

space, usually in one's pocket (but not, obviously, the chronicle roll in Figure 84). When there is a dire need to take information on the go with you, medieval readers were quite inventive, as Chapter 30 shows. Interestingly, the expandable information carrier lives on in our own day. Not only are there still book designers who produce accordion books in the medieval fashion, but the foldaway almanac described here has actually become ubiquitous in the form of pocket maps, displaying such information as the layout of cities and subway stations. In the same way as for our medieval peers, ease of use and portability are the driving forces behind getting plenty of information onto an object with a tiny footprint. "Doing more with less" is clearly a universal urge.

Per tibi ego hunc iuro castum fortemque cruorem
Perque tuos manes qui mihi numen erunt
Tarquinium profuga penas cum stirpe daturum
Iam satis est virtus dissimulata diu.
Illa iacens ad verba oculos sine lumine movit
Visaque concussa dicta probare coma.
Fertur in exequias animi matrona virilis
[& secum] fetus lacrimas invidiamque trahit.
Vulnus inane patet. brutus clamore quirites
Concitat. et regis facta nefanda refert.
Tarquinius cum prole fugit. capit annua consul — tunc primum ceperunt fieri annui consules
Iura. dies regnis illa suprema fuit.
Fallimur. an veris prenuntia venit hyrundo
Nec metuit ne qua versa recurrat hiemps.
Sepe tamen progne nimium properasse quereris
Virque tuo tereus frigore letus erit.
[iii kl. m. equiria martis] Iamque duo restant noctes de mense secundo — due
Marsque citos iunctis curribus urget equos
Ex vero positum permansit equiria nomen — ab equis qui tunc habebantur in curru
Que deus in campo (i. martio) prospicit ipse suo.
Iure venis gradive locum tua tempora poscunt
Signatusque tuo nomine mensis adest.
Venimus ad (anni) portum libro cum mense peracto
Naviget hinc alia iam mihi linter aqua.

Bellice depositis clipeo paulisper et hasta — [illegible] posuerat
Mars ades. et nitidas casside solve comas.
Forsitan ipse rogas quid sit cum marte poete.
A te qui canitur nomina mensis habet.
Ipse vides manibus peragi fera bella minerve
Num minus ingenuis artibus illa vacat.
Palladis exemplo ponende tempora sume
Cuspidis. invenies et quod inermis agas.
Tunc quoque inermis eras cum te romana sacerdos
Cepit. ut huic urbi semina magna dares.
Silvia vestalis quid enim vetat inde movere
Sacra lavaturas mane petebat aquas.
Ventum erat ad molli declive tramite ripam
Ponitur e summa fictilis urna coma.
Fessa resedit humo ventosque recepit aperto
Pectore turbatas restituitque comas.
Dum sedet umbrose salices volucresque canore
Fecerunt somnos. et leve murmur aque.
Blanda quies furtim victis obrepsit ocellis — obrepit
Et cadit a mento languida facta manus.
Mars videt hanc. visamque cupit potiturque cupita.
Et sua divina furta fefellit ope.
Somnus abit. iacet ipsa gravis. iam scilicet intra
Viscera romane conditor urbis erat.
Languida consurgit. nescit cur languida surgat.
Et peragit tales arbore nixa sonos.

[A silva enea de cuius prosapia fuit. silvius autem filius magni enee fuit. si[c] vocatur silvius quia in silva fuit natus. [illegible] enea in italia uxore [illegible]. quia mortuo enea [illegible] remansit timore ascanii [illegible] in silva fugiens ibi peperit]

Chapter 20

BOOKS ON A DIET

It is not just through expansion that a medieval manuscript can be tagged as uncommon or breaking with the norm. This chapter is devoted to a relatively rare kind of manuscript that is much *slimmer* than what you would expect (Figure 85). "Expect," because the relative proportions of manuscripts—the width in relation to the height—form a surprisingly stable feature in medieval book production. In fact, the vast majority of surviving manuscripts have the same relative proportions as our modern pages: their width is around 70 per cent of their height, which is about the same as our standard-format books today.[1]

This stability ought to surprise you. While readers of printed books have little choice as to the physical appearance of the object they read, owners of manuscripts handled a book that was usually made especially for them. Consequently, they would normally specify what it should look like, as explained in the General Introduction. You might think that medieval readers would go overboard and abuse this freedom of choice, ordering polka-dotted books with pink letters written upside down on triangle-shaped pages. The opposite turns out to be true. Book owners before print are predictable in that they mostly opted for regular features: their choices are typical, almost conforming to some unwritten rules. It is probable that scribes, who knew the rules, attempted to keep deviations from the norm at bay.

This striking act of conformation results from what is a driving force behind the chosen physical features: the anticipated use of the book. For example, if you anticipated that you would scribble an excessive number of notes in your book,

1 Gumbert, "The Sizes of Manuscripts."

Figure 85. Holster book with Ovid's *Fasti* produced for classroom use, twelfth century. Leiden, UB, VLQ 73, fol. 16v. With permission.

Figure 86. Ivory book plaque, Aachen, early ninth century. New York, Metropolitan Museum of Art, 1977.421. CC0 1.0 Universal. Source: www.metmuseum.org.

you would specify to the scribe to extend the size of the margins. And if you knew that you would take a book with you when you left the house, it would make sense to have that copy produced in a suitably small and light format. This strong link between form and function is good news for us: we may infer that narrow books—sometimes called holster books—were put on their diet for good reason.[2]

Ivory Decoration

One reason to slim books down had to do with their binding; or, more precisely, with its decoration. The most prestigious decorative element of a medieval binding was ivory plaques, slabs of elephant tusk into which elaborate scenes were cut. They were attached to the front and sometimes also to the back of a manuscript's binding, usually embedded in the wood of the boards. Book projects that involved this costly decoration sometimes produced manuscripts that were much narrower (or taller) than the norm. The plaques themselves had to be narrow given the limited width of the tusk (Figure 86). Interestingly, however, manuscript-makers sometimes made the book equally narrow. This was probably done for visual reasons: it looks better when the relative proportions of book and decoration are aligned. Moreover, keeping the book slim meant that more visible space was covered with ivory.

---

2 For this type of book, see Kwakkel, "'Dit boek heeft niet de vereiste breedte'"; Kwakkel and Newton, *Medicine at Monte Cassino*, chap. 4.

This tendency to keep a book narrow when ivory decoration was added is mentioned in a remarkable account by the historian Ekkehart of St. Gall (d. 1022). Referring to what is now St. Gall, Stiftsbibliothek, Cod. Sang. 53, he states that this manuscript was made tall and narrow for good reason (it measures 39.5 cm × 23.2 cm, meaning its width is 58 per cent of its height). Among the abbey's treasures, he reports in his chronicle, were two ivory plaques forming a diptych. According to Ekkehart, they once belonged to Emperor Charlemagne (d. 814), who used them as his wax tablet, which he kept next to his bed as part of his failed efforts to learn to write. When it was decided that the plaques would be used to decorate the bookbinding of a newly produced gospel book, the scribe—named Sintram according to Ekkehart—was asked to design the book in such a way "that it matched the height and width of the ivory," which another monk-artisan, Tuotilo, had beautifully carved with a scene of the abbey's namesake. Ekkehart calls the gospel book that is the result of Sintram and Tuotilo's labour the "Evangelium longum" (long Gospel book), the name by which it is still known today.[3] The relative width of the manuscript appears to have been so striking to him that he used this pronounced visible feature as an identifier of the book.

Books for Soloists

A second reason to produce a slim book in the Middle Ages is pragmatic rather than artistic. When one examines what these oddly tall manuscripts contain, it turns out that a fair number hold texts that were sung by soloists during Mass. Take the cantatorium and troper, for example, two frequently used musical books. When one limits the view to the period before 1200, it so happens that most surviving copies are formatted in the slim dimensions discussed here.[4] Another famous example is the St. Gall Processional (Cod. Sang. 360), which is not just very narrow at 25.5 cm × 8 cm (the width is only 30 per cent of the height), but also very thin: it holds only thirty-four pages. The manuscript is not held in a proper binding, but instead is stored in a book box, few of which survive from the Middle Ages.[5]

---

3 For this story, and on Tuotilo's carving, see De Wald, "Notes on the Tuotilo Ivories in St. Gall"; Duft and Schnyder, *Elfenbein-Einbände*, pp. 18–22. Cod. Sang. 53 has been digitized by the Virtual Manuscript Library of Switzerland (e-codices), and can be found at www.e-codices.unifr.ch/en/list/one/csg/0053.

4 Huglo, *The Cantatorium*, pp. 96 and 99, tables 3.1a and 3.2 (Cantatoria); p. 97, table 3.1b (Tropers).

5 Cod. Sang. 360 has been digitized by the Virtual Manuscript Library of Switzerland (e-codices), and can be found at www.e-codices.unifr.ch/en/list/one/csg/0360.

The reason why these musical books are designed so awkwardly (in that they break with the norms of medieval book production) is related to how they were used: while held in one hand. The effect of the narrow shape was that the weight of the book rested on the palm when it lay open in your hand. This meant that the soloist could easily hold it up for a long period of time. Also, the format allowed the reader to move about while holding the book, which was essential for such processionals as Cod. Sang. 360. Books with regular dimensions, by contrast, execute much more pressure on the fingertips and the thumb when held in one hand. This is unsurprising, of course, because they were not designed for holding: they were supposed to rest on a desk or podium while in use. Moreover, narrow books are often also quite thin, which reduces their weight. As with the shift in the pressure points, the weight loss helped the reader hold the book up for longer.

Classroom Use

For the same reason—easy holding—the narrow format also became popular in education in the monastic school.[6] A considerably high number of surviving holster books have texts that are known to have been popular in an educational context, especially the classics. The classical poets were used for teaching rhetoric, grammar, and dialectic, commonly in an oral teaching situation. The narrow format allowed the teacher to move around the classroom while holding a book in one hand. (With the coming of the university this changed: the teacher would now generally place his book on a lectern and teach from the front of the classroom.) The other hand was available for pointing out things, and perhaps even for slapping young novices over the head; corporal punishment was thriving in medieval education. These narrow books commonly have a width that is 50–60 per cent of their height. The example in Figure 85 at p. 162, a copy of Ovid's *Fasti* produced in ca. 1150–1200, measures 24 cm × 12 cm and thus has a relative width of only 0.5 (compared to the height, which is 1.0). This is evidently a teaching copy. Not only was Ovid particularly popular in teaching the *Trivium*, the manuscript also holds an *accessus*. This tool is an academic prologue that highlights to the student such things as the intention of the writer, the life of the poet, the title of the work, the quality of the poem, and the style of writing.[7]

6 Kwakkel, "'Dit boek heeft niet de vereiste breedte,'" pp. 40–44.

7 A discussion of the *accessus* and those made with the intention of later additions is found in Minnis, *Medieval Theory of Authorship*, p. 15.

A Long Tradition

While the examples given above focus on the period before 1200, the practice of making slim books thrived in the later medieval period as well. In the fifteenth century, for example, municipal clerks made narrow literary manuscripts, probably conforming to chancery practices. Moreover, there appears to be a real tradition of slender paper books in Middle English literary culture. Oxford, Bodleian Library, MS Douce 228, a copy of *The Romance of Richard Coeur de Lion*, is the slimmest manuscript I know. It has been argued that this particular manuscript was made for minstrels; this makes perfect sense, as they could hold it up with a single hand to read the text while they performed.[8]

Overall, ivory decoration and handheld use are two significant factors in this long tradition of making "slim" books. When faced with a slender book, we can therefore speculate: was the binding perhaps originally fitted with ivory decoration? After all, the precious material was often stolen from the books in later periods. Or, if this seems unlikely because the parchment and handwriting suggests a cheap production, perhaps it was made for handheld use, for example, by a performer or teacher.

A Librarian Speaks Up

While there were good reasons for making such slim medieval manuscripts, they were indeed regarded as unusual by people in the period. This is confirmed by the label "long Gospel book" given to St. Gall, Cod. Sang. 53, as discussed, but also by a striking remark by Hector of Moerdrecht (d. 1465), librarian of the Charterhouse Nieuwlicht in the Dutch city of Utrecht. In two narrow manuscripts, Utrecht, UB, 102 and 159, he critiqued their format. On the flyleaf of the first of these manuscripts he wrote:

> The Epistles of Paul with interlinear gloss [...], which we previously did not have in their entirety, in conformity with which the rest of the books were formed, so that it might be made into one volume and bound more conveniently, although it is not a good format since it is tall and not as broad as it should have been [...].
>
> (Item epistule pauli cum glosa interlineari [...] non ex toto quas antea habuimus, secundum quas libri ceteri formati sunt ut fieret unum volumen

---

8 Mills and Rogers, "Popular Romance," p. 51. MS Douce 228 has been partly digitized by Oxford's Bodleian Library, and can be found by searching for its shelfmark on their Luna Catalogue at http://bodley30.bodley.ox.ac.uk:8180/luna/servlet.

> et commodius ligarentur. licet non sit bona formacio cum sit longa et non secundum exigenciam eius lata.)[9]

Even though Hector was biased (he was the community's librarian and thus involved in book production on a "professional" level), his critique was precisely because the two books indeed broke the rules for medieval page proportions: their width is 63 per cent of their height. As Chapter 14 showed, Carthusians were keen on presenting text in a "proper" manner. It makes sense, in this light, that we encounter a librarian from the same monastic order who is a bit fastidious about a book's design.

9 Gumbert, *Utrechter Kartäuser*, p. 139 (citation); p. 141 for the similar remark in the other manuscript.

a b c d e f g h i j k l m n o p q
r ſ s t u v w x y z & a e i o u
A B C D E F G H I J K L M N O P Q
R S T U V W X Y Z

a e i o u	a e i o u
ab eb ib ob ub	ba be bi bo bu
ac ec ic oc uc	ca ce ci co cu
ad ed id od ud	da de di do du

In the Name of the Father, and of the Son, and of the Holy Ghoſt. *Amen.*

OUR Father, which art in Heaven, hallowed be thy Name; thy Kingdom come, thy Will be done on Earth, as it is in Heaven. Give us this Day our daily Bread; and forgive us our Treſpaſſes, as we forgive them that treſpaſs againſt us: And lead us not into Temptation, but deliver us from Evil. *Amen.*

Chapter 21

BOOKS ON A STICK

This chapter moves even further away from the normal medieval book. The main focus is a peculiar bookish object that thrived in the sixteenth through eighteenth centuries, but which has medieval roots, as this chapter shows. The object in question is the "hornbook" (Figure 87). Given the definition of "book" discussed in the General Introduction (see pp. 4–5), we have to conclude that the hornbook is not even a book (i.e., an object made out of quires). Nevertheless, it does emphasize the close connection between the design of objects used for reading and human anatomy. Speaking to the diversity of medieval written culture, this chapter shows that objects to read from were not just made from parchment or paper, but also from gingerbread.

Hornbooks

The hornbook is a primer: a text used by children as they were learning to read. It usually contains the alphabet and some additional short texts, such as the Lord's Prayer or Hail Mary, which the new readers—helpfully—should have already known by heart. These texts are found, for example, in the specimen in Figure 87, which measures only 11 cm × 6 cm. The hornbook's design reflects perfectly how artifacts to read from were customized for use by human beings—which is sensible, of course, because these were their consumers. This particular device, for example, enables those new to reading to hold it up at eye level, as close to the face as needed to examine the unfamiliar shapes in front of them. The other hand was free to practise writing the letters, perhaps with the help of a slate tablet.

Figure 87. Hornbook with printed text, seventeenth century. Boston, Public Library, Call No. G.Cab.3.52. Public domain. Source: www.digitalcommonwealth.org.

Materials

Most surviving hornbooks are made out of wood. In the Early Modern period the pupil's "required readings" were usually printed on a sheet of paper that was subsequently covered by a thin slice of animal horn for protection—hence the object's name. The result is a remarkably sturdy object, which could be dropped without damaging it; a minimum requirement, it seems, for any device used by young children.

Surviving hornbooks show that they were also used to teach adding and subtracting. The one seen in Figure 88, which dates from the eighteenth century and measures 28 cm × 18 cm, has a nifty add-on to this end: an abacus, which is mounted on top. This particular specimen shows the end of the hornbook's development, which appears to have become more sophisticated over time. The hornbook in Figure 88 contains another novel feature: the sheet of paper can be removed from behind the horn and reversed, or replaced by another sheet.

While hornbooks could also be made out of other materials, such as ivory or lead, one particularly unusual type is worth mentioning: a wooden mould survives that was used to produce a gingerbread version of the hornbook, handle and all (New York, Columbia University Library, RBML Plimpton Hornbook 20).[1] The tradition of this particularly tasty hornbook goes back to the eighteenth century. The English poet Matthew Prior (d. 1721) mentions it in one of his poems:

> To Master John the English maid
> A horn-book gives of ginger-bread
> And that the Child may learn the better,
> As he can name, he eats the letter;
> Proceeding thus with vast delight,
> He spells, and gnaws from left to right.[2]

The gingerbread hornbook arguably wins the prize for best pedagogical tool: what better reward for a pupil than to eat the letter successfully read aloud?

Medieval Period

While the heyday of the hornbook was no doubt the Early Modern period, the bookish device was also used during the Middle Ages. Although, unfortunately,

---

1 See Columbia University Libraries' Online Exhibition "Our Tools of Learning": George Arthur Plimpton's Gifts to Columbia University, at https://exhibitions.cul.columbia.edu/exhibits/show/plimpton/hornbooks.

2 Prior, *The Poems of Matthew Prior, Vol. 1*, p. 211.

Figure 88. Hornbook with abacus, eighteenth century. Washington, Library of Congress, Z1033.H8 W6 1800z. CC0 1.0 Universal. Source: https://lccn.loc.gov/2007700160.

none survive, there is sufficient visual evidence to support this claim. The oldest known scene that includes a hornbook is an Italian manuscript with an unidentified devotional text about the life of Mary, the mother of Christ (Oxford, Bodleian Library, MS Canon. Misc. 476, fol. 47v). Based on its script, the manuscript's

Figure 89. Hornbook in action, fifteenth century. New York, Columbia University Library, Plimpton 184, fol. 10v, detail. With permission.

production date can be placed around the middle of the fourteenth century.[3] The image shows Christ being brought to school by his mother. He is bringing his "textbook" with him to class: a hornbook, which dangles from his wrist by a string. (Surviving Early Modern specimens have a hole in the handle, probably to accommodate a similar manner of transportation.) While confirming that the hornbook is a medieval invention, intriguingly, we are also shown how young children carried their reading material to school.

The second visual evidence from the medieval period takes us to Germany in the 1440s–1460s. It concerns a scene in New York, Columbia University Library, Plimpton 184 (Figure 89) showing an allegory involving Algorism (who is the

---

3 MS Canon. Misc. 476 has been digitized by Oxford's Bodleian Library, and can be found by searching for its shelfmark on their Luna Catalogue at http://bodley30.bodley.ox.ac.uk:8180/luna/servlet.

teacher) and his pupil. Holding a hornbook displaying Arabic numerals, Algorism states (according to the text bubble in Eastern Upper German): "Ich pin algorismus genant | das raitt(e)n han ich in mein|ner hant" (My name is Algorismus and / I carry the reckoning tablet in my hand).[4] (Note that in this image, too, a string is visible at the end of the stick.) While this illustration was produced somewhat later than the Italian example discussed before, the setting in which the hornbook was used is the same: an educational environment where basic information about letters and digits is conveyed to young pupils. As with learning the ABC from eighteenth-century hornbooks, the device they were holding was perfectly suited for this task.

While the hornbook may defy our definition of "book," its design is as functional as regular manuscripts. Moreover, it emphasizes how much the objects we use for reading—then and today—were designed to accommodate the needs of our human bodies as we read. Regular books can be kept open with ease by applying gentle pressure on the outer margins of the pages. Release the pressure with your right hand and a page lifts up in the air, just enough to be conveniently flipped. The hornbook may not have pages, but its design works perfectly for the purpose for which it was made: handheld use. It is light and durable, both essential features of a device used by children, and it has a handle that enables the user to hold the text up, close to the eyes. The object may look a bit strange, but its design is both clever and, in many ways, timeless.

---

4 The citation of the German is taken (and slightly amended) from the manuscript description that can be found by searching for its shelfmark in Digital Scriptorium's catalogue at http://bancroft.berkeley.edu/digitalscriptorium. The correction in the second line (*hav* > *han*) is by Nigel Palmer (Oxford), who also localized the language and provided the translation.

Chapter 22

SLIPS, STRIPS, AND SCRAPS: MESSAGING

Leaving the world of actual and "almost" books behind, the concluding four chapters of this section deal with artifacts that have a casual relationship to manuscripts, but an evident affiliation to written culture. The present chapter and the next deal with flat materials of small proportions cut from larger sheets or lifted from the recycling bin. Because of their cheap (or even free) nature, many of the slips, strips, and scraps discussed here are ephemeral and written hastily: they were meant to be read and thrown out. Yet, fortunately for us, they were not. The text on them is often written in a special language of short and abbreviated words, and it was probably understood that they may contain "typos." The speed, short lifespan and cursory nature of the artifacts discussed here are familiar to us today: we send each other short, hastily written messages all day, and they are notoriously filled with abbreviations and typos. And we, too, use small, redundant scrap materials for drafting short lists and notes intended to have a short lifespan. This chapter observes the historical roots of this practice, while the next one explores another, more scholarly use for such slips.

Roots

Ephemeral written culture predates the Middle Ages. Early surviving examples are wooden tablets that were written on almost two thousand years ago, between 97 and 103 CE. The tablets were dug up in a Roman army camp called Vindolanda just south of Hadrian's Wall in Northern England, and they now rest in the British Museum. Some four hundred wooden tablets with correspondence were found in the house of Flavius Cerealis, prefect of the Ninth Cohort of Batavians. Remarkably,

Figure 90. Medieval and Early Modern waste material, fourteenth to eighteenth centuries. Maastricht, Regionaal Historisch Centrum Limburg, Box 384. Photo by the author.

Figure 91. Vindolanda tablet with birthday invitation, 97–103 CE. London, British Museum, 1986, 1001.64 (= Tab. Vindol. II 291). CC BY-SA 3.0. Source: Wikimedia Commons (Photo by Fae).

the Vindolanda tablets are only 1–3 mm thick and about the size of a modern postcard. An especially charming and personal one is Tab. Vindol. II 291 (Figure 91). It invites the commander's wife, Sulpicia Lepidina, to her sister's birthday party at a neighbouring fort. Claudia Severa writes:

> On 11 September, sister, for the day of the celebration of my birthday, I give you a warm invitation to make sure that you come to us, to make the day more enjoyable for me by your arrival, if you are present. Give my greetings to your Cerialis. My Aelius and my little son send him their greetings. Farewell, sister my dearest soul, as I hope to prosper, and hail.

Astonishingly, with this tiny object of about 22 cm wide we have in our hands a two-millennia-old text message sent from one sister to another, concerning a matter as routine but personal as a birthday party. As scholars have remarked, this tablet holds one of the oldest surviving specimens of a woman's handwriting.[1]

Produced with wooden pens with stuck-on nibs, the four hundred surviving Vindolanda tablets also include correspondence from the field, probably sent by courier. The sub-commander Masculus writes to Flavius Cerealis, his superior: "Please, my lord, give instructions as to what you want us to have done tomorrow. Are we to return with the standard to the crossroads all together or [only half of us? Also,] my fellow soldiers have no beer. Please order some to be sent" (Tab. Vindol. III 628).[2] This oldest known order for beer was no doubt meant

1 Information and citation from the British Museum's Collection online (search for the inventory number, 1986,1001.64, at www.britishmuseum.org).

2 Cuff, "King of the Batavians."

to be thrown out, yet it survives because the earth preserved the wood on which it was written.

Paper Slips

Similar short logistical messages survive from the Middle Ages, although their manner of survival is different. Figure 93 shows waste material discovered by my students in Leiden University's Book and Digital Media Studies programme. A total of 132 paper slips were pressed together to form a sort of papier-mâché "cardboard" which was used to support (and be covered with) the leather of the bookbinding (Figure 92 shows merely a selection of the slips). The material originates from quite an unusual place: the recycling bin of a small court near Heidelberg. It concerns ephemeral material that is generally lost from the Middle Ages, such as letters and scrap paper.

A particularly interesting category is the equivalent to our modern-day "yellow sticky notes": strips of paper that were sent from one servant to another. For example, one note in the pile requests that wild roses be purchased in Heidelberg, while making sure "to include some that are still in bud." The note was written on behalf of Philip, Count Palatine of the Rhine (d. 1508), and we may assume that the other recycled materials in this archive are also affiliated to his court.

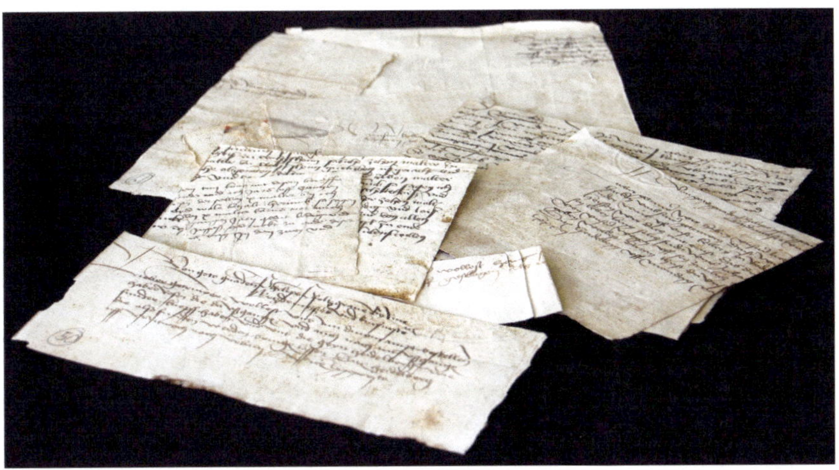

Figure 92. Part of archive found in bookbinding, fifteenth century. Leiden, Bibliotheca Thysiana, Inv. Nr. 2200 H. Photo by the author.

(a)

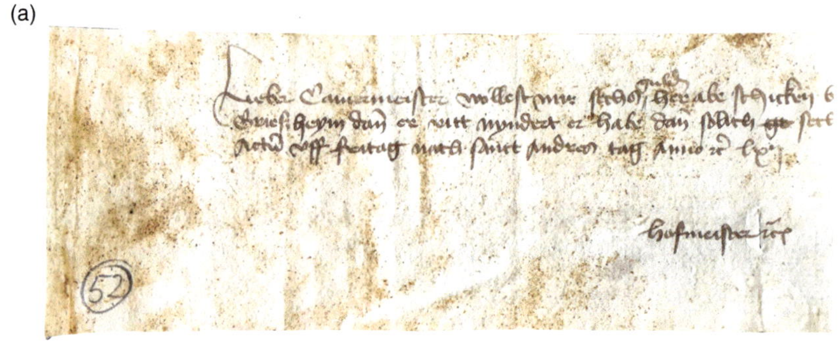

(b)

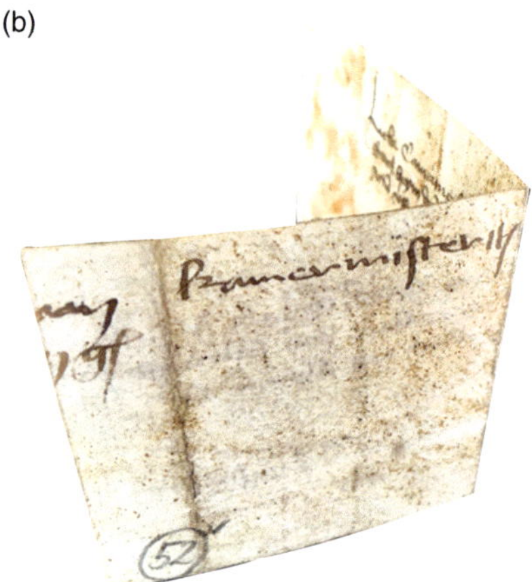

Figure 93. (a) Recto side, showing inside of note, asking chamberlain to fetch money; (b) Verso side, identifying the recipient: "kamermister" (chamberlain), fifteenth century. Leiden, Bibliotheca Thysiana, Inv. Nr. 2200 H, item 52. Photos by the author.

Another message was written by the housemaster ("hofmeister etc.") and it requests the amount of six guilders from the duke, whose servant, the "Camermeister" or chamberlain, is the recipient of the message (Figure 93a):

> Lieber Camermeister, wollest mir sechs gulden her abe schicken b[...]
> Griessheym dann er uitt nyndert er habe dann solich ge sech[s ...]
> Actum uff fritag nach sanct Andres tag anno etc. [14]61.
> hofmeister etc.[3]

---

3 Transcription by Ed van der Vlist (Royal Library The Hague).

The note was cut on the right side, which makes it impossible to provide a full transcription and gauge its precise meaning besides the request for money, which was apparently for somebody from Griesheim, a city a few kilometres to the west of Darmstadt in Germany.

The back of the message (Figure 93b) also adds to our understanding of this hidden world of medieval text messaging. It shows to whom the note needed to be delivered (the "kamermister"), but also that it was folded for transportation. Even today the slip still wants to take on the form of a folded message, as if the paper has muscle memory. Many of these slips were produced from recycled charters or account books. The messages were either written on their back, or on a strip that was cut from their margin, as is visible in on the back of the note in Figure 92b: note the half-words next to the word "kamermister." Why use a good sheet of paper if the message would be discarded immediately after use?

Time Capsule

The Vindolanda tablets and the medieval slips in Leiden form a time capsule in that they preserve ordinary conversations that do not normally survive from the past. We meet everyday people doing everyday things. Their manner of expressing themselves is untainted in that they do not try to be literary or witty, but merely convey a brief and routine message for short-term use and, ultimately, destruction. It makes perfect sense, therefore, that these "text messages" were written on surfaces that were easily available: pieces of wood and slips of waste paper from the recycling bin.

While the caches from Vindolanda and Leiden are remarkable, there are actually plenty of time capsules still out there. The average archive in Europe contains several boxes filled with medieval waste, which usually includes a wide range of recycled "transitory" material, such as letters and notes (Figure 90 at p. 176). The material seen here has never been studied systematically, nor, does it seem, have most comparable scraps. If such paper and parchment slips are the medieval equivalent of today's text messages, written in a cursory fashion and forgotten about almost immediately after receipt, these archival boxes are not unlike our phones' memories. They allow us to read conversations meant to be deleted hundreds of years ago.

Subsistentia aut uniuscuiusq; psonae hoc ipsum qd ex
stat et subsistit ostendat. Ideoq; ppter sabellium [illegible] sim
tres ee subsistentias confitendas qd quasi tres subsistentes
psonas significare uideretur. Candidus

Indagandum quid e essentia & essentialitas. quid existentia
et existentialitas quid substantia et quid substantialitas
sed aliud et aliud non recipitur circa dm. non est in alio ut
aliud est. ut accedens in subiecto. Differt aut existentia ab
existentialitate. qm existentia iam in eo est ut sit ei esse. at
uero existentialitas potentia est ut possit esse. nondu est ipsu
esse. Multo aut magis existentia a substantia differt. qm exis
tentia ipsum ee est & solum esse. & non in alio esse. aut
subiectu alterius. sed unu et solu ipsum esse. Substanti
a aut non ee solu hab& sed & quale aliquid esse
subiacet enim insepositis qualitatib; & idcirco di
citur subiectum ON. substantia dicitur ON
TOTHC. substantialitas. quae post geni
tas ab existentia & existentialita
te. deus aut ipse est unu & so

Chapter 23

SLIPS, STRIPS, AND SCRAPS: SCHOLARLY NOTES

While the medieval examples of ephemeral artifacts discussed in Chapter 22 involved paper, other examples, explored here, were made from parchment. In the Middle Ages, such slips were called *schedulae* (singular *schedula*). The ones discussed here were in essence the by-product of parchment production. While the waste material became used for the production of small books, which can be recognized by their uneven pages (Figure 94) and translucent patches (see Figure 4 at p. 9), the scraps were particularly popular for note-taking.[1] Before exploring a rare surviving scholarly note that I happened upon by chance in the collections of Leiden University Library, let's first explore how the material itself came to be.

From Skin to Parchment

In order to make an animal skin into parchment, it needed (among other steps) to be stretched taut on a frame. This stretching, combined with the natural shape of the animal's body, resulted in very uneven edges. The longer sides were slightly narrower in the middle where the animal's stomach had been, which gave them an elongated dent, while the shorter sides had various smaller dents around the locations where the head, tail, and legs had been. The edges needed to be removed to make a tidy sheet to write on. What was left over when this job was

1 For the use of offcuts, see Kwakkel, "Discarded Parchment" (note-taking at pp. 243–44). Kwakkel, "Classics on Scraps" presents a case study of classical manuscripts produced from offcuts.

Figure 94. Manuscript made from offcuts, showing uneven edge of page and discolouration, ca. 1000–1025. Leiden, UB, VLO 92, fol. 124r. With permission.

done were small pieces of parchment, called offcuts (see Figure 94 and the General Introduction, p. 8).

The strips were not only deemed unsuitable for book-making because of their odd size (long and skinny), but they were also riddled with deficiencies, such as stains, discolouration, and translucent patches, either by virtue of their location on the animal's body, or because of the stretching process. Unwieldy as they were, such "offcuts" were primarily acceptable for texts of limited length that did not need to look spiffy, such as notes, short draft texts, letters, horoscopes, wills, or addenda attached to charters.[2] When used as a writing support, offcuts have an informal air about them, which is also reflected by the grade of script with which they are filled. The texts are often written down in a cursive hand or in a book hand with a cursive element, showing that they were copied at high speed.

The casual appearance of the offcut matches the nature of the texts they hold: notes and drafts, and even letters, none of which were usually made to be kept permanently. This is why it was not seen as a problem to use scrap materials, although the small dimensions of the parchment offcuts did pose a particular problem for the letter writer: they had to be brief. Both Anselm of Bec and Bernard of Clairvaux apologize for the brevity of their letters: they would have loved to have written more, but were unable to. Knowing the materials they had to work with, we can perhaps guess why. Charles of Orléans states it even more plainly in one of his letters: "For lack of space, I am writing no more to you."[3] We have to take this very literally.

Scholarly Note

The ironic thing is, of course, that because they were intended to have short lives, offcuts that do survive are valuable. They shed light, after all, into corners of medieval written culture that have remained dark. A good example is a parchment strip of 5 cm × 10 cm discovered in Leiden University Library (Figure 95). The Leiden *schedula* is filled with notes made by a person affiliated to a medieval university. The text on the upper half of the scrap can be dated to the second half of the thirteenth century, while the lower part, written by a different person, is from ca. 1300. The slip was folded in the manuscript and the second writer was probably a later owner of the manuscript who added text to an existing note.

---

2 Kwakkel, "Discarded Parchment."
3 Kwakkel, "Discarded Parchment," p. 243.

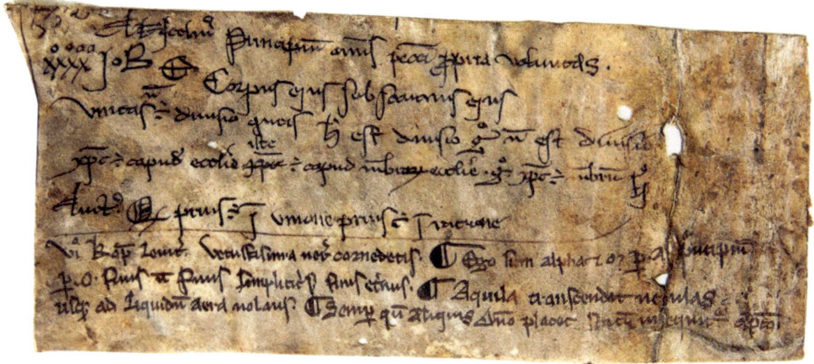

Figure 95. Parchment strip with notes, thirteenth century. Leiden, UB, BPL 191 D, unfoliated. Photo by Giulio Menna.

We can envision the scholar (perhaps it was a student?) pondering various themes that were popular at a thirteenth-century university. According to his notes, he is sparring with the notion of *propria voluntas* (self-will or personal choice) and how it relates to sin. We can also see how the student might have been struggling to keep up with his teacher's lecture; he wrote at high speed in a cursive hand and used many abbreviations. What it shows us is a welcome addition to what we already know about note-taking from primary sources. *De disciplina scholarum*, a study manual written by Pseudo-Boethius made in Paris in the 1230s, advises that students bring such *schedulae* with them to class for note-taking. Evidence suggests that the strips were kept with the textbook, folded into the quires like the Leiden specimen.

The Leiden scrap is right at home in the manuscript to which it is now appended. The host codex is dense with texts used in education, most of which are also heavily glossed. The most notable of these texts, the first in the manuscript, is the very study manual by Pseudo-Boethius that prescribes the use of *schedulae* for note-taking. Evidently, the users who filled this tiny parchment strip took the advice in that manual to heart.

Tradition

The tradition of using scrap material for taking notes (and subsequently sticking the note in the book) took off in the thirteenth century. Browsing through scholastic (that is, university) books from that period reveals these stowaways from time to time. The tradition was continued, however, into the age of paper (Figure 96).

Figure 96. Paper strip with annotation, fifteenth century. Leiden, UB, BPL 139 unfoliated. Photo by Giulio Menna.

This material came into common use during the fourteenth century, and during the production of paper books there were sometimes scraps left over (blank parts were sometimes cut from partly failed leaves), though not as systematically as in the production of parchment manuscripts. These paper leftovers were perfect for taking notes. Just like its parchment counterparts, the paper slip in Figure 96 has uneven edges (right side and bottom), which suggests that it, too, was a leftover from another job. The note is filled with text written in a quick cursive script and it is riddled with abbreviations: it was no doubt jotted down for personal and short-term use by the student or scholar who wrote it. Notably, the use of these paper strips is comparable to our modern use of scraps of paper fished out of the blue recycling bin: any snippet will do, even if it looks a bit scruffy, as long as it has a blank surface.

33

It ons is en kynt an ghekoemen sonder na[me]
des donnersdaech voer synte pieters dach
ad vyncula en wi hietten pieter
int jaer xv en .ii. en was ghelect in
onser frouwen kerc onder een banck

It ons is een kynt an ghecomen daech
na synte Wylliborts dach ao xv^c en t
in synte peters kerc by synte hubrechts
outaer en hadde een breif by hem
dat dat pieter soude hieten en was
een ongekerstent kynt

It ons is een kint an ghecomen saterdachs voer sint
katrinen dach ao xv^c ii yn wort ~~[illegible]~~ ghevonden
yn onser vrouwen kerck ~~[illegible]~~ en was out ontrent
iii jaer

Ons is een kint an gecomen [illegible] op die [illegible]
[illegible] dach anno xv^c en [illegible] en sinen naem is Jasper
en die hebben wy hem gegeven want hy gheen
naem by hem en hadde

Chapter 24

MEDIEVAL NAME TAGS

Extending the discussion of small ephemeral slips in the previous chapters, the focus remains on tiny objects that are not supposed to exist anymore. Kept in the massive vault of the regional archives in Leiden (*Erfgoed Leiden en Omstreken*), these tiny slips tell a powerful story. In fact, more than in any other medieval document I have encountered, no more personal and intimate view of medieval life is offered than the small name tags discussed here. A fair warning is appropriate, however; make sure you have a tissue at hand.

Name Tags

These fifteenth-century strips are written in Middle Dutch and are part of the archive of the medieval Holy Spirit Orphanage (Heilige Geest- of Arme Wees- en Kinderhuis) in the city of Leiden.[1] Founded in 1316, the orphanage was connected to the parish of St. Peter, and was in operation until the 1980s. The building survives and is situated less than a hundred metres from the massive Church of St. Peter (Hooglandse Kerk), which can be seen towering over the city from miles away. Until the middle of the twentieth century, the charitable organization was responsible for the care of foundlings and children.

The paper slips, some of which are as small as 1 cm × 3 cm, add a real-world dimension to what we know about medieval orphanages. The example shown

1 For a history of the orphanage (including a brief discussion of the name tags), see van der Wiel, *"Dit kint hiet Willem."*

Figure 97. Booklet describing intake of foundlings, dated 1502. Erfgoed Leiden en Omstreken, HGW, Archiefnr. 519, Inv. nr. 3384. Photo by the author.

here reads: "This child's name is William" ("*Dit kint hiet Willem*," Figure 98). Each slip shows a pair of holes as well as the indent of a pin, which explains what we are looking at: name tags pinned on a foundling's clothing as they entered the orphanage. As far as I know, this is the only surviving collection of medieval name tags, and it is a mystery why they were kept in the orphanage's archive for five centuries.

Who Wrote Them?

The tag collection can be divided into two categories. Some were probably written by one of the masters of the orphanage. The one seen in Figure 98, for example, is done by an experienced, professional hand. Others, however, are written in a less

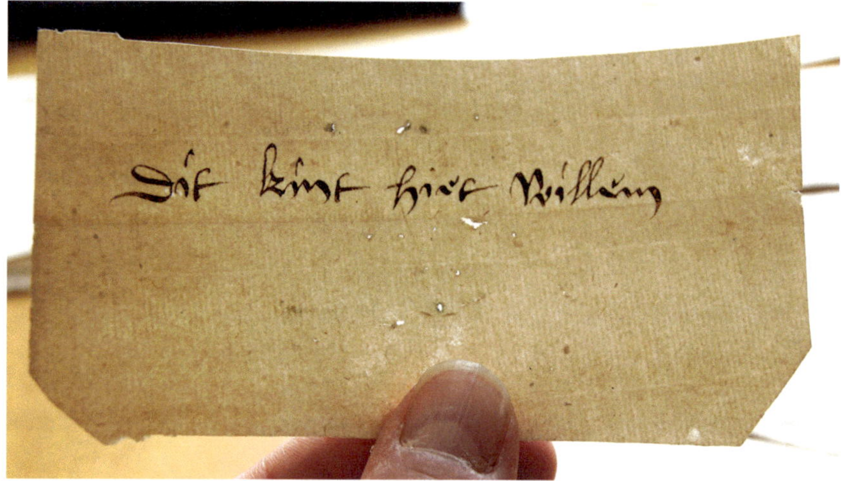

Figure 98. Name tag of foundling "Willem," fifteenth century. Leiden, Erfgoed Leiden en Omstreken, HGW, Archiefnr. 519, Inv. nr. 3384. Photo by the author.

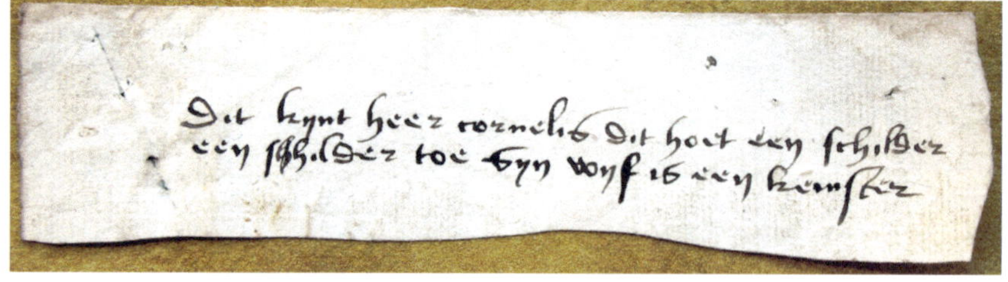

Figure 99. Name tag of foundling "Cornelius," fifteenth century. Leiden, Erfgoed Leiden en Omstreken, HGW, Archiefnr. 519, Inv. nr. 3384. Photo by the author.

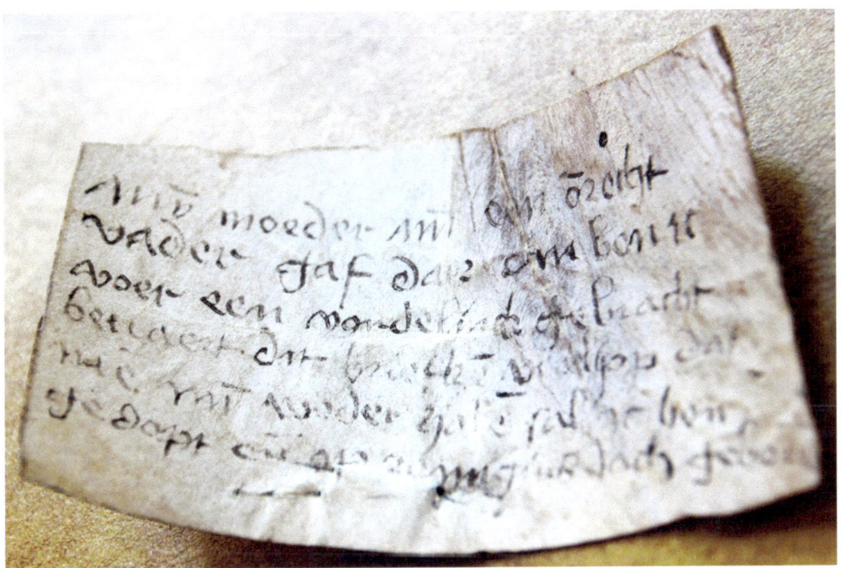

Figure 100. Name tag of anonymous foundling, fifteenth century. Leiden, Erfgoed Leiden en Omstreken, HGW, Archiefnr. 519, Inv. nr. 3384. Photo by the author.

experienced hand, less accustomed to writing. These were probably written by the children's parents. This is supported by the observation that these tags provide more details about the child.

The one in Figure 99 (again with a clear pin mark) reads: "This child is called Cornelius and belongs to a painter whose wife is a wool comber" ("*Dit kijnt heet cornelis dit hoet een schilder een schilder toe sijn wijf is een kemster*"). On another tag we read "This child is baptized and her name is Mariken" ("*Dijt kijnt is ghekorstent ende haerren name is mariken*"). Both show how some children—whether found in the street or dropped off at the orphanage—entered the orphanage with some family history literally attached to them.

The only parchment tag among these paper scraps provides a particularly detailed history (Figure 100). It reads "My mother gave me an illegal father, which is why I was brought here as a foundling. Keep this note so that they can pick me up again later. I was baptized and born on St. Remigius Day" ("*Mijn moeder min een onrecht vader gaf daer om ben ic voer een vondelinck gebracht, bewaert dit briefken v[...] opdat nae min weder halen sal ic ben gedopt ende op Remigius dach geboren*"). As in the case of the scrap in Figure 99, the information on this note was most likely to have been provided by the parents, probably as they dropped off their child.

Accompanying Booklet

The paper slips are kept together with a booklet of ca. 1500, in which they may, in fact, have travelled through time (Figure 97 at p. 188). The title on the booklet's first page tells us what we are dealing with: "The Child Book: How the Children Came Here" ("*Item dat kijnderbock hoe dat die kijnder hier ghecomen sijen*"). The booklet confirms the origins of the slips: they were indeed attached to the orphans. An entry for the year 1510 reports, "A child came into our care the day after St. Willebrord's day in the year 1510 in St. Peter's Church at the altar of St. Hubrecht and he had a note with him stating that his name was Peter. He was a newborn child" ("*Item ons is een kynt anghecomen daechs na Synte Wylleboerts dach anno [1510] in Synte pyters kerc by synte hubrecht outer ende hadde een brief by hem dat dat pyeter soude hyeten ende was een nuboren kynt*").

The booklet forms the counterpart to the labels, for it registers the orphans and provides information about the location where they were found. We may presume that the foundlings entered the house, often as babies, were tagged, and were then processed for care. However, the entries in the book also contain brief reports from people who found these children in public spaces and came by to drop them off at the orphanage. The stories on the fifty-odd pages are truly heartbreaking.

The top entry of page 33 features the following entry (Figure 97, p. 188):

> Item, a child came into our care without a name on the Thursday before the feast of St. Peter in Chains. And we named him Peter, in the year 1502, for he was found in the Church of Our Lady under a bench
>
> (*Item ons is en kijnt an ghekoemen sonder naem des donnersdacx voer sijnte pieters dach ad vynckula ende vij hietten pieter int jaer 1502 ende vas gheleit in onsser frouwen kerc onder een banck*)

On page 7 a story with an unhappy ending is penned by two scribes under the heading "anonymous" (*sonder naem*). The first writes "Item, a child was found in the Church of St. Peter and we named him Luke, on the Sunday before St. Luke [18 October] in the year 1491. He looked like a newborn child to us, and he had been placed on the altar of St. Agnes." A second scribe, using a slightly browner ink, added a short line, sometime later: "Luke died around St. Catharine's Day [November 25] in the same year." (Scribe 1: "*Item een kijnt ende vas ghevonden in sinte pieters kerc ende wij hietent Lucas op die zonnendach voer sinte Lucas anno 1491 ende was een nuo borun kijnt als ons dachten ende lach op sinte aegten altaer.*" Scribe 2: "*Lucas starf omtrent sinte katrinen dach actum voerseit.*") The second scribe then crossed out the entry in the register.

These narratives form a powerful accompaniment to the paper slips. They report how and where the foundlings were found, and when they came to the orphanage with paper name tags pinned to their clothes. Handling the paper slips in the archives is a touching experience: to think that they were made for the sole purpose of providing information about a child whose life was about to change dramatically. The handwriting underscores the emotions that must have been felt by the parents: the text is written in a scruffy manner, often with mistakes in spelling and grammar. For them it must have been a difficult task to write down these mini histories, in more ways than one.

The statute of wynchestre

This ys thassise of all maner of breade of what grayne of corne soever yt be. It shalbe wayed after the farthinge wastell. The symnell shall waye lesse then the wastle .ii d. because of the seythinge. And the farthinge white lofe shall way more then the wastle because of the branynge .ii d. And the halfpennye wheaten lofe shall waye .iii. farthinge white loaves. And the halfpennye loaf of all manner of corne .ii. halfpennye white loaves shall waye. And the baker shalbe allowed on evry quarter for bakinge for grounde and fournynge .iiii d. for wood .iii d. for the iorney men .ii d. ob. for .ii. pages .i d. ob. for salte ob. for Eyste ob. for candle ob. & his tiedynge ob. and ye brande to his advauntage

R. qrtr whet	R. q. symnell	R. farth. wastel	R. ob. white lofe	R. d. whete lof	R. d. housh
iiii s.	i li. vii oz. iiii d.	i li. viii oz. viii d.	iii li. vii oz. iiii d.	x li. ix oz. xii d.	xiiii li. iii oz. x
iiii s. vi d.	i li. iiii oz. xviii d.	i li. iii oz. ii d.	iii li. ii oz. xiii d.	ix li. viii oz.	xii li. x oz. xi
v s.	i li. iii oz. ii d.	i li. iii oz. vi d.	ii li. xi oz. i d.	viii li. ix oz. iii d.	xi li. viii oz. ii
v s. vi d.	i li. i oz. xii d.	i li. ii oz. xvii d.	ii li. viii oz. i d.	viii li. iiii d.	x li. viii oz. vi
vi s.	i li. viii d.	i li. i oz. xii d.	ii li. v oz. xii d.	vii li. iiii oz. xvii d.	ix li. x oz. viii
vi s. vi d.	xi oz. vii d.	i li. xi d.	ii li. iii oz. xii d.	vi li. x oz. x d.	ix li. ii oz.
vii s.	x oz. ix d.	xi oz. xiii d.	ii li. i oz. xiiii d.	vi li. v oz. iii d.	viii li. vi oz. x
vii s. vi d.	ix oz. xiii d.	x oz. xvii d.	ii li. iii d.	vi li. ix d.	viii li. xi oz. x
viii s.	ix oz.	x oz. iii d.	i li. x oz. xvi d.	v li. viii oz. viii d.	vii li. iii oz. iii
viii s. vi d.	viii oz. viii d.	ix oz. xii d.	i li. ix oz. xii d.	v li. iiii oz. xvi d.	vii li. ii oz. v
ix s.	vii oz. xvii d.	ix oz. i d.	i li. viii oz. x d.	v li. i oz. xi d.	vi li. x oz. ii
ix s. vi d.	vii oz. vii d.	viii oz. xi d.	i li. vii oz. xi d.	iiii li. x oz. xviii d.	vi li. vi oz. v
x s.	vi oz. xix d.	viii oz. iii d.	i li. iii oz. xiiii d.	iiii li. viii oz. iii d.	vi li. ii oz. xi
x s. vi d.	vi oz. xi d.	vii oz. xv d.	i li. v oz. xviii d.	iiii li. v oz. xvii d.	v li. xi oz. xv
xi s.	vi oz. iiii d.	vii oz. viii d.	i li. v oz. iiii d.	iiii li. iii oz. xiiii d.	v li. viii oz. xi
xi s. vi d.	v oz. xviii d.	vii oz. ii d.	i li. iiii oz. xii d.	iiii li. i oz. xvi d.	v li. vi oz. vi
xii s.	v oz. xii d.	vi oz. xvi d.	i li. iiii oz.	iiii li.	v li. iiii oz.
xii s. vi d.	v oz. vi d.	vi oz. x d.	i li. iii oz. ix d.	iii li. x oz. vii d.	v li. i oz. xvi
xiii s.	v oz. i d.	vi oz. v d.	i li. ii oz. xix d.	iii li. viii oz. xviii d.	iiii li. xi oz. x
xiii s. vi d.	iiii oz. xvii d.	vi oz. i d.	i li. ii oz. x d.	iii li. vii oz. x d.	iiii li. x oz. vi
xiiii s.	iiii oz. xii d.	v oz. xvi d.	i li. ii oz. i d.	iii li. vi oz. iii d.	iiii li. viii oz.
xiiii s. vi d.	iiii oz. viii d.	v oz. xii d.	i li. i oz. xiii d.	iii li. iiii oz. xix d.	iiii li. vi oz. x
xv s.	iiii oz. v d.	v oz. ix d.	i li. i oz. vi d.	iii li. iii oz. xviii d.	iiii li. v oz. iii
xv s. vi d.	iiii oz. i d.	v oz. v d.	i li. xviii d.	iii li. ii oz. xv d.	iiii li. iii oz. x
xvi s.	iii oz. xviii d.	v oz. ii d.	i li. xii d.	iii li. i oz. xvi d.	iiii li. ii oz. v
xvi s. vi d.	iii oz. xv d.	iiii oz. xix d.	i li. vi d.	iii li. xviii d.	iiii li. i oz. iii
xvii s.	iii oz. xii d.	iiii oz. xvi d.	i li.	iii li.	iiii li.
xvii s. vi d.	iii oz. ix d.	iiii oz. xiii d.	xi oz. xiiii d.	ii li. xi oz. iii d.	iii li. x oz. xv
xviii s.	iii oz. vi d.	iiii oz. x d.	xi oz. ix d.	ii li. x oz. viii d.	iii li. ix oz. x
xviii s. vi d.	iii oz. iiii d.	iiii oz. viii d.	xi oz. iiii d.	ii li. ix oz. xiii d.	iii li. viii oz.
xix s.	iii oz. ii d.	iiii oz. vi d.	xi oz.	ii li. ix oz.	iii li. vii oz. x
xix s. vi d.	ii oz. xix d.	iiii oz. iii d.	x oz. xvi d.	ii li. viii oz. vi d.	iii li. vii oz.
xx s.	ii oz. xviii d.	iiii oz. i d.	x oz. xi d.	ii li. vii oz. xvi d.	iii li. vi oz. ii

Chapter 25

POSTERS BEFORE PRINT

We remain in the realm of flat objects, albeit those under scrutiny now are quite a bit larger than the tiny pieces of parchment and paper explored in previous chapters. In the Middle Ages words were not just written in books and on small paper or parchment slips, but also on full—*plano*—parchment skins: the full animal skin was the largest writing surface available in medieval written culture. Many of these "posters" were produced to be mounted on walls. While very few survive, and even fewer in one piece, they show how (and what) information was put on public display, both indoors and outside.

Advertisements

Commercial scribes and Early Modern printers marketed their goods and services in order to draw a crowd to their shops. In Chapter 6 we encountered the commercial scribe Herneis, who tried to lure clients into his bookshop by adding spam to the books he produced. He identified the street where he was situated: Rue Neuve Notre Dame. Parisians would go to this street for their French books, whether to buy them or to have them decorated or bound. For Latin manuscripts they went to the Rue St. Jacques, in the Latin Quarter, where students and teachers lived.

Because medieval tradespeople kept their shops in the same neighbourhood as other artisans of the same craft, customers knew precisely where to go when they needed a book, a candle, a good chair—or all three, the perfect combination.

Figure 101. Full skin with regulations for bread-making in Winchester, England, sixteenth century. Philadelphia, University of Pennsylvania Libraries, LJS 238. Public domain. Source: www.openn.library.upenn.edu.

Figure 102. Advertisement sheet of professional scribe Herman Strepel, ca. 1447. The Hague, KB, 76 D 45 Nr. 4A-B. With permission.

In Brussels the commercial booksellers, scribes, and decorators were situated in the Bergstraat (or Rue Montagne). The street is strategically situated across from the city's cathedral, which is a location preferred by book artisans in other cities as well.[1] The canons of the cathedral chapter, as well as many of its visitors, could read and were, therefore, potential clients. This location-sharing by people selling the same goods also presented a problem: how to convince the reader to step into *your* shop and not your neighbour's. This is where the first poster comes in: the advertisement sheet (Figure 102).

This fragment was once part of a much larger sheet, which displayed many different types of scripts (The Hague, KB, 76 D 45 Nr. 4A). Another fragment from the same sheet also survives (Nr. 4B). Given that each fragment measures 25 cm × 33 cm, the full sheet must have been quite large. The poster states that it was made by Herman Strepel, probably of Münster. With this poster, Strepel could show off to his potential clientele how well he could write and just how many different scripts

1 Kwakkel, *"Dit sijn die Dietsche boeke,"* pp. 170–71 (Brussels) and 165n134 (examples of other cities).

he had mastered. Like a good businessman, he displayed the names of the scripts in gold: how can you resist ordering a book written in such pretty letters?

The back of such advertisement sheets are generally empty and in some cases their corners display rust-edged holes, which suggests they were pinned to a wall, like a menu in a fast-food restaurant today. A German sheet from 1516 invites the beholder to "come in," showing that this particular sheet acted as a mini window display outside the shop. Because such sheets also presented the names of the scripts, the client could simply enter and tell the scribe in what kind of script he wanted his book to be copied, for example in *fracta*, *rotunda*, or *modus copiistarum* (Figure 19 may show such a transaction between a commercial scribe and his client).[2] These posters show just how advanced the book trade was even before the invention of print: a jargon had emerged that united artisans and connected clients to commercial makers of books.

Maps

Another kind of poster is the wall map, though these, too, survive in small numbers. Perhaps the best-known specimen is the Hereford Mappa Mundi, which was produced around 1300 and measures an astonishing 1.59 × 1.34 metres (about 5.25 × 4.25 feet). This particular map was first put on display in Hereford Cathedral for the benefit of pilgrims, although references suggest that by the seventeenth century it was placed in the library, perhaps so it could be consulted for study purposes. The map contains over a thousand inscriptions and legends, such as that of the Mandrake, the creature immortalized by the Harry Potter series. The Hereford map is thought to have been made of a single sheet, but this is simply not possible.[3] As an inventory of skins has shown, animals used for the production of manuscripts in northwest Europe (mostly cows) usually measured around 68 cm × 48 cm, while the largest specimens measured around 80 cm × 56 cm.[4]

Much larger than the Hereford specimen is the older Ebstorf Mappa Mundi, which measured 3.6 × 3.6 metres and was produced in the late thirteenth century. This beast of a poster, which would cover a full wall in a modern bedroom, was produced from the skins of no fewer than thirty goats. The Ebstorf map, which was sadly lost in the Allied bombing of Hanover in October 1943, was produced for contemplative purposes for the inhabitants of the Benedictine nunnery of

2 For advertisement sheets, see Wehmer, "Die Schreibmeisterblätter," quotation at p. 154.
3 A dedicated website for the Hereford map is found at www.themappamundi.co.uk. The single-sheet claim is found here, among other places.
4 Gumbert, "Sizes and Formats," p. 236 (n. 17 for disputing sizes over 80 cm in height).

Ebstorf. It allowed the beholder to observe God's creation, the world, in all its details. Thankfully a full-size facsimile was made before its destruction, allowing this enormous map to live on in kind.[5]

Wall Catalogues and Inventories

Surviving artifacts highlight the existence of a third category of medieval posters: library catalogues and inventories. Again, these are fairly large sheets, sometimes composed of several animal skins. The information on these posters is of a most practical kind, given that it showed readers where in the library they could find copies of certain texts. The catalogue was one of a series of instruments that helped readers find their way around the collection of books in the monastery.

The poster in Figure 103 dates from ca. 1500 and originally measured 80 cm × 59 cm. It displays the books present in the library of the Abbey of St. Jerome (known as "Lopsen"), a community in the Congregation of Windesheim situated on the outskirts of Leiden. Considering the holes in its corners and its blank verso, it was apparently pinned to the wall, probably in the library. The inventory is divided into categories, such as *libri refectoriales* (books read during meals) and *libri devoti et utiles* (books for personal spiritual development). Within these categories books are numbered with Roman numerals. This is clearly an inventory more than a catalogue. The absence of proper shelfmarks, like the ones discussed in Chapter 17, meant the reader or librarian had to hunt for the copy they sought when they arrived at the lectern that held a certain category of books. Even if the copies in this particular library were fitted with a title shield (see pp. 89–90), effort was still required to track them down.

Regulations

The final poster artifact discussed here is a sixteenth-century government document from the city of Winchester, England (Figure 101 at p. 194). Under the heading "The statute of wynchestre" it provides detailed regulations for bread-making in the city. The document, now kept at the University of Pennsylvania Libraries as LJS 238, gives prescribed weights and costs for bread loaves produced from different grades of wheat, namely "quarter symnell" (the finest bread you

5 A searchable digital facsimile of the Ebstorf Mappa Mundi (Ebstorfer Weltkarte) is hosted online by Leuphana Universität Lüneburg at www2.leuphana.de/ebskart/ (in German).

could buy in medieval England), "farthing wastel," "white lofe," "wheten lof," and "household lof."[6] These categories are found in columns 2 through 5. The different breads are depicted above the relevant column (faintly visible in the image), while the first column shows a bag of grain.

Like the other specimens discussed in this chapter, the regulations were written on parchment. This material was ideally suited for displaying information on a wall: it was durable, it could handle moisture, and the full skin provided a more or less poster-sized format. Even though the Statutes of Winchester poster is smaller than the other examples (it measures 44 cm × 34 cm), the oddly shaped corners at the top of the statutes show that a full skin was used for its production. This narrower part of the parchment sheet was once the base of the animal's neck, an uneven area that was usually cut off. As described in Chapter 23, these offcuts and slips could subsequently be used to take down notes. For these regulations, however, this part of the skin remained in place because it was perfectly shaped to hold the clarifying prose that needed to be part of this medieval poster.

6 LJS 238 has been digitized by the University of Pennsylvania Libraries and can be found in its Lawrence J. Schoenberg Manuscripts online repository at http://openn.library.upenn.edu/Data/0001/html/ljs238.html, from which these details are gathered, together with Devine, "Food for Thought," *Unique at Penn* (blog), https://uniqueatpenn.wordpress.com/2013/04/08/food-for-thought.

Figure 103 (overleaf). Book inventory placed on wall in library of St. Jerome Abbey, Leiden, ca. 1500 (recycled as book cover). Leiden, Erfgoed Leiden en Omstreken, Kloosters 885 Inv. Nr. 208A. With permission.

libri [illegible]

j Prima ps biblie.
ij Secunda ps biblie.
iij Tercia ps biblie.
iiij liber cum [illegible].
v [illegible]
vi Omelie [illegible] hyemale [illegible]
vij Omelie [illegible] estivale de [illegible]
viij [illegible]
ix [illegible] de tpe [illegible]
x [illegible]
xi
xij
xiij [illegible] ps

Aurea legenda, p anni.

libri bti augustini epi ypponensis [illegible]

j [illegible]
ij [illegible] n. [illegible]
iij [illegible] et opibz, cu [illegible] alijs.
iiij [illegible]. De [illegible] cu [illegible]
v De [illegible] et aia. cu alijs.
vi Prima ps sup [illegible]
vij Secunda ps sup [illegible]
viij Sup sermone dni in monte
ix Ad fres de heremo.
x Ad bonifaciu comite epla, et [illegible]
xi Meditaciones. et Soliloqa beati [illegible]
xij Manuale.
xiij Sermones diversi.
xiiij Sermones alij sup veteris testamen[illegible]
xv Regula.
xvi Sup [illegible] quinquagena psalterij.
xvij [illegible]
xviij [illegible]
xix [illegible]

iij Sup ecclesiasten.
[illegible] Translatio [illegible] sup cantica canticoru.
v Translatio psalteri sedm hebraicam [illegible]
vi Sup ezechiam [illegible], cu quinq sequentibz.
vij Sup [illegible] et quinq sequentibz.
viij Sup danielem.
ix Sup matheum.
x Sup eplas ad galathas, ad titu, et philemone.
xi Sup eplam ad ephesios, cu textu [illegible] epte.
xij De illustribz viris, cu alijs.
xiij Contra [illegible] heretici, etc.
xiiij [illegible], sive flores iheronimi.
xv [illegible] in eplaribz no habentur.
xvi Sup marcu.
xvij [illegible] ad [illegible], cu ceteris.
xviij [illegible]
xix [illegible] ad [illegible]
xx [illegible]
xxi [illegible] sup [illegible]
xxij Regula ad eustochiu.
xxiij Epla ad amicu egrotu.
xxiiij Epla ad heliodoru.
xxv
xxvi

libri bti gregorij pape.

j Prima ps moraliu [illegible]
ij Secunda ps moraliu [illegible]
iij Tercia ps moraliu [illegible]
iiij Quarta ps moraliu [illegible]
v
vi
vij [illegible]
viij [illegible]
ix
x
xi [illegible]
xij [illegible]
xiij

libri bti iohis crisostomi.

j [illegible]
ij [illegible]
iij [illegible]
iiij [illegible]
v [illegible] nove.
vi Qd nemo leditur nisi a seipso, cu ceteris.
vij De compunctione cordis, cu alijs.
viij
ix
x

libri beati bernardi abbatis.

j Sermones hyemales de tpe et de [illegible]
ij Sermones estivales de tpe et de [illegible]
iij Prima ps sermonu sup cantica.
iiij Secunda ps sermonu sup cantica.
v Sermones de diversis.
vi Flores
vij Epistolae
viij Sermones sup Qui habitat.
ix Omelia sup Missus est.
x [illegible] ad [illegible]
xi Tractatus de [illegible] mor. et [illegible]
xij De duodecim gradibz humilitatis.
xiij De precepto et dispensatione.
xiiij Colloquiu simonis [illegible] et ihesu. cu sermo [illegible]
xv De diligendo deo, de caritate. et apologeticu
xvi Omelia de villico, cu ceteris.
xvij Ad eugeniu de consideratione.
xviij Meditationes, de institutione mor. etc.
xix
xx
xxi

libri richardi de sco victore.

j De duodecim patriarchis [illegible] contempla[illegible]
ij Sup cantica canticoru.
iij Sup Quid e tibi mare. etc.
iiij De statu interioris hois. etc.
v De sompno nabuchodonosor. etc.
vi Sup psalmu Afferte. cu alijs.
vij De contemplatione maior.
viij De trinitate. et sup misit herodes rex.
ix Sup apocalipsim.
x
xi
xij

libri ysidori hispalensis epi.

j Ethimologiaru libri viginti.
ij De summo bono. libri tres.
iij Sup veteris testamenti interpretationes.
iiij Sup cantica canticoru.
v Ad florentina sorore sua libri duo.
vi
vij
viij

libri bonaventure [illegible]

j Stimulus amoris de passione dni. [illegible] de eode.
ij Centiloquiu. De timore. exempla.
iij Soliloquiu.
iiij De modo confitendi. cu alijs.
v
vi

libri hugonis de sco victore.

j De disciplina claustraliu. Qui seqtur.
ij Comentu sup regula augustini. etc.
iij Speculu [illegible]. De tribz dietis.
iiij De vanitate reru mundanaru, cu ceteris.
v Didascalon.
vi
vij

libri nycolai de [illegible]

j Sup ecclesiasticu [illegible]
ij Sup eplas pauli. [illegible]
iij Sup psalteriu [illegible]
iiij Sup libros historiales [illegible]
v
vi

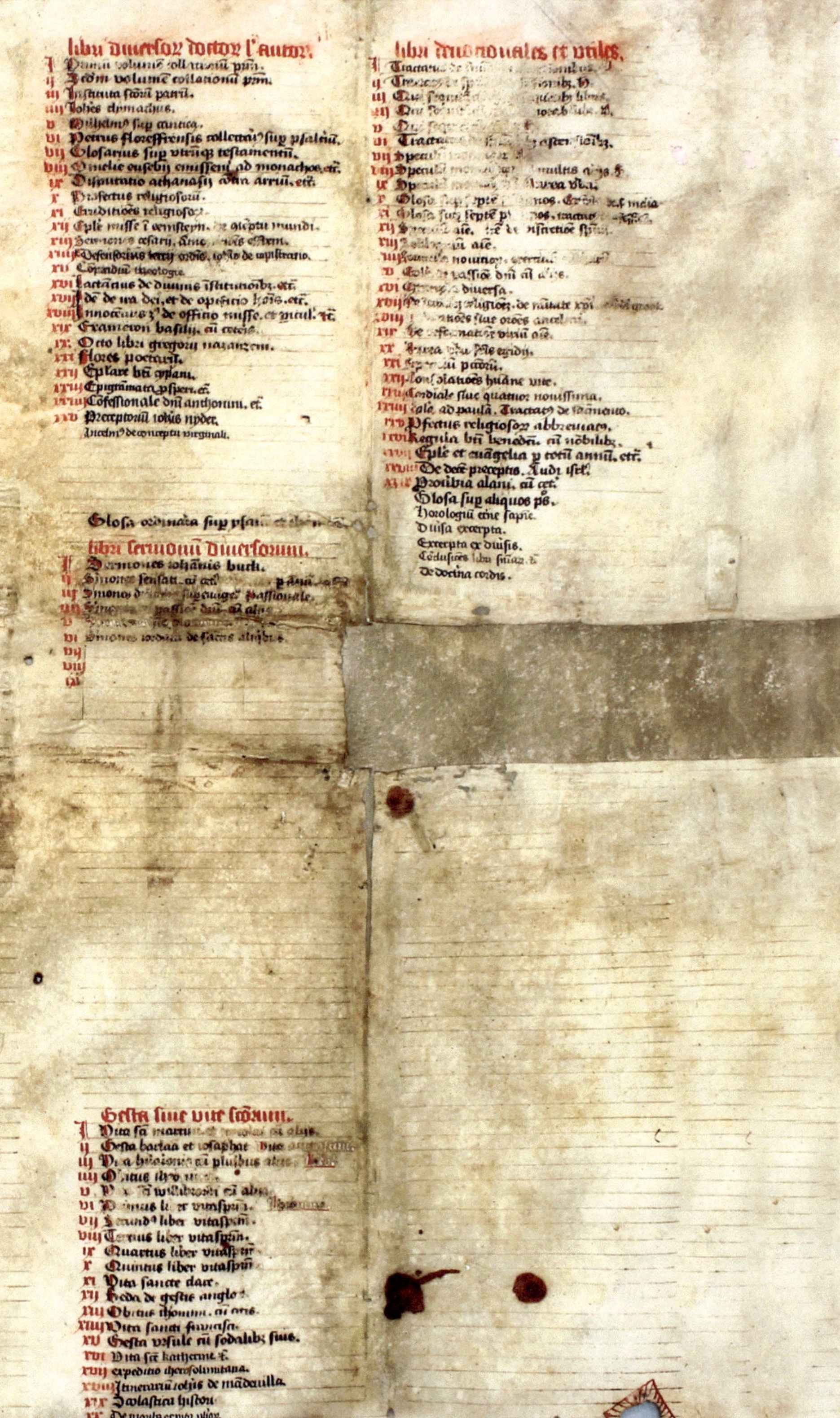

Meridies
Auster
Angulus
Aquarius
Capricornus
Sagittarius
Patri
Vita
Regis
Angulus
Boreas
Septentrio

Chapter 26

MEDIEVAL BOOK APPS

In the last chapter of this section the spectrum of medieval written culture expands once again, not just in the material sense, but also regarding the kind of book under scrutiny: for once, the discussion includes objects from the era of print. Here we examine books with remarkable tools and instruments physically attached to them, a genre that is both rare and versatile—and, frankly, a bit weird as well. Mounted onto the page or the bookbinding, these added instruments extended the book's primary function as an object that one reads into a utilitarian piece of hardware. Some of these add-ons functioned as a calculator, others—astonishingly—even allowed the reader to tell time. As unusual as this enhanced functionality was in the Middle Ages, to a modern person it seems very familiar. Apps on our smartphones, after all, do precisely the same: they extend the function of the phone far beyond its original parameters. Let's examine how medieval books were sometimes more than books.

The Volvelle

The most common piece of "hardware" added to the book is a calculation tool named a "volvelle." It breaks with the tradition that a book provides 2D information, because it consists of one or more rotating disks mounted on the page (Figure 104). Volvelles allowed the reader to make a variety of complex calculations, such as the position of the sun and the moon, or the precise date of Easter—which, like the volvelle, moved. The oldest volvelles are connected to the scientific explorations of Ramón Llull, a thirteenth-century scholar working in the kingdom of Majorca, who imported the clever device from Arabic scholarly culture. He introduced them in his *Ars Magna* (The Great Art) of ca. 1305. This explains why the earliest volvelles

Figure 104. Volvelle in housebook of Houcken family near Münster, ca. 1450–1500. Maastricht, Regionaal Historisch Centrum Limburg, 22.001A. Photo by the author.

date from the fourteenth century (there are no older manuscripts that hold them, as far as I am aware), as well as why the oldest ones are found in books holding works by Llull. The reason why he included these devices is very medieval but also speaks to the curiosity of scholars in the thirteenth century: Llull believed that they could provide logical answers about Creation. Llull's specimens, however, were less sophisticated than the ones shown in this chapter. They had only three discs and present less data on and around the dials.

Tools on Bookbindings

Other instruments were mounted *on* the manuscript rather than *in* it: they were part of the bookbinding. A particularly unusual one is found on the binding of a fourteenth-century Oxford manuscript with texts about fortune-telling and geomancy (Oxford, Bodleian Library, MS Digby 46). Geomancy is a method of divination that interprets random patterns, as produced, for example, by tossed soil or sand. The process could also be done with a series of random numbers, but where would one find this collection of numbers? This problem is solved by a device attached to the binding of the Bodleian manuscript.[1] Space was carved out in the wood of the front board, and two connected cogwheels were placed in this cavity. Turning these produces a number which could subsequently be used for geomancy: the series of numbers it generated became the basis for the necessary calculations, which were handily explained inside the book.

Another book in the Bodleian Library (MS Broxbourne 46.10) has a less elaborate tool added to its binding: its production did not involve a chisel but pen and ink. It belongs to a seventeenth-century printed book (to again move briefly out of our comfort zone) with a sheepskin binding. The front of the binding is not filled with blind-stamped decoration, as was often the case (see Chapter 9 and Figure 41 at p. 74), but is, rather, adorned with a working sundial.[2] The reader could carry the book into the sun and place a stylus on the cover, which would reveal what time it was. While it may not have been the most practical clock, the cover reveals that it was used to this end: the "footprint" of the stylus is still visible as a small circle and a black stain near the letters IHS close to the bottom of the cover. Moreover, the severity of the stain suggests that the book was frequently used to tell the time.

---

1 MS Digby 46 has been partly digitized by Oxford's Bodleian Library, and can be found by searching for its shelfmark on their Luna Catalogue at http://bodley30.bodley.ox.ac.uk:8180/luna/servlet.

2 An image of the binding of MS Broxbourne 46.10 has been digitized by Oxford's Bodleian Library, and can be found in their *Digital.Bodleian* repository listed under "Broxb. 46.10" at http://digital.bodleian.ox.ac.uk/shelfmarks.html.

Pop-Up Sundials

While this sundial was probably added to the book by an Early Modern reader, there are also sundials that were actually part of the printed text by the printer. The 1624 edition of Salomon de Caus's *La pratique et démonstration des horloges solaires*, a tract on measuring time, includes several "pop-up" sundials. The most elaborate one, found at page 23 of the text, consists of two pieces of cardboard, a square and a triangle (Figure 105). To use the clock, the larger (square) component is placed in an upright position. A printed illustration, showing the hours of the day, was pasted to each side. The smaller triangle was then slipped through an incision in the square. Not only did this keep the component with the dial upright, but the tip of the triangle also functioned as the needle in its centre.

Remaining in the age of print for another moment, printers also embraced the medieval volvelle and included it in a variety of publications. Petrus Apianus's *Astronomicum Caesareum* (Imperial Astronomy), a work he printed in 1550 with the financial support of Emperor Charles V, includes twenty-two of them, some with as many as six spinning discs (Figure 106). This edition even includes tiny coloured strings that, when pulled taut, make it easier to read the values at the edge of the discs. Pearls were strung onto the ends of these strings, giving the book the looks befitting its reading audience: Apianus gave most copies away to kings and heads of state. The copy seen here once belonged to Henry VIII of England.

Figure 105. Pop-up sundial in work on time calculation by Salomon de Caus, printed in 1624. Leiden, UB, 676 A 6. Photo by the author.

Figure 106. Luxury volvelle with six discs in Petrus Apianus's *Imperial Astronomy*, printed in 1550. Leiden, Bibliotheca Thysiana, 1625. Photo by the author.

Invasive

While adding these tools was an invasive procedure that involved cutting holes in pages and adding glue to them (and in some cases even hacking into the wooden binding), they are sometimes encountered in books from the medieval and Early Modern periods. As important as volvelles were to some readers in these periods, from a material point of view the crude computers have one big downside: they added volume to the book and made it bulky, especially when more than one was added. Books are not designed to include bulky objects made from cardboard, because it produces dents on the facing pages. The fifteenth-century volvelle shown in Figure 104 even includes decorated pieces of wood which form the dials. They add to the thickness of the manuscript significantly, and the pins that hold them together even stab the facing pages. Still, it appears that the user of this remarkable book—and those of other such book-contraptions—could live with this bulkiness. In that sense, too, medieval books with attached utilitarian applications are like our smartphones today: new functions may add volume, but we don't care because the applications are so very useful.

Figure 107. Girdle book carried on body by Queen Anne Boleyn, ca. 1540 (discussed at p. 229). London, BL, Stowe 956. CC0 1.0 Universal. Source: www.bl.uk/catalogues/illuminatedmanuscripts.

INTRODUCTION

This final section moves away from the production of written artifacts and the culture of reading, which have been the main ingredients of the narrative so far. Various contexts of medieval written culture are briefly highlighted. Our first stop is the monastic scriptorium: **Chapter 27** deals with the intriguing observation that this environment, the kitchen in which medieval books were made, is not depicted in surviving manuscripts. While there is plenty of medieval art showing individual scribes producing a manuscript, there is none—at least not convincingly so—that shows several artisans at work in the same room. This observation is all the more striking because decorators presumably had only to look around for inspiration and a model of how to depict a scriptorium. While it does not solve this mystery, the chapter does highlight the limited way in which scribes at work are presented in medieval iconography.

Chapter 28 stays in the vicinity of scribes at work and inquires about the appearance of their working spaces. What can we learn from depictions of their desks? How did they handle having several books open at the same time (at least their exemplar and the parchment they copied it onto) with limited desktop space? Examining scribes at work in medieval images—one of the few sources available to us—teaches us a variety of things. For example, different types of desks appear to have been used by people making books (scribes) and those composing texts (translators). Likewise, decoration also provides a close-up look at readers in the process of reading. Both scribes and readers had to negotiate the restricted space provided by the medieval desk, but both had solutions at their disposal to increase the value of the real estate in front of them.

The next two chapters again return to readers, but focus not on the consumption of books, which is the focus of the section Reading in Context, but on different aspects of book ownership. **Chapter 29** sheds light on the second-hand book market, a difficult task given the limited tangible evidence left behind by this thriving business. We tend to regard manuscripts as precious objects, not as second-hand goods. Perhaps this is the result of the somewhat negative connotation that "used books" have today: they are often poor-looking objects, beaten and scruffy, and nearing the end of their lives. Nevertheless, every surviving medieval manuscript is a second-hand book: most of them, in fact, would have been traded in this market many times over. Moreover, the dynamics we tend to connect to the notion of second-hand—used and trampled, perhaps even tatty-looking—*does* apply to manuscripts, as many of the case studies discussed in this book have shown.

Chapter 30 examines a different dynamic of medieval book ownership: how books moved about. The long life of medieval books makes it probable that they were relocated at some point—or points—in their lives. Owners died and new owners were not necessarily living in the same city, or even country. Furthermore, owners would take their books as they travelled, for example, because they were merchants, who, devout as they were, brought their religious or mystical texts with them, or students who carted their textbooks to universities far afield. The prospect of travel also inspired owners to have their books made portable, either by asking scribes to adopt a portable format or by fitting the book with a binding that facilitated movement.

The topic of parchment is revisited in **Chapter 31**, which homes in on imperfections found in and on animal skins. The context of damage and imperfection, it turns out, can be quite insightful of how parchment was made (by parchment-makers) and processed into books (by scribes). An interesting notion that emerges in this chapter is the difference between how we modern observers tend to perceive holes, rips, and repairs, and what medieval book artisans thought about them. While we tend to regard sheets with holes as unusable, scribes, it seems, were very matter-of-fact about these inevitable shortcomings. They simply wrote around those parts of the page that were unsuitable, perhaps because it contained a tear or a particularly dense hair implant. This lenient approach to imperfections makes sense, because they were part and parcel of using the skins of once-living creatures, as this chapter shows.

The last chapter of the book, **Chapter 32**, turns to destruction. When they were made, handwritten books were the latest and greatest. They were expensive objects produced for the happy few who could read and afford such luxury items. Their status changed dramatically, however, when a new, quicker-to-produce medium entered the European book scene: the printed book. In many cases, the only perceived value of medieval manuscripts was to recycle their leaves. Sliced and diced, they came to be used for a variety of purposes. Appropriately for the conclusion of a book on manuscripts, the last chapter outlines this sad story of systematic destruction. However, it also shows how the end of a manuscript's life offers a beginning of new scholarly research.

SCRIPTOR SRIPTORUM PRINCEPS EGO NEC OBITURA DEINCEPS LAUS MEA NEC FAMA QUIS
SIM MEA LITTERA CLAMAT LITTERE TE TUA SRIPTURA QUEM SIGNAT PICTA FIGURA
PREDICAT EADWINUM FAMA PER SECULA VIUUM INGENIUM CUIUS LIBRI DECUS IND
ICAT HUIUS QUEM TIBI SEQUE DATUM MUNUS DEUS ACCIPE GRATUM

Chapter 27

WHERE ARE THE SCRIPTORIA?

Our first stop is a visit to the centre of medieval book production: the scriptorium. This chapter's primary tool for looking through the keyhole into this room are miniatures. Decoration on the medieval page shows us human figures handling or making books. While being careful not to take the iconography too literally, such images help us paint a picture of what the medieval world of the book looked like, practically speaking. The well-known depiction of Eadwine, for example, shows this "Prince of Scribes" (according to the description that accompanies his portrait) holding both pen and knife (Figure 108). What such bookish scenes surviving in manuscripts do *not* show, and this is remarkable, are *groups* of scribes at work.

While the monastic scriptorium is the location where manuscripts were made—at least until ca. 1200, when commercial scribes began to take over the monks' role as book producers—it turns out that medieval images of scriptoria are rare, or perhaps even non-existent. While an intense search across various online and offline platforms reveals images with several book-makers at work, none of the surviving images I encountered unquestionably presents a scriptorium. This observation prompts an intriguing question, which is explored in this chapter: where are the scriptoria?

Teaming Up

Bremen, Staats- und Universitätsbibliothek, b. 21 is a richly decorated devotional book produced at Echternach Abbey in Luxemburg. It was made as a monumental gift for Emperor Henry III (d. 1056), and at fol. 124v we encounter an extraordinary

Figure 108. Eadwin, called Prince of Scribes in the Latin text in the frame, ca. 1160–1170. Cambridge, Trinity College, R.17.1, fol. 283v. With permission of the Master and Fellows of Trinity College, Cambridge.

scene. The image shows a peculiar blend of two worlds: on the right, the miniature shows a monk, who is probably copying the text, while the person on the left, whose clothes show he is not a monk but a layperson, is producing the manuscript's decoration.[1] For important books like this, professionals from the outside world were sometimes hired to decorate the pages. Is the place where they are working a scriptorium? Not likely. What the image really shows is how this particular book came to be, namely with the help of a hired hand. Perhaps this image was added to show the Emperor, who is depicted receiving the book on the facing page, that a professional had decorated it. No expense was spared, it expresses. There is another reason to infer we are not shown the inside of a scriptorium. When lay scribes were asked to enter an abbey for the duration of a book project, which did happen from time to time, they appear to have been separated from the local monks.[2]

A similar scenario is depicted in two related copies of Beatus of Liébana's Commentary on the Apocalypse, now known as the Beatus of Tábara (Madrid, Archivo Histórico Nacional, 1097 B, ca. 968–970) and the Las Huelgas Apocalypse (New York, Morgan Library and Museum, M.429, ca. 1220). The first was created by a monk named Magius and his assistants at Tábara de León, a monastery in Spain. Magius also worked on the earlier Morgan Beatus (New York, Morgan Library and Museum, M.644, ca. 960), but died while working on the Beatus of Tábara. It was then finished by his pupil Emeterius, who drew himself and Magius (labeled as "Senior") working in a tower scriptorium. Behind Emeritus, another monk cuts parchment. All this is much easier to see in the later Morgan copy, where the scene is depicted at fol. 183r.[3]

Both versions of the scene raise questions rather than answer them. Are we looking at a realistic representation of a scriptorium? If these two images do show us a real scriptorium, it is a surprisingly tiny space, not a vast room with rows of desks. Or, did the illustrator instead choose to sacrifice a realistic view of a spacious room in order to show multiple people in the small space of a miniature? The same issues—the limited size of the space and whether we are looking at a scriptorium—are encountered in a tenth-century ivory cutting that once decorated a binding (Figure 109). The three people in the lower part appear to be

1 Images of the Gospel Lectionary of Henry III can be seen online by entering "Gospel Lectionary of Henry III" in the 'title' field of the Web Gallery of Art's search tool, www.wga.hu/index.html.

2 An inventory of monastic regulations is found in Kwakkel, *"Dit sijn die Dietsche boeke,"* p. 36; cases from the twelfth century are available in Gullick, "Professional Scribes."

3 M.429, fol. 183r has been digitized by the Morgan Library and Museum, and can be found in their Online Exhibition "Apocalypse Then: Medieval Illuminations from the Morgan," at www.themorgan.org/collection/Las-Huelgas-Apocalypse/49.

Figure 109. Ivory plaque from bookbinding showing Gregory the Great and three scribes at his feet, late tenth century. Vienna, Kunsthistorisches Museum, Inv. Nr. Kunstkammer, 8399. CC0 1.0 Universal. Source: Wikimedia Commons.

involved in copying text: they have pens in their hands and one of them holds an inkwell. The figures are placed in a cramped space underneath the main character, Gregory the Great, who is towering over the scribes squeezed into the register below him to copy his works. Three scribes producing manuscripts in a confined space do not constitute a scriptorium. Or do they?

A Spanish Scriptorium?

There is one last image to discuss here. It is found in the *Book of Games* (*Libro de los Juegos*), a text commissioned by Alfonso X of Spain. The sole surviving copy kept in Madrid's Bibliotheca de San Lorenzo de El Escorial includes a scene of a room furnished with benches that are occupied by scribes copying books, while a supervisor looks on.[4] While it is tempting to identify this room as a scriptorium, there are issues here, too: none of the people shown here appear to be monks, as is evident from both their hairstyle and clothes.

With these observations in mind, the initial question still stands: where are the scriptoria? After all, a search on the web and in my bookcase produced no more than a handful of scenes with more than one scribe working on a book in the same physical space. None of them, however, convincingly show us the inside of a monastic scriptorium. Moreover, there are very few depictions of multiple scribes working together, period. The latter observation is especially remarkable given the fact that the books that might have included such images were produced in the very environment that is so conspicuously absent from our view. It is almost as if the monastic artisans preferred to keep out of view the environment in which they and their fellow monks produced books.

---

4 On the *Libro de los Juegos* manuscript, see Musser, *Los libros de acedrex dados e tablas.*

DEANO

Chapter 28

DESKTOPS

While miniatures may not show us groups of scribes collaborating to make a manuscript, they do depict, in detail, scribes at work, as the previous chapter outlined. Let's stay with these images of individual scribes and examine what we can learn about the practical context of producing a manuscript. To do so, this chapter zooms in on one particular element of scenes showing the copying scribe: his desk. Desk space was a bit of a thing in the Middle Ages. Not all desks were as small as the one shown in the frontispiece at the very beginning of this book, which looks like a small podium. Bigger desks were sometimes a necessity. Manuscripts can easily have a wingspan of half a metre when open. The scribe who used such a book to copy from also had to have space, however, for the empty sheets that would contain the copied text. As this was challenging, special scribal desks were invented, as becomes clear here. Others fought the same battle for space, such as readers and translators, who might also have had several books open at the same time. Let's examine medieval depictions of desktops and the strategies of increasing one's desk space.

Scribes

The first group of people who had to manage multiple books were scribes. By definition, a scribe had to have at least two books on his desk: the one he was making (a growing pile of quires filled with text) and the one he was copying from, called the "exemplar." While keeping track of the loose quires may have been challenging,

Figure 110. Translator Simon de Hesdin at work at a broad desk consisting of two parts placed next to one another, 1479. London, BL, Royal 18 E.III, fol. 24r. CC0 1.0 Universal. Source: www.bl.uk/catalogues/illuminatedmanuscripts.

of those discussed here, the scribe had it easiest. After all, he was only technically reading one book: the one being copied from. This explains why a scribe's desk was of limited size, at least judging from surviving depictions. In most cases their working surfaces were also slanted rather than flat. There are two well-known images of author and scribe Jean Miélot at work (Brussels, KBR, 9278, fol. 10r), which show how his desktop rested at a forty-five-degree angle.[1] In fact, in both depictions his desk is also split in half: he uses the lower half for writing and as his tools (ink pots and pens), while the upper level holds the exemplar he copies from.

Notably there are also broader desks, more like today's artist or drafting tables. The translator Simon de Hesdin is shown using such a table (Figure 110 at p. 216). Although the working side is out of sight, the desk clearly provides room for two books placed *next* to one another. This may have been especially beneficial for a translator, who needed to carefully read one or more source texts and subsequently scribble down his translation in loose quires or on loose sheets. This way, whatever books he needed would be right in front of him: there was no need to look up at a high book platform. A similar desk layout is seen in a fifteenth-century portrait of Jean Wauquelin translating Jacques de Guyse's *Annals of Hainaut* from Latin to French (Valenciennes, Bibliothèque municipal, 772, fol. 168r). Perhaps this was a favoured set-up of translators, since it allowed them to keep careful tabs on their place on all pages open before them as they worked.

Readers

While it is easy to find images of scribes with a desk full of books, it is less common to encounter readers in similar situations. That is to say, there are relatively few medieval scenes in which someone is reading but not writing, where books are present but pens are not. In part, this has to do with medieval study practices. Readers would usually have a pen nearby even when they were just reading: after all, remarks and critiques needed to be added to the margin at the spur of the moment (see Chapter 14). Less common "penless" images often show a crowded desktop. Several medieval manuscript portraits of Christine de Pizan show her with multiple books at a big, messy desk. The absence of the pen may result from an urge to depict Christine as an avid reader.

From the late medieval period a special tool was available for readers who did not like the clutter shown on Christine's desk: the book carousel. The example in Figure 63 at p. 119, found in a fifteenth-century copy of Jean de Meung's *La consolation de Boèce*, is a relatively small one which turned horizontally. These

---

1 Illustrations of Jean Miélot at his desk writing can be seen at "Jean Miélot" in Wikipedia at https://en.wikipedia.org/wiki/Jean_Miélot.

carousels allowed readers to consult multiple manuscripts in a very convenient fashion, by spinning (slowly!) the movable top part. The oldest one I could find is in a portrait of Petrarch from the fourteenth century (Darmstadt, Universitäts- und Landesbibliothek, Inventar-Nr. Cod. 101), but it is possible they were used even earlier.

Book Wheel

The medieval "book spinner" in Figure 63 circumvented the constrictions of the limited space a regular desktop provided. However, what if you needed even more real estate than the turning desktop could offer? The answer to this question is perhaps one of the most intriguing pieces of book furniture that survive from the past: the book wheel. This image shows the book wheel invented by the Renaissance engineer Agostino Ramelli, whose concept was based on medieval designs (Figure 111). The upside to the carousel is obvious: there is space for many books. This practice is not unlike deciding to hook up a second monitor to your computer, except that the reader is actually watching twelve monitors at the same time, like a trader on Wall Street. I have sat behind one from the seventeenth century at Leiden's Bibliotheca Thysiana, and it is truly a majestic feeling to spin the wheel. The click-click sound of the gears hidden inside the device is simply mesmerizing.

Laptop

While desktops (in their great variety) are representative of how most scribes and readers handled their books, there is also a surface space that is more exceptional, and that can only be referred to as a "laptop." The use of such portable desks, which sat on the scribe's lap, is well documented in the Early Modern period and beyond. They were used, for example, by noblemen or secretaries drafting documents and letters while on the road. These laptop desks are essentially boxes with a slightly angled surface, inside which the writing materials were stored, including paper, pen, and ink. Interestingly, this practice—and tool—goes back to at least the twelfth century. These are seen, for example, in the right portal of Chartres Cathedral's west facade of ca. 1150 (Figure 112). There we encounter several classical thinkers, including mathematician Pythagoras and the grammarian Donatus, crouched over their lap desks with a pen in their hand and inkhorns on the wall beside them. They could set the pot they were using into a hole in their desktop (see the figure on the right), which may, incidentally, have held blank sheets inside, like the portable kits from the Renaissance.

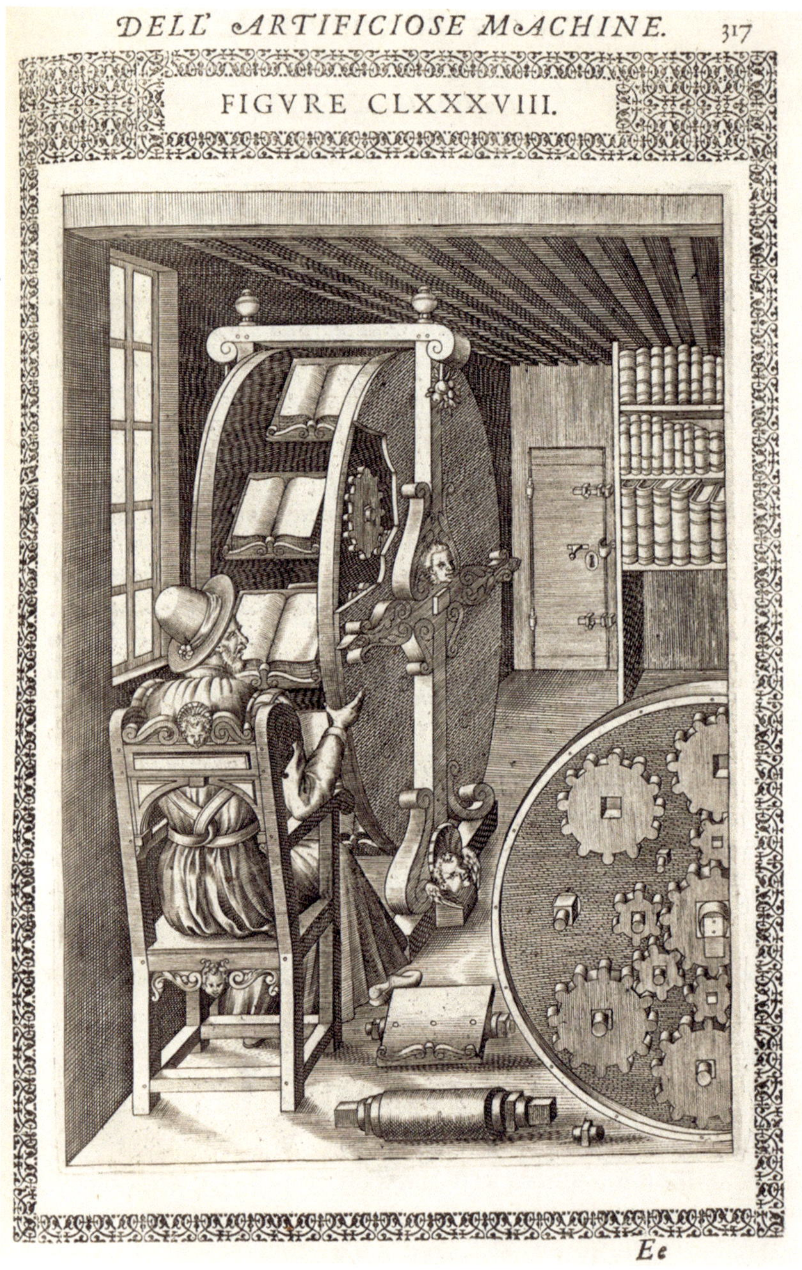

Figure 111. Large book wheel with vertical orientation, as depicted in *Le diverse et artificiose machine del Capitano Agostino Ramelli*, 1588. New Haven, Beinecke Rare Book and Manuscript Library, Yale University, Eliz+47, fig. CLXXXVIII. Public domain. Source: http://beinecke.library.yale.edu/tags/digital-collections.

Figure 112. Chartres Cathedral, west portal, twelfth century. Pythagoras (left) and Donatus writing on small desks placed on their laps. Source: Flickr (copyright Matthias Haupt, with permission).

Apart from the fact that the actual desk space was more limited than what we are used to, medieval desktops were not so different from ours, including how messy they could get. They contained books, both open and closed, as well as writing tools. However, more so than in our present time, desktops were a necessary tool: the medieval quill, after all, needed a stable and even surface.

MACROBIUS

IN

SOMNIUM SCIPIONIS

Chapter 29

SECOND-HAND BOOKS BEFORE PRINT

This chapter and the next again focus on the medieval reader; not to examine how the manuscript reflects reading practices, as is done in the section Reading in Context, but to deal with aspects of book ownership. Like modern readers, medieval people owned two types of books: some were bought new, others second-hand. The two are very different entities, as we all know. New copies are expensive, pristine, and probably present a current publication, while second-hand ones, by contrast, are damaged, may smell of cigars, and potentially present an older edition of the text. Apart from the cigar smell, not much has changed in this regard since the Middle Ages. In that era, too, books were bought both new and pre-owned. And like most books today, their value differed greatly. We know this in part thanks to a familiar piece of information that is sometimes encountered in a medieval book: price tags.

Valuing Books

Medieval booksellers carefully set a value on both the new and the second-hand books that they offered for sale. Mind you, while they had the second-hand copies in stock, ready to be browsed by potential clients, the new ones still needed to be made. For these, arrangements awaited, regarding both material features and price. While it is difficult to deduce precisely which factors were in play in the appraisal process of second-hand books, availability and looks were probably deemed important. Manuscripts with illustrations or with a decorative binding, for example, may have been more expensive than plain copies bound in a parchment wrapper. Unlike today, the text's edition was unimportant (there were

Figure 113. Fifteenth-century price in thirteenth-century text (top of page). Leiden, UB, BPL 168, fol. 56v. With permission.

no publishers, editions, or even title pages), nor was the pristine preservation of the copy in question: it was common for medieval readers to jot down notes in the margins anyway, so few copies were truly pristine for long.

Surviving price tags, while rare, add a real-world dimension to these inferences and assumptions. The tags are usually found on the first or last page of the book, commonly at the very top so that they could be easily found (Figure 113). These prices were sometimes added next to individual copies listed in book inventories, which were made if an owner planned to sell, or if he or she had died. These inventories provide a great source of information about the value of books at particular times, even when the copies themselves no longer exist. Some of these lists acted as a kind of sales catalogue. On a blank leaf in a fourteenth-century historical book in the British Library (Royal 14 C.CXIII, fol. 13v), Symonis Bouzon (d. 1352), prior of the Benedictine cathedral priory at Norwich, listed all the books he personally owned.[1] Next to the thirty-odd titles, he wrote down their value, perhaps with the intention of selling them.

Simple Price Tags

There are two types of price indicators. First there is the plain one, which merely presents a number expressing how much money needed to be forked over in order to own the book. The one in Figure 113, found at the top of the page, reads "8 s[olidi]" (shillings), while the manuscript in Figure 114 was sold for "15 s[olidi]," meaning that it was considerably more expensive.

That these two manuscripts were sold second-hand can be determined from the handwriting: while the pictured price tags date from the fifteenth century, the books themselves were copied in the twelfth and thirteenth centuries, respectively. This means, of course, that the copies were several centuries old when the bookseller wrote these prices in.[2] It also shows that the texts they contain—Macrobius's commentary on Cicero's *Dream of Scipio* (Figure 113) and excerpts from Priscian (Figure 114)—remained valuable, even though reading and learning practices had evolved considerably between the moments of production and resale.

1 Royal 14 C.CXIII has been digitized by the British Library, and can be found by searching for its shelfmark in their Catalogue of Illuminated Manuscripts at www.bl.uk/catalogues/illuminatedmanuscripts/welcome.htm.

2 Another example of such an old medieval second-hand volume is discussed in Kwakkel, "Commercial Organisation and Economic Innovation," pp. 176–77.

Figure 114. Fifteenth-century price in thirteenth-century text. Leiden, UB, BPL 104, fol. 1r. Photo by the author.

Complex Price Tags

The second type of price tag, which is even more rare, brings us to the heart of the commercial book trade. Rather than presenting a single price placed by a bookseller, it provides an itemized bill that covers all stages of the book's production. One found in Cambridge, Peterhouse College, manuscript 110, reads:

> Pro pergamo 27 quat. precium quaterni iii d. Summa vi s. ix d.
> Pro scriptura eorundem viz. xvi d. pro quaterno. Summa xxxvi s.
> Pro luminacione viii d.
> Pro ligacione ii s.[3]

This bill provides a wealth of information. It shows us how much was paid for the parchment (line 1: three pence per quire, or six shillings and nine pence total), for the copying of the text (line 2: sixteen pence per quire, or thirty-six shillings total), for the illumination (line 3: eight pence) and for binding the book (line 4: two shillings). In this case it was the book's owner who wrote these expenses down (he did so in other manuscripts, too), probably to keep track of how much he paid the artisans who executed the different production stages of his custom book. It was more common, however, for such itemized bills to be drawn up by the individual

---

3 Quoted from James, *A Descriptive Catalogue*, p. 128. This case is discussed in Kwakkel, "Commercial Organisation and Economic Innovation," pp. 175–76.

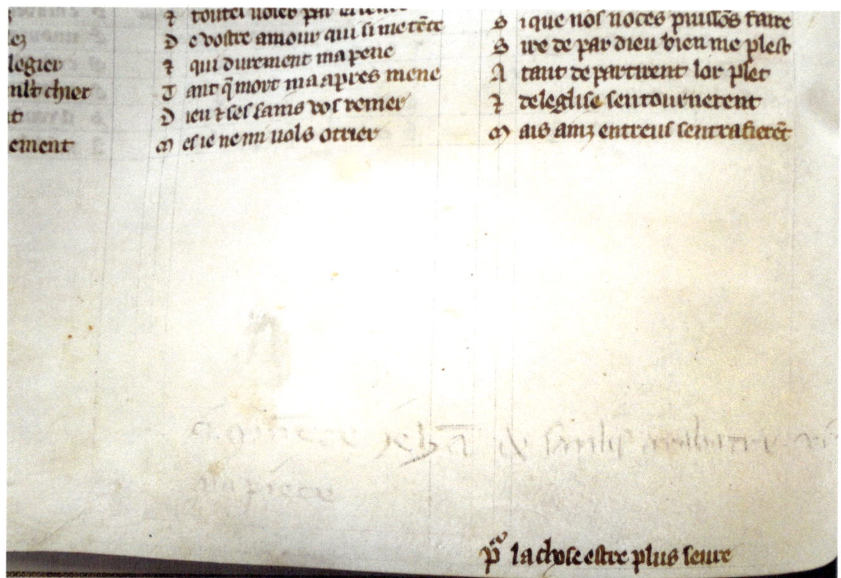

Figure 115. "Invoice" of professional scribe pencilled in lower margin, thirteenth century. The Hague, KB, 71 A 24. Photo by Ed van der Vlist.

who coordinated the book project, a person called "libraire" in medieval French account books and "stationer" in English ones.

To provide such tallies, the artisan who copied or decorated had to keep track of how many quires he had already completed. From time to time we encounter pencilled notes that helped him do just that. In The Hague, KB, 71 A 24 (Figure 115), the professional scribe Jehan de Sanlis jotted down how much money he was owed by the bookseller. The "invoice" is written in graphite and is barely visible just above the line in ink at the very bottom: *ci [com]me[n]ce Jeha[n] de Sanlis a ratable VI d. a la piece* ("Here starts Jehan de Sanlis at the rate of 6 pence per piece [= quire]"). As a subcontractor working for different booksellers, Jehan had to make sure he got paid for his toil. The book was to have a royal owner, incidentally, because the bookseller, a person by the name of Thomas de Maubeuge, had it made for King Charles V of France (d. 1328).[4]

4 Rouse and Rouse, *Manuscripts and Their Makers*, pp. 173–202 (Maubeuge); 189 and 137 (MS 71 A 24). The transcription of Sanlis' note is by Ed van der Vlist (The Hague, Koninklijke Bibliotheek).

The Value of Price Tags

Price tags add considerably to our understanding of the medieval book trade. They not only show how much medieval books differed in price, but also allow us to relate these differences to specific material and textual features of the books in which they survive. Perhaps the most striking thing about medieval price tags, however, is that they allow us to trace second-hand copies and observe how much cheaper they were than new ones, a dimension that remains understudied in current scholarship. The irony, of course, is that these once-cheap second-hand books usually fetch enormous sums of money at auction today.

Chapter 30

MANUSCRIPTS ON THE MOVE

Manuscripts shed light to another contextual aspect of medieval book ownership: movement of manuscripts. In their owner's backpack, on wagons, and in boats: medieval books were keen travellers. With them they carried texts and ideas across Europe, disseminating the sciences, spreading romances, and passing on historical narratives. Short texts may have moved from A to B because they were committed to memory, by troubadours, for example, but longer texts more likely travelled in the guise of ink on a parchment or paper page. Texts that were made for travel were often fitted in special bindings, as Figure 116 shows (more about this manuscript in a moment). If a book was not going very far, its reader may even carry it on his or her body, like the girdle book in Figure 107 at p. 207, which belonged to Queen Anne Boleyn, the second wife of Henry VIII.[1] The tiny manuscript contains the Psalms in English in the translation of John Croke and features a stern-looking Henry. But what if a movable book is not secured in a typical portable binding? What other clues are there to indicate that a medieval text had been on the move? This chapter takes a closer look at the transportation of books in the Middle Ages.

1 Stowe 956 has been digitized by the British Library, and can be found by searching for its shelfmark in their Catalogue of Illuminated Manuscripts at www.bl.uk/catalogues/illuminatedmanuscripts/welcome.htm.

Figure 116. Portable girdle book with knot to clip behind belt (plastic strips hold book open for photo), fifteenth century. New Haven, Beinecke Rare Book and Manuscript Library, Yale University, MS 84, fol. 6v–7r. Public domain. Source: http://beinecke.library.yale.edu/tags/digital-collections.

Moving Books

Occasionally we get glimpses into the transportation of books and the rationale behind it. Court records show, for example, that when in 1423 a boat with commercial goods was seized in Nice, a batch of paper prayer books was among the confiscated items.[2] When in 1334 war broke out near the city of Affligem, the Benedictine monks had to flee and their books became travellers, as reported by the fourteenth-century Middle Dutch author Jan van Boendale: "Then the monks took their belongings, their books and relics, and left their beautiful abbey, to go and live in Brussels" ("*Die moencke haer goet [eigendommen] doe namen, / Haer boeke ende haer reliquien tsamen, / Ende lieten den cloester scoene / Ende maecten te Brusele hare wone*").[3]

Remarkably, while it must have been quite normal for books to physically move between monastic communities, cities, and even countries, the phenomenon is almost completely hidden from our sight. The only pronounced evidence we have are book formats and bindings that were specially designed for portability. Folding books, for example, were developed to reduce dimensions (see Figure 82 at p. 156). Another means to facilitate transport was affixing a special binding to the book so it could be attached to the reader's belt with a clip or a knob, like the copy of Boethius's *The Consolation of Philosophy* (Figure 116 at p. 228), kept at the Beinecke Library, Yale University (MS 84). The owner even managed to place some annotations in the margins, which must have been difficult given the lumpy binding.[4]

Mystical Texts on the Move

Even with such exceptionally clear visual evidence, medieval books themselves reveal surprisingly little about their itinerary. After all, they would have to display evidence from both location A and B. An unusual exception are three booklets that would ultimately find a home in Rooklooster Priory just outside Brussels. All three include important mystical tracts. Two booklets in Paris, Bibliothèque Mazarine, 920 contain tracts by the Middle Dutch mystical authors Jan van Ruusbroec (booklet 1, fols. 2–45) and Hadewijch (booklet 6, fols. 120–44). The first of the twelve booklets in Brussels, KBR, 3067–73 (fols. 2–14) includes a sermon by the German mystic Eckhart. All three were copied ca. 1350, and the

---

2 Skemer, *Binding Words*, p. 163.

3 Mantingh, *Een monnik met een rol*, p. 267.

4 This manuscript has been digitized by the Beinecke library and can be found by searching for the shelfmark at http://beinecke.library.yale.edu/tags/digital-collections.

ex-libris inscriptions they hold (see also for such inscriptions Chapter 5), entered on their flyleaves by Rooklooster librarian Arnold de Short, tell us that they had become part of the priory's library in the early fifteenth century. Their journey to the priory was long and winding, however, and included crossing the border several times.

Their itinerary is evidenced by German glosses and excerpts that were added to the Middle Dutch texts two or three decades after the latter were copied down into the slim booklets. The 3067–73 booklet contains just a few glosses, suggesting that a German reader had difficulties reading Middle Dutch. For example, next to the Dutch "alte gadre" (together) the reader wrote in the margin: "alzesammen" (Figure 117). A few lines below, the Dutch "scout" (fault) was glossed with the German "schult."[5]

The German reader probably knew Dutch quite well (there are not many German equivalents found in the margins of this manuscript), but these particular Dutch words were written in the dialect of the Duchy of Brabant, which apparently posed a problem. Similar additions are found in the first of the two booklets in the Paris manuscript. The first two pages alone (fols. 1r–1v) contain as many as forty German glosses, but all of them were later erased (you can still read some of them if you hold the book at a certain angle). The foreign contribution in the other Paris booklet is more elaborate and complex. It entails several short excerpts from religious texts in Latin and German, which were added to pages that were left blank in the last quire of the booklet. All of these additions date from ca. 1350–1375.[6]

The Dutch booklets bear witness to a network through which mystical texts were exchanged between the duchy of Brabant (in particular Brussels) and cities in Germany (Cologne) and Switzerland (Basel).[7] Research has shown that the Brussels booklet was probably commissioned from a professional scribe by a patrician in town, who also had another part of the composite manuscript made (Part 4, with more Eckhart).[8] After one or two decades the tiny booklets travelled to a German reader or community. The latter seems the more likely scenario for the Paris booklets, considering they hold the additions of not just one but several different people. By the early fifteenth century, the booklets had returned to Brabant and were placed in Rooklooster Priory.

This intriguing case of the travelling mystical booklets raises important questions. How were the objects actually transported? They are small (about

---

5 Kwakkel, *"Dit sijn die Dietsche boeke,"* pp. 184–86.

6 Kwakkel, *"Dit sijn die Dietsche boeke,"* p. 256; the German additions in the second Paris booklet are discussed in Jonker, "Teksten op reis."

7 Jonker, "Teksten op reis."

8 Kwakkel and Mulder, "Quidam sermones."

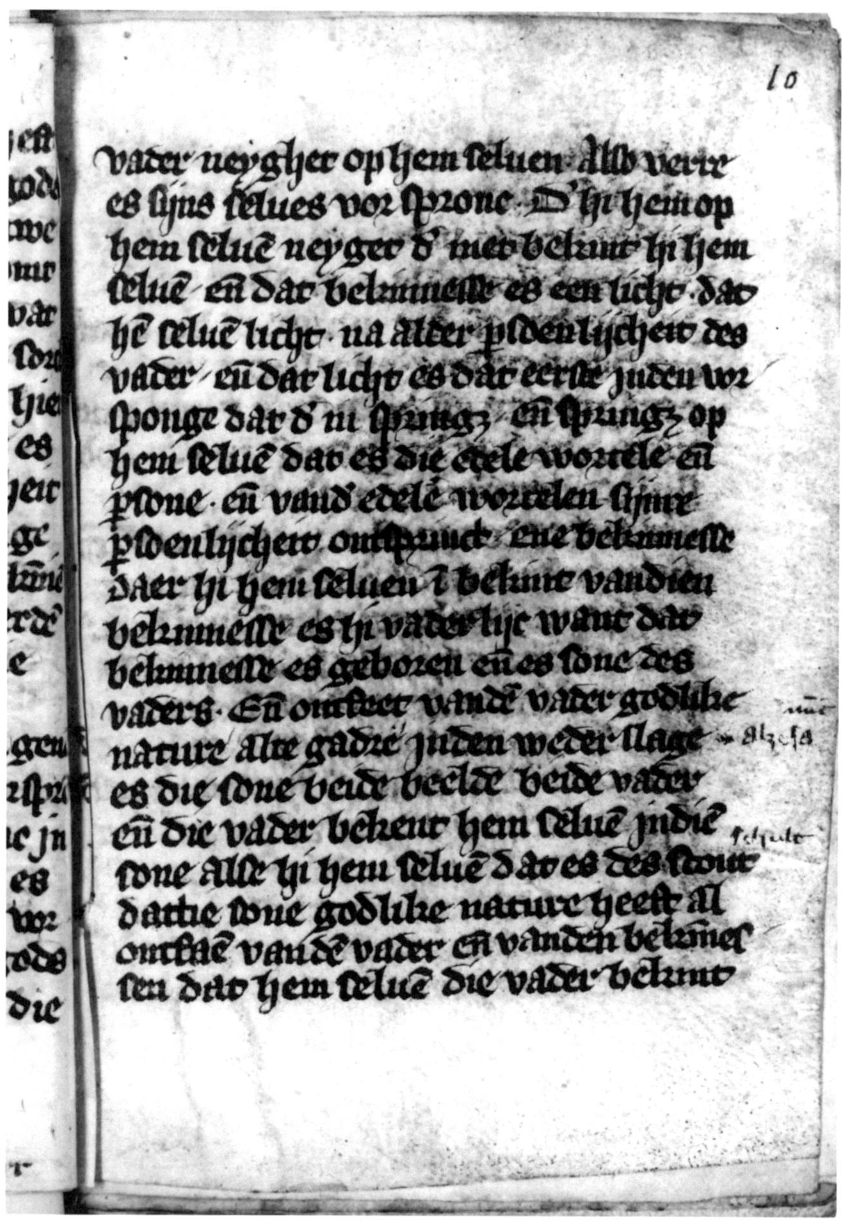

Figure 117. Middle Dutch mystical book with German equivalents in right margins, ca. 1325–1350. Brussels, KBR, 3067–73, fol. 10r. With permission.

13 cm in height, encompassing only a few quires), so perhaps they were put in a backpack. Were they made this small because the scribe knew they would be on the move? And why did they travel to a different region? Did they accompany their owner because he or she could not part with the mystical texts as they travelled abroad? Despite a lack of answers, the three thin booklets are tangible—though rare—evidence of the transportation of vernacular mystical works in fourteenth-century Europe.

ab· una

equo

xin

illa

menco

nnis

Chapter 31

THE SKINNY ON BAD PARCHMENT

While the main goal of this book has been to show how the material features of manuscripts can be used to provide insight into medieval written culture, one aspect, the most tangible one even, has not yet been exhausted: the materials from which medieval books were made. The focus in this chapter is on parchment, which is the most telling—culturally speaking—of the two materials used in manuscripts. The great thing about studying parchment manuscripts is that they attack the senses: you can touch and smell them, and hear the crackling sound of their pages. There is also much the material can tell you about the history of a manuscript: like the physician, the book historian can make a diagnosis by carefully observing skin. Good skin, which feels just like velvet and has an even all-over colour, may provide details about the reader. If the expensive kind of parchment was chosen, for example, he or she may have been affluent. Also, such good parchment shows that an experienced parchment-maker and optimal parchment animals were apparently in the reader's vicinity. However, it is material at the lower end of the scale that tells the most powerful and detailed story, shedding light on the book's production and providing clues about its use and storage post-production. Here's the skinny on bad medieval parchment.

Parchment-Maker

The parchment-maker was to blame for many of the imperfections encountered on the medieval page. Preparing parchment was an elaborate but also delicate business (see the General Introduction, pp. 7–8). In order to clear the skin of flesh and hair, it was attached to a wooden frame, tightly like a drum. If the round knife

Figure 118. Thirteenth-century strip used to repair an eleventh-century page. Leiden, UB, BPL 28, fol. 96v. Photo by the author.

Figure 119. Hole in parchment showing text two pages over, ninth century. Leiden, UB, VLF 94, fol. 10r. Photo by the author.

of the parchment-maker (the *lunellum*) cut too deep during this scraping process, elongated rips or holes would appear. We encounter such holes frequently in medieval books, which suggests that readers were not particularly bothered by them. Many scribes must have shared this sentiment, because they usually simply wrote around a hole (Figure 119). Some even placed a little line around them, playfully, as if to prevent people from falling in (see Figure 103 at pp. 200–1, lower right corner).

The hole in Figure 119 is quite extensive: you can even read text from two pages over through it, providing the reader with an unexpected sneak peek of the text that follows. The pages of this manuscript are filled with peculiar-looking symbols known as Tironian notes, a kind of shorthand in popular use among scholars (see Chapter 2).

The jabs of parchment-makers—and the resulting holes—were sometimes stitched together (Figure 120). Repairing holes was sometimes done more eloquently, for example, with embroidery stitches and coloured threads, such as one fourteenth-century manuscript masterfully repaired by the nuns of Vadstena Convent in Sweden (now Uppsala, Universitetsbiblioteket, C 371). In this case the repairs were executed not by the parchment-maker but by users of the book. In some monastic communities this must have been common practice, given that

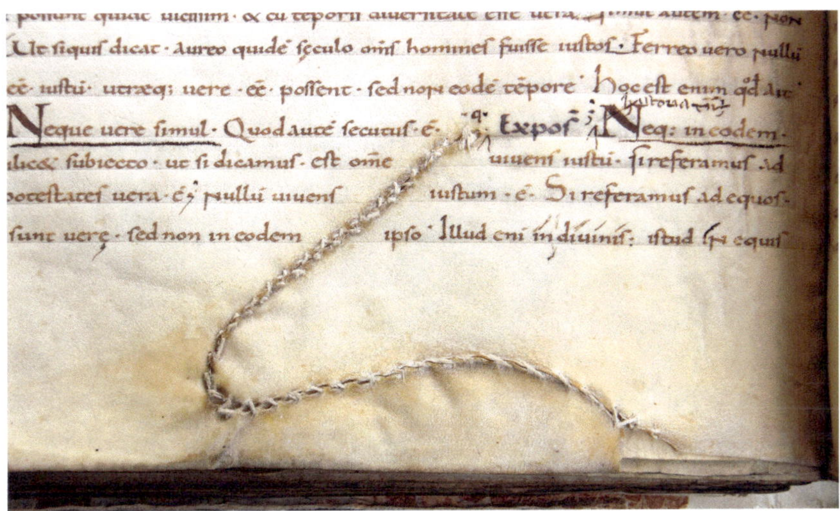

Figure 120. Repaired rip in parchment, twelfth century. Leiden, UB, BPL 25, fol. 25v. Photo by the author.

they repaired numerous books with such embroidery. The practice turned defect into art: good-looking bad skin.[1]

Another skin problem encountered by scribes during a book's production was the animal's hair follicles (the skin organs that produce and hold hair). These follicles appear as pronounced black dots on the white page. Often parchment-makers or scribes were able to sand them away, producing the desired smooth and cream-coloured surface. However, if the follicles had been too deep in a calf or sheep (especially one with dark hair), no dermatologist could have removed the imperfection, let alone the instruments of the scribe (Figure 121).

Follicles are helpful because they sometimes allow us to determine, based on the distance between the hairs, whether the animal was a cow or calf, a sheep, or a goat. This, in turn, may shed light on where the manuscript was produced: the use of goat, for example, usually points to Italy.

Reader

Bad skin may also tell us something about the people who owned, read, and stored manuscripts. The presence of holes and rips may indicate the cost of the materials.

1 Examples of these repairs can be viewed at Kwakkel, "Broidery on a medieval page," *Erik Kwakkel* (Tumblr blog), http://erikkwakkel.tumblr.com/post/52258862048/broidery-on-a-medieval-page-holes-in-the-pages-of.

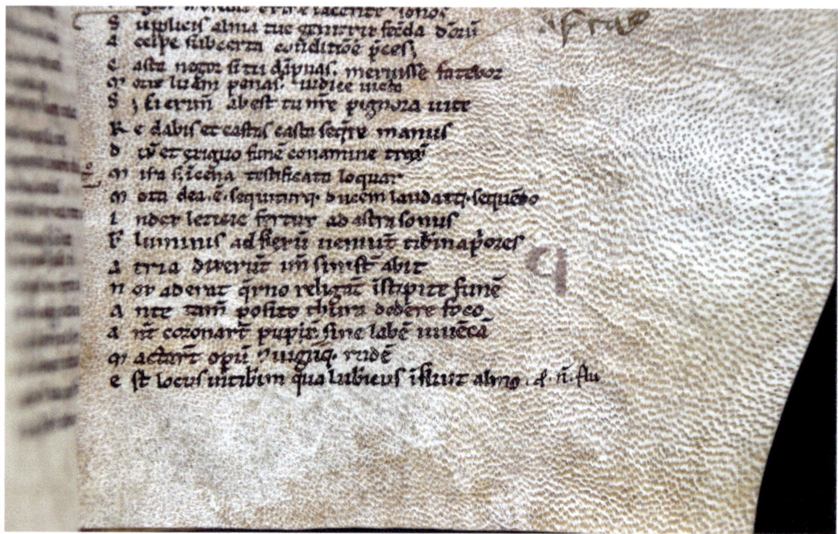

Figure 121. Pronounced follicle pattern of the animal's skin, twelfth century. Leiden, UB, VLQ 73. Photo by the author.

Studies suggest that parchment was sold in four different grades in some places, which implies that sheets with and without visible deficiencies may have been sold at different rates.[2] If this was indeed the case, an abundance of elongated holes in a manuscript may point to an attempt to economize on the cost of the writing support. In other words, bad skin may have come at a good price.

There were also cases where the reader was actually responsible for the damage to the page, for example, because the book was stored in an unsuitable location. Damp places, for one, would leave a mark on the manuscript's skin, as is clearly seen in a manuscript I call the "Mouldy Psalter" (Figure 122). On nearly every page the top corner shows a purple rash from the mould that once attacked its skin. It is currently safe and the mould is gone, but the purple stains show just how dangerously close the book came to destruction; some corners have actually been eaten away.

A final example of damage produced by the reader has nothing to do with neglect, but results from his or her love for the book. Frequent use could wear out the binding. Especially limp binding, "soft covers" that came without wooden boards (see the General Introduction, pp. 21–23), were not always able to withstand the

2 Gullick, "From Parchmenter to Scribe," p. 151.

Figure 122. Page turned purple from mould, eleventh century. Leiden, UB, BPL 2896. Photo by the author.

Figure 123. Well-used limp binding with damaged back, fifteenth century. Leiden, UB, BPL 138. Photo by the author.

pressure of frequent use (Figure 123). This manuscript from the fifteenth century looks worn and beaten. It is so happy to be retired that you can almost hear a groan of disappointment when you take it out of its box. It is filled with school texts and it was heavily used over a long period of time. At some point the binding gave in and began to arch, like an old man with a painful back.

Librarian

Some parchment manuscripts include what I like to call a "Frankenstein page," meaning that it consists of skin from different animals (Figure 118 at p. 234). This page is clearly composite. While the page itself is from the eleventh century, the very top part was cut from a thirteenth-century page. It was pasted onto the older sheet because it was short at the very top of the page. The repair job was probably undertaken by a medieval librarian (modern-day conservators do not tend to repair manuscript damage like this). The librarian used a sheet from a redundant book to make the fix.

Such reuse of redundant books is not an unusual scenario in the Middle Ages. In an age where materials were often not abundant, it made sense to put the strong parchment leaves to good use. Books that were past their due date were also recycled for the production of bookbindings, as the next chapter explains. In some other manuscripts, composite leaves like this (produced from the skin of different animals) were put together in a far less subtle fashion: by stitching (in the same fashion as in Figure 120 at p. 237). These repairs have even more of a "Frankenstein" feel to them.

A page like this shows us two things: that scribes (in this case someone from the eleventh century) did not mind using a folium that was imperfect and short on one side; and that people tasked with looking after books in the Middle Ages (librarians) took their work seriously. Tracts survive from the later Middle Ages that discuss how books should be treated (don't leave them open at night, because the mice may eat them), including how librarians ought to check all books in the library once a year.[3] This one obviously did.

Thief

Knives can be handy instruments. Scribes and readers were fond of them because they helped them erase text, either because the reading was wrong or because

---

3 For annual inspections, see Schreiber, "Die Karthäuser als Bücherfreunde," pp. 19–20; Marks, *The Medieval Manuscript Library*, vol. 1, pp. 29–36.

Figure 124. One of many initials cut from manuscript in medieval period, fourteenth century. Leiden, UB, BPL 59, fol. 45v. Photo by the author.

they disagreed with it. The parchment-maker, too, was fond of the knife, because it helped clean the skin—scrape off hair and pieces of flesh in what must have been the most smelly stage of a manuscript's production. There is also a much less noble wielder of the knife: the thief. Like parchment-makers, they wielded the instrument and scarred a book for life (Figure 124).

The spots of gold around the hole show that the thief removed an illuminated initial letter, the tail of which is still visible on the page. This particular thief was not very picky, because most initial letters have been cut from this fourteenth-century manuscript. Because of his deed, the book is also lacking passages from the text, namely the omitted words written on the verso of the stolen initial letters. The result is a story with gaps in its plot line, which must have been extremely disappointing to later medieval readers. Ironically, or better, perhaps, appropriately, it concerns a copy of Seneca's *Tragedies.*

Chapter 32

DESTROYING MEDIEVAL BOOKS (AND WHY THAT'S USEFUL)

The final chapter of this book deals with destruction and misery for the manuscripts in question, but at the same time with research opportunities and hope for those who study them. Appropriately for a last chapter in a book on manuscript culture, the story starts with the birth of printing. This invention made manuscripts old-fashioned and subsequently sparked a "recycling program" of handwritten books across Europe. Indeed, as surprising as it may seem if you have never heard of it, thousands of manuscripts were sliced, diced, and stripped for parts on a systematic basis until well into the eighteenth century. Let's give the medieval manuscript a final curtain call and observe what happened to many of them when their role as the primary carrier of texts was played out.

Culprit 1: The Bookbinder

Many manuscripts fell victim to recycling at the hands of binders, who cut them up to use for added support in the bookbindings of new printed copies. Like cars at a scrap yard, many medieval manuscripts were mutilated and plundered for parts until almost nothing was left. Single pages and small strips were cut away from handwritten books and pasted onto the spines of their printed cousins (see Figure 126). There the fragments remained, hidden out of sight, covered by the leather of the binding. Additionally, fragments of manuscripts were also used to cover the bindings of printed books (or sometimes other manuscripts).

Figure 125. Binding of printed book covered by redundant printed leaf, fifteenth century. Leiden, Bibliotheca Thysiana, 1178. Photo by the author.

Figure 126. Twelfth-century fragment inside binding of sixteenth-century printed book. Leiden, UB, 583 E 24. Photo by the author.

In spite of their mutilated appearance, manuscript fragments can be of great importance. The early history of the Bible, for example, could not have been written without the fragmentary evidence retrieved from Early Modern bindings. Fragments are interesting even for historians of printed texts, because printed books were also cut up to serve as binding material. The seventeenth-century book in Leiden's Bibliotheca Thysiana shown in Figure 125, for example, has a large fragment of an early printed book (perhaps even an incunabulum) pasted on the outside of its binding. The reason for reusing this page has to do with the material it was made from—parchment—which was deemed tough enough to protect the binding and withstand daily use in a library. Durability is also the reason why most fragments cut from medieval manuscripts are made out of parchment, like the parchment strips from a twelfth-century Latin manuscript glued inside a sixteenth-century binding of a printed book (Figure 126).

Culprit 2: The Tailor

The strength and durability of parchment made medieval pages ideal for supporting bookbindings. Tailors loved to recycle the material for the same reason. Medieval manuscript pages have been found as linings of bishops' mitres, to which a layer of cloth was subsequently pasted. The practice is observed in mitres held in Copenhagen (Arnamagnæanske Samling, AM 666 b 4^{0}), Berlin (Kunstgewerbemuseum, Staatliche Museen zu Berlin, K 6156), and Nuremberg

(Germanischen Nationalmuseums, KG709). What's really remarkable about the first of the mitre linings mentioned here is not so much that the poor bishop who wore it had a bunch of stiff, hidden medieval pages on his head, but that they were cut from an Old Norse translation of Old French love poetry (called "lais").[1] Lovers were chasing each other through dark corridors, maidens were frolicking in the fields, knights were butchering each other over nothing, and all the while the oblivious bishop performed the rites of the Holy Mass.

There are other examples where garment-makers used leaves from medieval manuscripts to stiffen cloth. A special case is recycling undertaken in the Cistercian nunnery in Wienhausen, Germany. In order to produce the liturgical vestments for statues of Christ, Mary, and the angels, the nuns cut up a number of Latin and German manuscripts, the leaves of which they used as lining.[2]

Culprit 3: The Scribe

Last—but actually first—among the book-predators are scribes. Not those working after the invention of print, but those from the Middle Ages. Their recycling activities show that the destruction of manuscripts by Early Modern binders was part of a long tradition. In the Middle Ages, too, something useful was done with a manuscript whose life was spent, for example, because its contents were no longer needed or the copy was worn out.

Surrounded by used books and with penknives in their hands, medieval bookmakers were bound to do some damage. There are several ways in which old pages could be put to good use in the monastic scriptorium or library. You can make note material out of them, for example (see Chapter 23). A more discreet way of recycling concerns what's called a "palimpsest," where words were scraped off a page and a new text copied down on it. In monasteries it would commonly have been librarians who undertook this scraping job, because it was they who provided the scribes with the material to write on.

In the early Middle Ages entire books were made of palimpsests. There was a definite upside to this practice from a supply point of view: it provided, albeit with a lot of effort, a pile of parchment to fill with something new. There was a downside as well. The scraped-away lower text usually never fully disappeared from sight

---

1 A description of the Copenhagen mitre is available in the National and University Library of Iceland's *handrit.is* repository, at https://handrit.is/en/manuscript/view/AM04-0666-b. An image is located at Kwakkel, "A love story hidden in a hat," *Erik Kwakkel* (Tumblr blog), http://erikkwakkel.tumblr.com/post/55554381477/a-love-story-hidden-in-a-hat-you-are-looking-at-a.

2 More on these recycled items in Klack-Eitzen, Haase, and Weissgraf, *Heilige Röcke*.

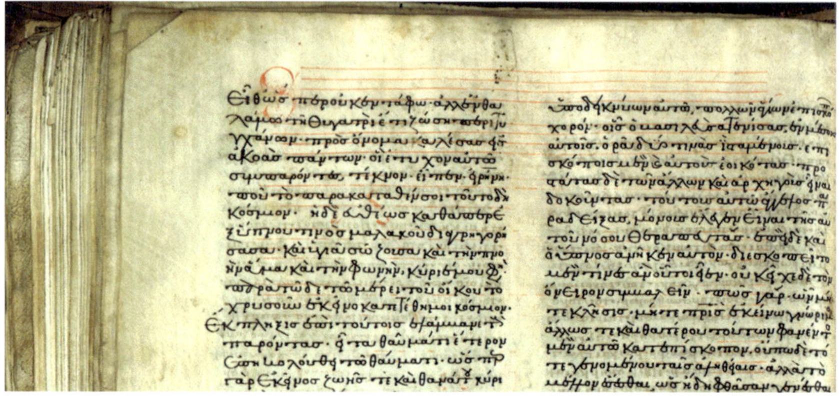

Figure 127. Greek manuscript written on leaves of palimpsested Latin missal. Eleventh- or twelfth-century upper text, tenth- or eleventh-century lower text. Cambridge, Trinity College, B.9.3, fol. 122v.

and tends to pop up unexpectedly. The upper text in Figure 127 is a collection of Greek saints' lives written in the eleventh or twelfth century. Underneath it, however, is an older text copied in the tenth or eleventh century. It appears to concern a Latin work used for liturgical purposes, perhaps a missal.[3] All that is visible of this text, however, are the rubrics: note the staves for the musical notation at the very top of the page.

While this is a Greek text written over a Latin work, the opposite also occurred: Wolfenbüttel, Herzog August Bibliothek, Guelf. 64 Weiss. contains an eighth-century copy of Isidore of Seville's *Etymologies* (upper text), yet to produce it a fifth-century Greek copy of St. Paul's Epistle to the Romans was palimpsested (lower text).[4]

Useful Destruction

Cases of recycling point out how very fruitful the afterlife—the second life, really—of a manuscript can be: old books could be put to new use as binding support. As bad as the destruction by medieval and post-medieval binders and scribes may seem, it is also something to be grateful for. Their activities give us,

3 James, *Western Manuscripts*, pp. 261–62.

4 A digital edition and facsimile of Guelf. 64 Weiss. is available: see Schassan, Gehrke, and Schwabe, "Digitale Edition der Handschrift Cod. Guelf. 64 Weiss.," *Herzog August Bibliothek*, http://diglib.hab.de/edoc/ed000006/index.php.

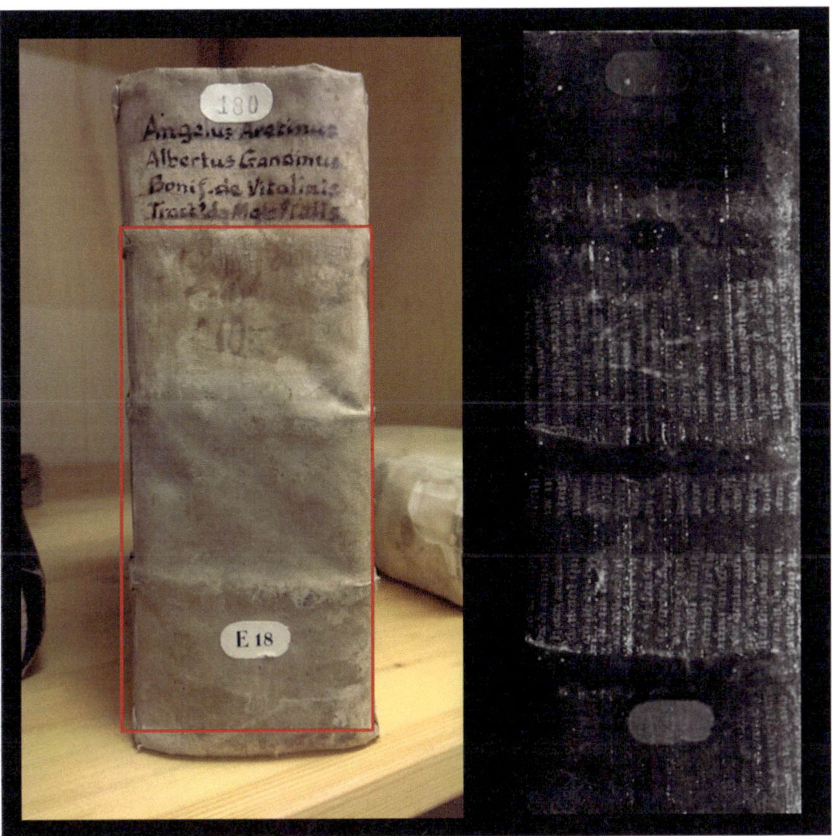

Figure 128. Fragment hidden in binding as revealed by MA-XRF scanner. Leiden, UB, 180 E 18. Photo by Anna Käyhkö (binding).

after all, pages or strips from manuscripts that would otherwise have completely disappeared. The alternative was much worse: in the two centuries after the Middle Ages, thousands of parchment manuscripts were boiled down to produce glue and have completely disappeared from sight. Fragments resulting from cutting down books, however, at least still show part of the once complete and thriving volume.

New medieval fragments are discovered every day in libraries across the world: encountering them and solving their mysteries (when and where were they made, and what text do they contain?) is both a satisfying and an exciting experience. There is now even a technique available—called Macro X-ray Fluorescence Spectrometry (or MA-XRF) scanning—with which the snippets in bookbindings can be seen and studied without opening up the binding. A thin beam of X-rays is used to scan for metal elements below the cover material of the binding (leather, parchment, cloth). Medieval iron-gall ink contains various of these elements, such as iron (Fe), copper (Cu), and zinc (Zn), and when a fragment is present under the covering material, the beam will thus return inky shapes—letters. Seeing invisible manuscripts emerge on a computer screen is a mesmerizing experience (Figure 128).[5]

Tracking and identifying medieval fragments, whether with a scanner or the naked eye, is currently undertaken by scholars around the globe. Seeing a few words or lines is often enough to identify the text via Google. An identified fragment, even a small one, is usually immediately made part of a scholarly discussion of a given text. Notably, medieval text traditions are not just represented by many full manuscripts, but also by fragments. In fact, the oldest stages of medieval text are normally represented by fragments, not by full manuscripts. In that way, fragments add significantly to the study of medieval literary and scholarly culture: even damaged and in pieces, books before print have an important story to tell.

5 The method we developed is published as Duivenvoorde, Käyhkö, Kwakkel, and Dik, "Hidden Library."

EPILOGUE: THE LEGACY OF THE MEDIEVAL BOOK

Figure 129. Parchment leaves, side view showing variation in colour and shape, ninth century. Leiden, UB, SCA 28, fol. 130r. Photo by the author.

What can reveal more about the culture of a milieu or of an epoch than the style of its books? It is this exciting rhetorical question, posed by Leon Delaissé in his landmark article published posthumously in 1976, which captures the spirit of the explorations undertaken in *Books Before Print.*[1] Its chapters show that medieval books are not merely objects that played a given role in society, for example, as tools or resources in religious practices and in education, but also that they themselves, through their material design, act as vehicles for the preferences and habits of the people who made up medieval society. As the case studies on the previous pages have shown, captured in the materiality of manuscripts are the data enabling us to make sense of their medieval users and settings of use. This is an important and advantageous legacy of the manuscript: that its observable features act as built-in historical evidence of a culture that has long vanished.

That this is even possible is because each medieval manuscript represents a single, custom-tailored production process, resulting in a one-of-a-kind—truly unique—book, as explained in the General Introduction. The motivations of scribes to opt for certain features were in large part sparked by the culturally and financially inspired preferences of the reader or the community that was to own the manuscript. Their needs were communicated, often verbally, and translated into specific material features.[2] This system is unique to handwritten books. Printed volumes can also contain features that are unique to a specific copy, but to a much lesser extent. Readers in the age of print could write annotations in the margin and perhaps add a custom-tailored binding, but they could not mould the individual printed book to their own tastes and preferences. It was the printer who decided what physical features to include (dimensions, design, typeface) and he or she did so, obviously, for the entire print-run at the same time, probably without direct input from individual readers. In other words, printers designed a book with an ideal, not a real, reader in mind: true personalization arguably stopped when the quill was replaced by the press.

The approach of *Books Before Print* assigns great research potential to the material book of the medieval period: we have only just started to explore how manuscripts as objects contribute to our understanding of disciplines other than book-history in the narrow sense. For example, physical features of surviving manuscripts give us a sense of how medieval society dealt with information, how its inhabitants consumed knowledge, how they applied it, and even how popular certain information was and why. It is quite a legacy that an object that has been obsolete for over six centuries can act as a vibrant and versatile tool to explore the

1 Delaissé, "Toward a History of the Medieval Book," p. 78.
2 Kwakkel, "Decoding the Material Book."

precursor of our modern "information society." The thirty-two chapters of *Books Before Print* all show how we may tap into such historical evidence: they teach how medieval manuscripts may be "read" in addition to the texts they hold.

Books Before Print also highlights a different legacy of the manuscript, equally pragmatic, but less evident unless you know where to look. The chapters in this book show that human beings' interaction with written information has deep historical roots. Sending a short message on a scrap of parchment, meant for one-time and vivid consumption, is not so different from our modern equivalent: texting (Chapter 22). Nor is adding additional functions—apps—to existing devices, extending their range of functionality (Chapter 26), or the urge to mark our favourite content with clever bookmarks (Chapter 16). These and many other chapters highlight what is read in between the lines throughout the book as a whole, namely that a division between "before print" and "after print" (or even of "digital" versus "analogue" book culture) promotes a somewhat artificial understanding of the book. Its history may have entered a new chapter with the introduction of Gutenberg's printing press, but it is still a chapter of the same story, just like our e-readers are.

The constancy in the history of the book and of reading is, of course, us—its readers. Despite the many innovations in book technologies—from roll, to handwritten book, to printed book, to e-book—our desire to absorb knowledge and entertainment through the written word is enduring: the handwritten book, its ancestors, and its successors demonstrate our drive to do this in ways that best fulfill our ever-changing needs, across cultures, regions, and indeed millennia. It should hardly be surprising, in this light, that we encounter familiar features in old books: that we recognize our modern books and manners of reading in such distant objects produced with quill and animal skin is the ultimate legacy of the medieval manuscript.

RECOMMENDED READING BY SECTION

Introduction to Manuscripts

Bischoff, *Paläographie* (English translation: Bischoff, *Latin Palaeography*)
Brown, J., *A Paleographer's View*
Brown, M. P., *Guide to Western Historical Scripts*
———. *Illuminated Manuscripts*
Burns, "Paper Comes to the West"
Cambridge History of the Book in Britain: c. 400–1100, vol. 1
Cambridge History of the Book in Britain: 1100–1400, vol. 2
Cambridge History of the Book in Britain: 1400–1557, vol. 3
Clemens and Graham, *Manuscript Studies*
Delaissé, "Toward a History of the Medieval Book"
Febvre and Martin, *The Coming of the Book*
Gumbert, "Fifty Years"
de Hamel, *The Book*
———. *History of Illuminated Manuscripts*
———. *Meetings with Remarkable Manuscripts*
History of Reading, Cavallo and Chartier, eds.
History of the Book, vol. 1, Roberts and Robinson, eds.
Howard, *The Book*
Kelly, *Capturing Music*
Kwakkel, "Decoding the Material Book"
Kwakkel and Menna, *Quill: Books Before Print*. www.bookandbyte.org/quill
Lemaire, *Introduction à la codicologie*
Lyall, "Materials: the Paper Revolution"
Making the Medieval Book, Brownrigg, ed.
Palazzo, *History of Liturgical Books*
Parisse, "Writing in the Middle Ages"

Parkes, *Scribes, Scripts and Readers*
———. *Their Hands Before Our Eyes*
Robinson, "The Format of Books"
Role of the Book, Ganz, ed.
Rouse and Rouse, *Authentic Witnesses*
Schneider, *Paläographie und Handschriftenkunde*
Shailor, *The Medieval Book*

Filling the Page: Script, Writing, and Page Design

Brown, *Writing and Scripts*
Calligraphy of Medieval Music, Haines, ed.
Clanchy, *From Memory to Written Record*
Cyrus, *The Scribes for Women's Convents*
Derolez, *Palaeography of Gothic Manuscript Books*
Ganz, "Book Production in the Carolingian Empire"
Gullick, "How Fast Did Scribes Write?"
Gumbert, "The Sizes of Manuscripts
———. "The Speed of Scribes"
———. " 'Typography' in the Manuscript Book"
de Hamel, *Scribes and Illuminators*
Kwakkel, "Behind the Scenes of a Revision"
———. "Biting, Kissing and the Treatment of Feet"
———. "Late Medieval Text Collections"
———. "Towards a Terminology"
Palmer, "Zur mittelalterlichen Zisterzienserinterpunktion"
Parkes, *Pause and Effect*
Roberts, *Guide to Scripts*
Robinson, "The Format of Books"
Rouse and Rouse, "The Vocabulary of Wax Tablets"
Smith, *Masters of the Sacred Page*
Teaching Writing, Learning to Write, Robinson, ed.
Tether, "*Mise en page, mise en écran*"

Enhancing the Manuscript: Binding and Decoration

Binding

de Bray, *Binding of Books*
Clarkson, "English Monastic Bookbinding"
Foot, *Bookbinders at Work*
———. *History of Bookbinding*

Gnirrep, Gumbert, and Szirmai, *Kneep en binding* (in Dutch, but with a multilingual (including English) glossary)
"Medieval Manuscripts: Bookbinding Terms, Materials, Methods, and Models"
Reed, *Ancient Skins, Parchments and Leathers*
Szirmai, *The Archaeology of Medieval Bookbinding*

Decoration

Alexander, *The Decorated Letter*
———. *Medieval Illuminators*
Backhouse, *The Illuminated Manuscript*
Cahn, *Romanesque Bible Illumination*
Camille, *Image on the Edge*
———. "Seeing and Reading"
The Göttingen Model Book. www.gutenbergdigital.de/gudi/eframes/mubu/mubufset.htm
Gullick, "Self-referential Portraits of Artists and Scribes"
de Hamel, *History of Illuminated Manuscripts*
———. *Manuscript Illumination: History and Techniques*
Lehmann-Haupt, *The Göttingen Model Book*
Mayr-Harting, *Ottonian Book Illumination*
Scheller, *Model-Book Drawings*

Reading in Context: Annotations, Bookmarks, and Libraries

Birrell, *English Monarchs*
Budny, *Assembly Marks*
Clark, *The Care of Books*
Emms, "Medieval Rotating Column-Indicators"
Grotans, *Reading in Medieval St. Gall*
Gumbert, "Points and Signposts"
Haines, "The Origins of the Musical Staff"
Leclerq, *Love of Learning*
Lowe, "The Oldest Omission Signs"
Overgaauw, "Where are the Colophons?"
Petrucci, *Writers and Readers in Medieval Italy*
Reynolds, *Medieval Reading*
Robertson, *Lectio Divina*
Saenger, *Space Between Words*
Teeuwen, "Marginal Scholarship"
Thompson, *The Medieval Library*

The Margins of Manuscript Culture

Blair, *Too Much to Know*
Ebstorfer Weltkarte, hosted by Leuphana Universität Lüneburg. www2.leuphana.de/ebskart/
Gumbert, *Bat Books*
———. "Sizes and Formats"
Huglo, *The Cantatorium*
Kwakkel, "Classics on Scraps"
———. " 'Dit boek heeft niet de vereiste breedte' "
Mappa Mundi, Hereford Cathedral, *Mappa Mundi Ltd*. www.themappamundi.co.uk
Orme, *Medieval Schools*
Robinson, "The Format of Books—Books, Booklets and Rolls"

Contextualizing the Medieval Manuscript

Christianson, *London Stationers and Book Artisans*
———. "Rise of London's Book-Trade"
Doyle, "Book Production by Monastic Orders"
———. "The English Provincial Book Trade"
Doyle and Parkes, "Copies of the *Canterbury Tales* and the *Confessio Amantis*"
Duffy, *Marking the Hours*
Duivenvoorde, Käyhkö, Kwakkel, and Dik, "Hidden Library"
Early Medieval Bible, Gameson, ed.
Gullick, "Professional Scribes"
Gumbert, *The Dutch and Their Books*
de Hamel, *Glossed Books of the Bible*
Horn and Born, "The Medieval Monastery"
Insular Manuscript Culture 500–1200, Kwakkel, ed.
Interpreting and Collecting Fragments, Brownrigg and Smith, eds.
Kwakkel, "Classics on Scraps"
———. "Commercial Organisation"
Manuscripts of the Latin Classics 800–1200, Kwakkel, ed.
McKitterick, *The Carolingians*
Michael, "Urban Production"
Mooney, "Professional Scribes?"
Munk Olsen, "The Production of Classics"
Production of Books in England, Gillespie and Wakelin, eds.
Reynolds, *A Survey of Latin Classics*
Rouse and Rouse, "Commercial Production"
———. *Manuscripts and Their Makers*
Taylor, "Authors, Scribes, Patrons, and Books"
Voights, "Scientific and Medical Books"

BIBLIOGRAPHY

Alexander, J. J. G. *The Decorated Letter*. New York: G. Braziller, 1978.

———. *Medieval Illuminators and Their Methods of Work*. New Haven: Yale University Press, 1992.

Backhouse, Janet. *The Illuminated Manuscript: The Craft of the Scribe*. London: Phaidon Press, 1979.

van den Berg, M. K. A. *De Noordnederlandse historiebijbel. Een kritische editie met inleiding en aantekeningen van Hs. Ltk 231 uit de Leidse Universiteitsbibliotheek*. Hilversum: Verloren, 1997.

Birrell, T. A. *English Monarchs and Their Books from Henry VII to Charles II*. Panizzi Lectures 1986. London: British Library, 1987.

Bischoff, Bernhard. *Latin Palaeography: Antiquity and the Middle Ages*. Translated by Dáibhí Ó Cróinín and David Ganz. Cambridge: Cambridge University Press, 1990.

———. *Paläographie des römischen Altertums und des abendländischen Mittelalters*. 2nd ed. Grundlagen der Germanistik 24. Berlin: Erich Schmidt, 1986.

Blair, Ann M. *Too Much to Know: Managing Scholarly Information before the Modern Age*. New Haven: Yale University Press, 2010.

de Bray, Dirk. *A Short Instruction in the Binding of Books*. Amsterdam: Nico Israel, 1977.

Brown, Julian. *A Paleographer's View: The Selected Writings of Julian Brown*. Edited by Janet Bately, Michelle P. Brown, and Jane Roberts. London: Harvey Miller, 1993.

Brown, Michelle P. *The British Library Guide to Writing and Scripts: History and Techniques*. British Library Guides. Toronto: University of Toronto Press, 1998.

———. *A Guide to Western Historical Scripts from Antiquity to 1600*. 3rd ed. London: British Library, 2002.

———. *Understanding Illuminated Manuscripts: A Guide to Technical Terms*. "Looking At" series. Malibu: J. Paul Getty Museum, 1994.

Brownrigg, Linda, ed. *Making the Medieval Book: Techniques of Production*. Los Altos Hills: Anderson-Lovelace, 1995.

Brownrigg, Linda L., and Margaret M. Smith, eds. *Interpreting and Collecting Fragments of Medieval Books*. Seminar in the History of the Book to 1500. Conference, Oxford, 1988. Los Altos Hills: Anderson-Lovelace, 2000.

Budny, Mildred. "Assembly Marks in the Vivian Bible and Scribal, Editorial, and Organizational Marks in Medieval Books." In *Making the Medieval Book: Techniques of Production. Proceedings of the Fourth Conference of the Seminar in the History of the Book to 1500, Oxford July 1992*, edited by L. L. Brownrigg, pp. 199–239. Los Altos Hills: Anderson-Lovelace, 1995.

Burns, R. I. "Paper Comes to the West, 800–1400." In *Europäische Technik im Mittelalter, 800 bis 1200: Tradition und Innovation, ein Handbuch*, edited by Ula Lindgren, pp. 413–22. Berlin: Gebr. Mann, 1996.

Busby, Keith. *Codex in Context: Reading Old French Verse Narrative in Manuscript.* 2 vols. Amsterdam: Rodopi, 2002.

Cahn, Walter. *Romanesque Bible Illumination.* Ithaca: Cornell University Press, 1982.

Camille, Michael. *Image on the Edge: The Margins of Medieval Art. Essays in Art and Culture.* Cambridge, MA: Harvard University Press, 1992.

———. "Seeing and Reading: Some Visual Implications of Medieval Literacy and Illiteracy." *Art History* 8 (1985): 26–49.

Cavallo, Guglielmo, and Roger Chartier, eds. *A History of Reading in the West.* Cambridge: Polity, 1999.

Christianson, C. Paul. *A Directory of London Stationers and Book Artisans, 1300–1500.* New York: Bibliographical Society of America, 1990.

———. "The Rise of London's Book-Trade." In *The Cambridge History of the Book in Britain: 1400–1557*, edited by Lotte Hellinga and J. B. Trapp, pp. 128–47. Vol. 3 of *The Cambridge History of the Book in Britain.* Cambridge: Cambridge University Press, 1999.

Clanchy, Michael. *From Memory to Written Record: England 1066–1307.* 3rd ed. Hobeken: Wiley-Blackwell, 2012.

Clark, John Willis. *The Care of Books.* Cambridge: Cambridge University Press, 1909. Reprint, Mansfield Center: Martino, 2005.

Clarkson, Christopher. "English Monastic Bookbinding in the Twelfth Century." In *Ancient and Medieval Book Materials and Techniques: Erice, 18–25 September 1992.* Studi e Testi 2, edited by Marilena Maniaci and Paola F. Munafò, pp. 181–200. Vatican City: Biblioteca Apostolica Vaticana, 1993.

Clemens, Raymond, and Timothy Graham. *Introduction to Manuscript Studies.* Ithaca: Cornell University Press, 2007.

Colclough, Stephen, and Alexis Weedon, eds. *The History of the Book in the West:1800–1914.* Vol. 2 of *The History of the Book in the West: A Library of Critical Essays.* Aldershot: Ashgate, 2010.

Cuff, David B. "The King of the Batavians: Remarks on Tab. Vindol. III, 628." *Britannia* 42 (2011): 145–156.

Cyrus, Cynthia J. *The Scribes for Women's Conventss in Late Medieval Germany.* Toronto: University of Toronto Press, 2009.

Delaissé, L. M. J. "Toward a History of the Medieval Book." In *Codicologica: Towards a Science for Handwritten Books*, vol. 1, edited by A. Gruijs and J. P. Gumbert, pp. 75–83. Leiden: Brill, 1976.

De Meyïer, K. A., *Codices Vossiani Latini, Pars III: Codices in Octavo*. Leiden: Universitaire Pers Leiden, 1977.

Derolez, Albert. *The Palaeography of Gothic Manuscript Books. From the Twelfth to the Early Sixteenth Century*. Cambridge Studies in Palaeography and Codicology 9. Cambridge: Cambridge University Press, 2003.

De Smet, Jos, A. Vandewalle, and Carlos Wyffels. *De rekeningen van de stad Brugge, 1280–1319*. Brussels: Paleis der Academiën, 1965.

De Wald, E. T. "Notes on the Tuotilo Ivories in St. Gall." *Art Bulletin* 12 (1933): 202.

Doyle, A. I. "Book Production by Monastic Orders in England (c. 1375–1530): Assessing the Evidence." In *Medieval Book Production: Assessing the Evidence. Proceedings of the Second Conference of the Seminar in the History of the Book to 1500, Oxford, July 1988*, edited by Linda Brownrigg, pp. 1–19. Los Altos Hills: Anderson-Lovelace, 1990.

———. "The English Provincial Book Trade before Printing." In *Six Centuries of the Provincial Book Trade in Britain*, edited by Peter Isaac, pp. 13–29. Winchester: St. Paul's Bibliographies, 1990.

Doyle, A. I., and Malcolm B. Parkes. "The Production of Copies of the *Canterbury Tales* and the *Confessio Amantis* in the Early Fifteenth Century." In *Medieval Scribes, Manuscripts and Libraries: Essays Presented to N. R. Ker*, edited by Malcolm B. Parkes and Andrew G. Watson, pp. 163–210. London: Scolar, 1978.

Duffy, Eamon. *Marking the Hours: English People and Their Prayers, 1240–1570*. New Haven: Yale University Press, 2006.

Duft, Johannes, and Rolf Schnyder. *Die Elfenbein-Einbände der Stiftsbibliothek St. Gallen*. Beuron: Beuroner Kunstverlag, 1984.

Duivenvoorde, Dorien, Anna Käyhkö, Erik Kwakkel, and Joris Dik. "Hidden Library: Visualizing Fragments of Medieval Manuscripts in Early-Modern Bookbindings with mobile Macro-XRF Scanner." *Heritage Science* 5 (2017): 1–10.

Emms, Richard. "Medieval Rotating Column-Indicators: An Unrecorded Second Example in a Thirteenth Century Bible (Cambridge, Corpus Christi College MS 49)." *Transactions of the Cambridge Bibliographical Society* 12 (2001): 179–84.

Febvre, Lucien, and Henri-Jean Martin. *The Coming of the Book: The Impact of Printing 1450–1800*. Translated by David Gerard. London: Verso, 1976.

Foot, Mirjam. *Bookbinders at Work: Their Roles and Methods*. London: British Library, 2006.

———. *Studies in the History of Bookbinding*. Brookfield: Scolar, 1993.

Freeman Sandler, Lucy. "Pictorial and Verbal Play in the Margins: The Case of British Library, Stowe MS 49." In *Illuminating the Book: Makers and Interpreters: Essays in Honour of Janet Backhouse*, edited by Janet Backhouse, Michelle P. Brown, and Scot McKendrick, pp. 52–68. London: British Library, 1998.

Friedman, John Block, and Kristen Mossler Figg, with Scott D. Westrem and Gregory G. Guzman. *Trade, Travel, and Exploration in the Middle Ages: An Encyclopedia*. New York: Routledge, 2000.

Gameson, Richard, ed. *The Cambridge History of the Book in Britain: c. 400–1100*. Vol. 1 of *The Cambridge History of the Book in Britain*. Cambridge: Cambridge University Press, 2011.

———. ed. *The Early Medieval Bible: Its Production, Decoration and Use*. Cambridge Studies in Palaeography and Codicology. Cambridge: Cambridge University Press, 1994.

Ganz, David. "Book Production in the Carolingian Empire and the Spread of Caroline Minuscule." In *The New Cambridge Medieval History, Vol. 2: c. 700–c. 900*, edited by Rosamond McKitterick, pp. 786–808. Cambridge: Cambridge University Press, 1995.

Ganz, Peter, ed. *The Role of the Book in Medieval Culture: Proceedings of the Oxford International Symposium 26 September–1 October 1982*. 2 vols. Bibliologia, part 3. Turnhout: Brepols, 1986.

Gillespie, Alexandra, and Daniel Wakelin, eds. *The Production of Books in England, 1350–1500*. Cambridge: Cambridge University Press, 2011.

Glorieux-de Gand, Thérèse. *Het woord van de kopiist: Colofons van gedateerde handschriften*. Brussels: Koninklijke Bibliotheek Albert I, 1991.

Gnirrep, W. K., J. P. Gumbert, and Janos A. Szirmai. *Kneep en binding: Een terminologie voor de beschrijving van de constructies van oude boekbanden*. The Hague: Koninklijke Bibliotheek, 1992.

Grafton, Anthony. *The Footnote: A Curious History*. Cambridge, MA: Harvard University Press, 1999.

Grotans, Anna. *Reading in Medieval St. Gall*. Cambridge Studies in Codicology and Palaeography. Vol. 13. Cambridge: Cambridge University Press, 2006.

Gullick, Michael. "From Parchmenter to Scribe: Some Observations on the Manufacture and Preparation of Medieval Parchment Based upon a Review of the Literary Evidence." In *Pergament: Geschichte, Struktur, Restaurierung, Herstellung*, edited by Peter Rück, pp. 145–57. Historische Hilfswissenschaften. Vol. 2. Sigmaringen: Jan Thorbecke, 1991.

———. "How Fast Did Scribes Write? Evidence from Romanesque Manuscripts." In *Making the Medieval Book: Techniques of Production. Proceedings of the Fourth Conference of the Seminar in the History of the Book to 1500, Oxford, July 1992*, edited by Linda L. Brownrigg, pp. 39–58. Los Altos Hills: Anderson-Lovelace, 1995.

———. "Professional Scribes in Eleventh- and Twelfth-Century England." In *English Manuscript Studies 1100–1700*, vol. 7, edited by Peter Beal and Jeremy Griffiths, pp. 1–24. London: British Library, 1998.

———. "Self-referential Portraits of Artists and Scribes in Romanesque Manuscripts." In *Pen in Hand: Medieval Scribal Portraits, Colophons and Tools*, edited by Michael Gullick, pp. 97–114. Los Altos Hills: Anderson-Lovelace, 2006.

Gumbert, J. P. *Bat Books: A Catalogue of Folded Manuscripts Containing Almanacs or Other Texts*. Bibliologia 41. Turnhout: Brepols, 2016.

———. *The Dutch and Their Books in the Manuscript Age*. The Panizzi Lectures 1989. London: British Library, 1990.

———. "Fifty Years of Codicology." *Archiv für Diplomatik, Schriftgeschichte, Siegel- und Wappenkunde* 50 (2004): 505–26.

———. "The Irish Priscian in Leiden." *Quaerendo* 4 (1997): 280–99.

———. "Points and Signposts: Whom Do They Help?" *Scriptorium* 63 (2009): 231–37.

———. "Sizes and Formats." In *Ancient and Medieval Book Materials and Techniques: Erice, 18–25 September 1992*. Studi e Testi, edited by Marilena Maniaci and Paola F. Munafò, pp. 227–63, 357–58. Vatican City: Biblioteca Apostolica Vaticana, 1993.

———. "The Sizes of Manuscripts: Some Statistics and Notes." In *Hellinga Festschrift/Feestbundel/Mélanges. Forty-three Studies in Bibliography Presented to Prof. Dr. Wytze Hellinga on the occasion of his retirement from the Chair of Neophilology in the University of Amsterdam at the End of the Year 1978*, edited by A. R. A. Croiset van Uchelen, pp. 277–88. Amsterdam: Nico Israel, 1980.

———. "The Speed of Scribes." In *Scribi e colofoni: Le Sottoscrizioni di Copisti dalle origini all'Avvento della stampa, atti del seminario di Erice X Colloquio del Comite International de Paleographie Latine (23–28 ottobre 1993)*, edited by Emma Condello and Giuseppe De Gregorio, pp. 57–69. Biblioteca del Centro per il Collegamento degli Studi Medievale e Umanistici in Umbria 14. Spoleto: Centro italiano di studi sull'alto medioevo, 1995.

———. "Thick Quires in Italy." In *Vernacular Manuscript Culture 1000–1500*, edited by Erik Kwakkel. Studies in Medieval and Renaissance Book Culture. Leiden: Leiden University Press, 2018.

———. " 'Typography' in the Manuscript Book." *Journal of the Printing Historical Society* 22 (1993): 5–28.

———. *Die Utrechter Kartäuser und ihre Bücher im frühen fünfzehnten Jahrhundert*. Leiden: Brill, 1974.

Haines, John, ed. *The British Library Guide to Manuscript Illumination: History and Techniques*. The British Library Guides. Toronto: University of Toronto Press, 2001.

———. *The Calligraphy of Medieval Music*. Musicalia Medii Aevi 1. Turnhout: Brepols, 2011.

———. *Glossed Books of the Bible and the Origins of the Paris Booktrade*. Woodbridge: Brewer, 1984.

———. *A History of Illuminated Manuscripts*. 2nd ed. London: Phaidon, 1994.

———. *Meetings With Remarkable Manuscripts*. London: Penguin Random House, 2016.

———. "The Origins of the Musical Staff." *Musical Quarterly* 91 (2008): 327–78.

de Hamel, Christopher. *The Book: A History of the Bible*. London: Phaidon, 2001.

———. *Scribes and Illuminators*. Medieval Craftsmen. Toronto: University of Toronto Press, 1992.

Hellinga, Lotte, and J. B. Trapp, eds. The *Cambridge History of the Book in Britain: 1400–1557*. Vol. 3 of *The Cambridge History of the Book in Britain*. Cambridge: Cambridge University Press, 1999.

Horn, Walter, and Ernest Born. "The Medieval Monastery as a Setting for the Production of Manuscripts." *Journal of the Walters Art Gallery* 44 (1986): 16–47.

Howard, Nicole. *The Book: The Life Story of a Technology*. Greenwood Technographies Series. Westport: Greenwood, 2005.

Huglo, Michel. *The Cantatorium: From Charlemagne to the Fourteenth Century*. Woodbridge: Boydell, 2001.

———. "The Cantatorium: From Charlemagne to the Fourteenth Century." In *The Study of Medieval Chant: Paths and Bridges, East and West. In Honor of Kenneth Levy*, edited by Peter Jeffery, pp. 89–103. Cambridge: Boydell, 2001.

James, Montague Rhodes. *A Descriptive Catalogue of the Manuscripts in the Library of Peterhouse*. Cambridge: Cambridge University Press, 1899.

———. *The Western Manuscripts in the Library of Trinity College, Cambridge: A Descriptive Catalogue*. Vol. 1. Cambridge: Cambridge University Press, 1900.

Johnson, William Allan. *Bookrolls and Scribes in Oxyrhynchus*. Toronto: University of Toronto Press, 2004.

Jonker, Esther. "Teksten op reis: Handschriftelijke getuigen van betrekkingen tussen Brabant en Bovenrijn in de veertiende eeuw." *Ons Geestelijk Erf* 83 (2012): 243–65.

Kelly, Thomas Forrest. *Capturing Music: The Story of Notation*. New York: W. W. Norton, 2014.

Kilpiö, Matti. "Two Medieval English Inscriptions in the Collections of the National Library of Russia, St. Petersburg." In *Western European Manuscripts and Early Printed Books in Russia: Delving into the Collections of the Libraries of St. Petersburg*, edited by Leena Kahlas-Tarkka and Matti Kilpiö. Varieng 9. Helsinki: University of Helsinki Press, 2012.

Klack-Eitzen, Charlotte, Wiebke Haase, and Tanja Weissgraf. *Heilige Röcke: Kleider fur Skulpturen in Kloster Wienhausen*. Regensburg: Schnell and Steiner, 2013.

Kwakkel, Erik. "Behind the Scenes of a Revision: Michael Scot and the Oldest Manuscript of his *Abbreviatio Avicenne*." *Viator* 40 (2009): 107–32.

———. "Biting, Kissing and the Treatment of Feet: The Transitional Script of the Long Twelfth Century." In *Turning over a New Leaf: Change and Development in the Medieval Book*, edited by Erik Kwakkel, Rosamond McKitterick, and Rodney Thomson, pp. 79–126, 206–08. Leiden: Leiden University Press, 2012.

———. "Book Script." In *The European Book in the Twelfth Century*, edited by Erik Kwakkel and Rodney Thomson, pp. 24–42. Cambridge: Cambridge University Press, 2018.

———. "Classics on Scraps: Classical Manuscripts Made from Parchment Waste." In *Manuscripts of the Latin Classics 800–1200*, edited by Erik Kwakkel. Studies in Medieval and Renaissance Book Culture, pp. 131–66. Leiden: Leiden University Press, 2015.

———. "Commercial Organisation and Economic Innovation." In *The Production of Books in England, 1350–1530*, edited by Alexandra Gillespie and Daniel Wakelin, pp. 173–91. Cambridge Studies in Palaeography and Codicology 14. Cambridge: Cambridge University Press, 2011.

———. "Decoding the Material Book: Cultural Residue in Medieval Manuscripts." In *The Medieval Manuscript Book: Cultural Approaches*, edited by Michael Van Dussen and Michael Johnson, pp. 60–76. Cambridge: Cambridge University Press, 2015.

———. "Discarded Parchment as Writing Support in English Manuscript Culture." In *English Manuscripts Studies 1100–1700*, vol. 17, edited by A. S. G. Edwards, pp. 239–61. London: British Library, 2012.

———. "'Dit boek heeft niet de vereiste breedte.' Afwijkende bladdimensies in de elfde en twaalfde eeuw." *Jaarboek voor Nederlandse Boekgeschiedenis* 19 (2012): 33–49.

———. *"Dit sijn die Dietsche boeke die ons toebehoeren": De kartuizers van Herne en de productie van Middelnederlandse handschriften in de regio Brussel (1350–1400)*. Miscellanea Neerlandica 27. Leuven: Peeters, 2002.

———. "Hidden in Plain Sight: Continental Scribes in Rochester Cathedral Priory, 1075–1150." In *Writing in Context: Insular Manuscript Culture 500–1200*, edited by Erik Kwakkel. Studies in Medieval and Renaissance Book Culture, pp. 231–61. Leiden: Leiden University Press, 2013.

———. "Late Medieval Text Collections: A Codicological Typology Based on Single-Author Manuscripts." In *Author, Reader, Book. Medieval Authorship in*

Theory and Practice, edited by Stephen Partridge and Erik Kwakkel, pp. 56–79. Toronto: University of Toronto Press, 2012.

———. ed. *Manuscripts of the Latin Classics 800–1200*. Studies in Medieval and Renaissance Book Culture. Leiden: Leiden University Press, 2015.

———. "The Margin as Editorial Space: Upgrading *Dioscorides alphabeticus* in Eleventh-Century Monte Cassino." In *The Annotated Book in the Early Middle Ages: Practices of Reading and Writing*, edited by Irene van Renswoude and Mariken Teeuwen, pp. 357–74. Utrecht Studies in Medieval Literacy. Turnhout: Brepols, 2018.

———. "A Meadow Without Flowers: What Happened to the Middle Dutch Manuscripts from the Charterhouse Herne?" *Quaerendo* 33 (2003): 191–211.

———. "Meer vensters op de Middeleeuwen." In *Het beste idee van 2014*, pp. 97–98. Tilburg: Uitgeverij de Wereld, 2014.

———. "Ouderdom en genese van de veertiende-eeuwse Hadewijch-handschriften." *Queeste* 6 (1999): 23–40.

———. "Towards a Terminology for the Analysis of Composite Manuscripts." *Gazette du Livre Médiéval* 41 (2002): 12–19.

———. ed. *Vernacular Manuscript Culture 1000–1500*. Studies in Medieval and Renaissance Book Culture. Leiden: Leiden University Press, 2018.

———. ed. *Writing in Context: Insular Manuscript Culture 500–1200*. Studies in Medieval and Renaissance Book Culture. Leiden: Leiden University Press, 2013.

Kwakkel, Erik, and Herman Mulder. "Quidam sermones: Geestelijk proza van de Ferguut-kopiist (Brussel, Koninklijke Bibliotheek, hs. 3067–73)." *Tijdschrift voor Nederlandse Taal- en Letterkunde* 117 (2001): 151–65.

Kwakkel, Erik, and Francis Newton. *Medicine at Monte Cassino: Constantine the African and the Oldest Manuscript of his 'Liber pantegni'*. Turnhout: Brepols, forthcoming.

Leclercq, Jean. *The Love of Learning and the Desire for God: A Study of Monastic Culture*. Translated by Catharine Misrahi. 3rd ed. New York: Fordham University Press, 1982.

Lehmann-Haupt, Hellmut. *The Göttingen Model Book: A Facsimile Edition and Translations of a Fifteenth-Century Illuminators' Manual*. 2nd ed. Columbia: University of Missouri Press, 1978.

Leitschuh, Friedrich, and Hans Fischer. *Katalog der Handschriften der Königlichen Bibliothek zu Bamberg*. Bamberg: Staatsbibliothek Bamberg, 1887–1912, 1966.

Lemaire, Jacques. *Introduction à la codicologie*. Louvain: Université catholique de Louvain, 1989.

Lowe, E. A. "The Oldest Omission Signs in Latin Manuscripts: Their Origin and Significance." In *Miscellanea Giovanni Mercati*, vol. 6, pp. 36–79. Studi e testi 126. Biblioteca Apostolica Vaticana, 1946.

Lyall, R. J. "Materials: The Paper Revolution." In *Book Production and Publishing in Britain 1375–1475*, edited by Jeremy Griffiths and Derek Pearsall, pp. 11–30. Cambridge: Cambridge University Press, 1989.

Mantingh, Erwin. *Een monnik met een rol. Willem van Affligem, het Kopenhaagse "Leven van Lutgart" en de fictie van een meerdaagse voorlezing*. Middeleeuwse Studies en Bronnen 73. Hilversum: Verloren, 2000.

Marks, Richard Bruce. *The Medieval Manuscript Library of the Charterhouse of St. Barbara in Cologne*. 2 vols. Analecta Cartusiana. Salzburg: Universität Salzburg, 1974.

Mayr-Harting, Henry. *Ottonian Book Illumination*. 2 vols. Turnhout: Harvey Miller, 1999.

McKitterick, Rosamond. *The Carolingians and the Written Word*. Cambridge: Cambridge University Press, 1989.

Michael, M. A. "Urban Production of Manuscript Books." In *The Cambridge History of the Book in Britain: 1100–1400*, edited by Nigel Morgan and Rodney M. Thomson, pp. 168–94. Vol. 2 of *The Cambridge History of the Book in Britain*. Cambridge: Cambridge University Press, 2008.

Mills, Maldwyn, and Gillian Rogers. "The Manuscripts of Popular Romance." In *A Companion to Medieval Popular Romance*, edited by Raluca L. Radulescu and Cory James Rushton, pp. 49–66. Woodbridge: Brewer, 2009.

Minnis, Alastair. *Medieval Theory of Authorship: Scholastic Literary Attitudes in the Later Middle Ages*. Philadelphia: University of Pennsylvania Press, 1988.

Mooney, L. R. "Professional Scribes? Identifying English Scribes Who Had a Hand in More Than One Manuscript." In *New Directions In Later Medieval Manuscript Studies. Essays From the 1998 Harvard Conference*, edited by Derek Pearsall, pp. 131–41. York: York Medieval Press, 2000.

Morgan, Nigel, and Rodney M. Thomson, eds. *The Cambridge History of the Book in Britain: 1100–1400*. Vol. 2 of *The Cambridge History of the Book in Britain*. Cambridge: Cambridge University Press, 2008.

Mudridge, Alan. *Copying Early Christian Texts: A Study of Scribal Practice*. Tübingen: Mohr Siebeck, 2016.

Munk Olsen, Birger. "The Production of Classics in the Eleventh and Twelfth Centuries." In *Medieval Manuscripts of the Latin Classics: Production and Use. Proceedings of the Seminar in the History of the Book to 1500, Leiden, 1993*, edited by Claudine A. Chavannes-Mazel and Margaret Smith, pp. 1–18. Los Altos Hills: Anderson-Lovelace, 1996.

Musser, Sonja. "Los libros de acedrex dados e tablas: Historical, Artistic and Metaphysical Dimensions of Alfonso X's Book of Games." Dissertation. Arizona: University of Arizona, 2007.

Orme, Nicholas. *Medieval Schools: From Roman Britain to Renaissance England.* New Haven: Yale University Press, 2006.

Overgaauw, E. A. "Where are the Colophons? On the Frequency of Datings in Late-Medieval Manuscripts." In *Sources for the History of Medieval Books and Libraries*, edited by Jos M. M. Hermans, Rita Schlusemann, and Margriet Hoogvliet, pp. 81–93. Groningen: Egbert Forsten, 1999.

Palazzo, Eric. *A History of Liturgical Books from the Beginning to the Thirteenth Century.* Translated by Madeleine Beaumont. Collegeville: Liturgical Press, 1998.

Palmer, Nigel F. "Simul canternus, simul pausernus: Zur mittelalterlichen Zisterzienserinterpunktion." In *Lesevorgänge: Prozesse des Erkennens in mittelalterlichen Texten, Bildern und Handschriften*, edited by E. C. Lutz, Martina Backes, and Stefan Matter, pp. 483–569. Zurich: Chronos, 2010.

Parisse, Michel. "Writing in the Middle Ages." In *A History of Writing: From Hieroglyph to Multimedia*, edited by Anne-Marie Christin, pp. 287–306. Paris: Flammarion, 2002.

Parkes, Malcolm B. "The Literacy of the Laity." In *Literature and Western Civilization II: The Medieval World*, edited by David Daiches and Anthony Thorlby, pp. 555–77. Vol. 2 of *Literature and Western Civilization*. London: Aldus Books, 1974. Reprint, *Scribes, Scripts and Readers*, pp. 275–97.

———. *Pause and Effect: An Introduction to the History of Punctuation in the West.* Farnham: Ashgate, 1992.

———. *Scribes, Scripts and Readers: Studies in the Communication, Presentation and Dissemination of Medieval Texts.* London: Hambledon, 1991.

———. *Their Hands Before Our Eyes: A Closer Look at Scribes. The Lyell Lectures Delivered in the University of Oxford, 1999.* Farnham: Ashgate, 2008.

Petrucci, Armando. *Writers and Readers in Medieval Italy.* Studies in the History of Written Culture. New Haven: Yale University Press, 1995.

Prior, Matthew. *The Poems of Matthew Prior, Vol. 2.* The British Poets Including Translations In One Hundred Volumes 31. Chiswick: Whittingham, 1822.

Reed, Ronald. *Ancient Skins, Parchments and Leathers.* London: Seminar Press, 1972.

Reynolds, L. D. *Texts and Transmission: A Survey of Latin Classics.* Oxford: Clarendon, 1983.

Reynolds, Suzanne. *Medieval Reading: Grammar, Rhetoric and the Classical Text.* Cambridge: Cambridge University Press, 1996.

Roberts, Jane. *Guide to Scripts used in English Writings up to 1500.* London: British Library, 2015.

Roberts, Jane, and Pamela Robinson, eds. *The History of the Book in the West: 400–1455.* Vol. 1 of The History of the Book in the West: A Library of Critical Essays. Aldershot: Ashgate, 2010.

Robertson, Duncan. *Lectio Divina: The Medieval Experience of Reading*. Cistercian Studies 238. Collegeville: Liturgical Press, 2011.

Robinson, P. R. "The Format of Books: Books, Booklets and Rolls." In *The Cambridge History of the Book in Britain: 1100–1400*, edited by Nigel Morgan and Rodney M. Thomson, pp. 39–54. Vol. 2 of *The Cambridge History of the Book in Britain*. Cambridge: Cambridge University Press, 2008.

———. ed. *Teaching Writing, Learning to Write, Proceedings of the XVIth Colloquium of the Comité International de Paléographie Latine*. Kings College London Medieval Studies 22. Woodbridge: Boydell & Brewer, 2010.

Römer, Gerhard, and Gerhard Stamm. *Raimundus Lullus—Thomas Le Myésier, Electorium Parvum seu Breviculum, 1: Vollständiges Faksimile der Handschrift St. Peter perg. 92 der Badischen Landesbibliothek Karlsruhe; 2: Kommentar zum Faksimile*. Wiesbaden: Dr. Ludwig Reichert, 1988.

Rouse, Richard H., and Mary A. Rouse. *Authentic Witnesses: Approaches to Medieval Texts and Manuscripts*. Publications in Medieval Studies 17. Notre Dame: University of Notre Dame Press, 1991.

———. "The Commercial Production of Manuscript Books in Late Thirteenth- and Early Fourteenth-Century Paris." In *A Potencie of Life: Books in Society. The Clark Lectures, 1986–1987*, edited by Nicolas J. Barker, pp. 45–61. London: British Library, 1993.

———. *Manuscripts and Their Makers: Commercial Book Producers in Medieval Paris, 1200–1500*. Studies in Medieval and Early Renaissance Art History 25. Turnhout: Harvey Miller, 2000.

———. "The Vocabulary of Wax Tablets." *Harvard Library Bulletin* (1990): 220–30.

Saenger, Paul. *Space Between Words: The Origins of Silent Reading*. Stanford: Stanford University Press, 1997.

Savage, Ernest A. *Old English Libraries: The Making, Collection and Using of Books during the Middle Ages*. London: Methuen, 1911.

Scheller, Robert W. *Exemplum: Model-Book Drawings and the Practice of Artistic Transmission in the Middle Ages (ca. 900–ca. 1470)*, translated by Michael Hoyle. Amsterdam: Amsterdam University Press, 1995.

Schneider, Karin. *Paläographie und Handschriftenkunde für Germanisten: Eine Einführung*. Sammlung kurzer Grammatiken germanischer Dialekten 8. Tübingen: Max Niemeyer, 1999.

Schreiber, Heinrich. "Die Karthäuser als Bücherfreunde." *Sankt Wiborada. Bibliophiles Jahrbuch für Katholisches Geistesleben* 1 (1933): 16–21.

Shailor, Barbara A. *The Medieval Book: Illustrated from the Beinecke Rare Book and Manuscript Library*. Toronto: University of Toronto Press, 1991.

Skemer, Don C. *Binding Words: Textual Amulets in the Middle Ages*. University Park: Penn State University Press, 2006.

Smith, Lesley. *Masters of the Sacred Page: Manuscripts of Theology in the Latin West to 1274*. Notre Dame: University of Notre Dame Press, 2001.

Szirmai, Janos A. *The Archaeology of Medieval Bookbinding*. Aldershot: Ashgate, 2000.

Taylor, Andrew. "Authors, Scribes, Patrons, and Books." In *The Idea of the Vernacular: An Anthology of Middle English Literary Theory, 1280–1520*, edited by Jocelyn Wogan-Browne, Nicholas Watson, Andrew Taylor, and Ruth Evans, pp. 353–65. University Park: Pennsylvania State University Press, 1999.

Teeuwen, Mariken. "Marginal Scholarship: Rethinking the Function of Latin Glosses in Early Medieval Manuscripts." In *Rethinking and Recontextualizing Glosses: New Perspectives in the Study of Late Anglo-Saxon Glossography*, edited by Patrizia Lendinara, Loredana Lazzari, and Claudia Di Sciacca, pp. 19–37. Textes et Etudes du Moyen Age 54. Turnout: Brepols, 2011.

Tether, Leah. "*Mise en page, mise en écran*: What Medieval 'Publishing' Practices Can Tell Us About Reading in the Digital Age." *LOGOS* 25 (2014): 21–36.

Thompson, James Westfall. *The Medieval Library*. University of Chicago Studies in Library Science. New York: Hafner, 1957.

Trentelman, Karen, Koen Janssens, Geert van der Snickt, Yvonne Szafran, Anne T. Woollett, and Joris Dik. "Rembrandt's 'An Old Man in Military Costume': The Underlying Image Re-examined." *Applied Physics A* (2015): 801–11.

Voights, Linda E. "Scientific and Medical Books." In *Book Production and Publishing in Britain 1375–1475*, edited by Jeremy Griffiths and Derek Pearsall, pp. 345–402. Cambridge Studies in Publishing and Printing. Cambridge: Cambridge University Press, 1989.

Wehmer, Carl. "Die Schreibmeisterblätter des späten Mittelalters." In *Miscellanea Giovanni Mercati*, vol. 6, pp. 147–61. Studi e testi 126. Vatican City: Biblioteca Apostolica Vaticana, 1946.

van der Wiel, Kees. *"Dit kint hiet Willem." De Heilige Geest in Leiden: 700 jaar vondelingen, wezen en jeugdzorg*. Leiden: Primavera Pers, 2010.

Online Resources

BBC News, Unique Book Goes on Display, May 26, 2003, http://news.bbc.co.uk/go/pr/fr/-/2/hi/europe/2939362.stm

Beinecke Library, Yale University, New Haven. Gregorius Bock's *Scribal Pattern Book*, 1510–1517. MS 439. http://beinecke.library.yale.edu/tags/digital-collections

Bibliothèque national de France (National Library of France). *Gallica*. http://gallica.bnf.fr

British Library Catalogue of Illuminated Manuscripts. www.bl.uk/catalogues/illuminatedmanuscripts/welcome.htm

British Library Press Office. "British Library Acquires the St Cuthbert Gospel—the Earliest Intact European Book." April 16, 2012. www.bl.uk/press-releases/2012/april/british-library-acquires-the-st-cuthbert-gospel--the-earliest-intact-european-book

British Museum. Collection Online. www.britishmuseum.org

Columbia University Libraries. " 'Our Tools of Learning': George Arthur Plimpton's Gifts to Columbia University." Online exhibition, curated by Jennifer B. Lee. https://exhibitions.cul.columbia.edu/exhibits/show/plimpton/hornbooks

Devine, Alexander. "Food for Thought." *Unique at Penn* (blog), University of Pennsylvania Libraries. April 8, 2013. https://uniqueatpenn.wordpress.com/2013/04/08/food-for-thought

Ebstorfer Weltkarte. Hosted by Leuphana Universität Lüneburg. www2.leuphana.de/ebskart

Ferguson, Stephen. "15th Century Bookmark With Column Indicator." *Notabilia* (blog), Princeton University. July 12, 2014. https://blogs.princeton.edu/notabilia/2014/07/12/15th-century-bookmark-with-column-indicator

Gutenberg Digital. *The Göttingen Model Book*. www.gutenbergdigital.de/gudl/eframes/mubu/mubufset.htm

Institut de recherche et d'histoire des textes. *Inititale: Catalogue de manuscrits enluminés*. http://initiale.irht.cnrs.fr/

Kennedy, Maev. "British Library Seeks £9m to Buy Oldest Book in Europe." *The Guardian* online. July 14, 2011. www.theguardian.com/books/2011/jul/14/british-library-seeks-buy-oldest-book

Kwakkel, Erik. *Erik Kwakkel* (Tumblr). 2012–2015. http://erikkwakkel.tumblr.com

———. *Erik Kwakkel* (blog). 2014–2016. http://medievalbooks.nl

Kwakkel, Erik, and Giulio Menna, *Quill: Books Before Print*. www.bookandbyte.org/quill

Mappa Mundi, Hereford Cathedral. *Mappa Mundi Ltd*. www.themappamundi.co.uk

Massachusetts Collections Online. "Chronique anonyme universelle." *Digital Commonwealth*. www.digitalcommonwealth.org/search/commonwealth: np193j76j

"Medieval Manuscripts: Bookbinding Terms, Materials, Methods, and Models." Compiled by the Special Collections Conservation Unit of the Preservation Department of Yale University Library (July 2013). https://travelingscriptorium.files.wordpress.com/2013/07/bookbinding-booklet.pdf

Metropolitan Museum of Art. www.metmuseum.org/art

Morgan Library and Museum. "Apocalypse Then: Medieval Illuminations from the Morgan." www.themorgan.org/collection/Las-Huelgas-Apocalypse/49

National and University Library of Iceland. *handrit.is*. https://handrit.is

Schassan, Torsten, Stefanie Gehrke, and Fabian Schwabe. "Digitale Edition der Handschrift Cod. Guelf. 64 Weiss." *Herzog August Bibliothek*, 2007–2010. http://diglib.hab.de/edoc/ed000006/index.php

University of California, Berkeley Library. Digital Scriptorium. http://bancroft.berkeley.edu/digitalscriptorium

University of Michigan, Ann Arbor. Advanced Papyrological Information System (APIS UM). https://quod.lib.umich.edu/a/apis

University of Oxford, Bodleian Library. Digital.Bodleian. http://digital.bodleian.ox.ac.uk

———. Luna Catalogue. http://bodley30.bodley.ox.ac.uk:8180/luna/servlet

University of Pennsylvania Libraries. Lawrence J. Schoenberg Manuscripts. http://openn.library.upenn.edu

Virtual Manuscript Library of Switzerland (e-codices). www.e-codices.unifr.ch

Web Gallery of Art. Edited by Emil Krén and Dániel Marx. http://www.wga.hu/index.html

Wikimedia Commons. "Karolingischer Buchmaler um 820." https://nl.wikipedia.org/wiki/Bestand:Karolingischer_Buchmaler_um_820_001.jpg

Wikipedia. "Jean Miélot." https://en.wikipedia.org/wiki/Jean_Miélot

INDEX OF MATERIAL FEATURES

Page numbers in **bold** indicate where the term is defined in this volume. Page numbers in *italics* indicate related images. Entries may also refer to terms listed in the General Index.

MANUSCRIPT INDEX

Page numbers in *italics* indicate images.

GENERAL INDEX

Page numbers in *italics* indicate related images. Entries may also refer to terms listed in the Index of Material Features.

Printed in the United States
by Baker & Taylor Publisher Services